"Countless research studies have shown that one of the most important factors to influence successful treatment outcomes is the therapeutic relationship. There's no intervention more powerful than using the present-moment interaction between client and therapist to experiment with new behaviors and promote behavioral flexibility. This book teaches clinicians how to effectively use the therapeutic relationship as a tool for behavioral change, and is a must-read for every clinician regardless of their theoretical orientation. This book provides practical tools for guiding clinicians on how to use the therapeutic interaction to foster behavioral change; offers specific steps to identify, track, and monitor both client and therapist's targeted behaviors for treatment, and modify them in the moment; and with its many worksheets, exercises, and sample dialogues, this book is the perfect resource for any clinician who wants to help clients build authentic and more fulfilling relationships."

> —**Avigail Lev, PsyD**, director of the Bay Area CBT Center, and coauthor of *Acceptance and Commitment Therapy for Interpersonal Problems*, *The Interpersonal Problems Workbook*, and *Acceptance and Commitment Therapy for Couples*

"*Functional Analytic Psychotherapy Made Simple* clearly and elegantly describes an approach that is incredibly useful for therapists and coaches. The authors explain how to consciously create a context that intentionally nurtures growth. The skill of functional analysis can be applied broadly, and this book explains this skill in a way that is easy to understand and apply. Functional analytic psychotherapy (FAP) is about consciously moving into conversation with courage, awareness, and love. This book embodies this beautifully."

> —**Rachel Collis**, executive coach; MBA lecturer, Queensland University of Technology, Australia

"For clinicians who want their therapy relationships to improve their clients' lives, this book is the place to start. A delight to read, *Functional Analytic Psychotherapy Made Simple* provides a clear and compassionate guide to helping therapists be present, supportive, and responsive to clients. The book is chock-full of vivid clinical examples, tools and worksheets, and helpful solutions for getting unstuck in therapy. The result is an excellent foundation for therapists to develop powerful curative relationships with clients, while being seamlessly grounded in the principles of behaviorism that underlie this therapy. Coming over a quarter century since the seminal book on FAP was released, and distilling the authors' forty-plus years of wisdom and experience, the book is a true achievement. *Functional Analytic Psychotherapy Made Simple* is destined to become a gem in any clinician's library. I wish I had this book when I first learned FAP many years ago."

> —**Jonathan B. Bricker, PhD**, behavioral scientist, psychology professor, and practicing FAP therapist

"After haunting psychotherapy theory for a century, the personal relationship between therapist and client has come to its own as the most powerful tool for therapeutic change. This book explains why and how the personal relationship is essential in the treatment of psychological problems. Seldom has a single volume covered such a broad array of skills and such depths of understanding. Weaving samples of clinical conversation into theory, it makes the complexities of the psychotherapy process—not so much simple, but rather—crystal clear. Its wisdom will cross cultural barriers because it speaks directly to what is at the heart of being human."

> —**Luc Vandenberghe**, psychotherapist in private practice and faculty member at the Pontifical Catholic University of Goias, Brazil

The *Made Simple* Series

Written by leaders and researchers in their fields, the *Made Simple* series offers accessible, step-by-step guides for understanding and implementing a number of evidence-based modalities in clinical practice, such as acceptance and commitment therapy (ACT), dialectical behavior therapy (DBT), compassion-focused therapy (CFT), functional analytic psychotherapy (FAP), and other proven-effective therapies.

For use by mental health professionals of any theoretical background, these easy-to-use books break down complex therapeutic methods and put them into simple steps—giving clinicians everything they need to put theory into practice to best benefit clients and create successful treatment outcomes.

Visit www.newharbinger.com for
more books in this series.

FUNCTIONAL ANALYTIC PSYCHOTHERAPY
made simple

A Practical Guide to Therapeutic Relationships

GARETH HOLMAN, PhD
JONATHAN KANTER, PhD
MAVIS TSAI, PhD
ROBERT KOHLENBERG, PhD

New Harbinger Publications, Inc.

Publisher's Note

Distributed in Canada by Raincoast Books

Copyright © 2017 by Gareth Holman, Jonathan Kanter, Mavis Tsai, and Robert Kohlenberg
New Harbinger Publications, Inc.
5674 Shattuck Avenue
Oakland, CA 94609
www.newharbinger.com

Excerpts from THE ESSENTIAL RUMI by Jalal al-Din Rumi, translated by Coleman Barks. Copyright © 1997 by Coleman Barks. Used by permission.

"Session Bridging Form" adapted from A GUIDE TO FUNCTIONAL ANALYTIC PSYCHOTHERAPY by Mavis Tsai, Robert J. Kohlenberg, Jonathan W. Kanter, Barbara Kohlenberg, William C. Follette, and Glenn M. Callaghan. Copyright © 2009 by Robert J. Kohlenberg. Reprinted by permission of Springer Publishers.

Cover design by Amy Shoup

Acquired by Catharine Meyers

Edited by James Lainsbury

Indexed by James Minkin

Library of Congress Cataloging-in-Publication Data on file

19   18   17

10   9   8   7   6   5   4   3   2   1   First Printing

For John Avery (Granddad):

"Every day, make someone laugh."

Awareness, courage, love, and humor.

Contents

Treating Others with Awareness, Courage, and Love

Human beings evolved in small groups and bands. We are social beings, and the importance of others is as basic to our psychology as breathing is to our physiology.

As a scientific matter we know that others are key to our functioning, but we can also *feel* how important that is in our daily lives. If you look at what is most important to you and what is most painful to you, it is likely that people are involved in both of those reactions. We may be tormented by rejection, or loneliness, or shame, or relationship problems: but all of these are examples of both the importance of others and other people as a focal point of our psychological pain. We may hope to achieve, or create, or contribute, or love—but these too will implicitly involve people to share with.

Most clinical problems are reflected in our relationships with others. This is true etiologically: experiences such as a lack of nurturance, interpersonal abandonment, neglect, and trauma are among the most toxic experiences known, and in the opposite direction, social support, intimacy, and caring are among the most uplifting. Is it any wonder then that the quality of the therapeutic relationship is related to the outcomes of most forms of therapy, including those that are evidence based?

If social processes are central to the development of human problems, we should expect to see psychopathology appear in the relationship between clients and therapists; and in many if not most cases, we do. This is a problem if it is not handled correctly, but also an opportunity if it is, since the therapist is able to work *directly* with the problem behavior of interest in the therapeutic consulting room.

To do this, however, you need a clear set of guiding principles. You need to see the function of social events, not just their form. Most clients have social relationships of importance outside of psychotherapy, but often these are not curative because people accidentally reinforce the wrong things or support unhelpful rules. If merely being in the presence of others was enough, then people would not usually need to seek out professional help. The automatic reactions that we have to others may not be what they need therapeutically. A therapist needs to be genuine, but also needs to be thoughtful and strategic. That is a tricky balance that needs to be based on principles.

What functional analytic psychotherapy (FAP) offers is a small set of clear guidelines that help therapists keep their eye on the features of the therapeutic relationship that most predict positive outcomes. FAP can be used as a stand-alone treatment in many cases, but it can also be used to support the deployment and augmentation of other treatment methods—especially those drawn from the same behavioral roots.

This book positions FAP as part of contextual behavioral science (CBS). In so doing, it invites the reader to harmonize FAP principles with modern behavioral analysis, including relational frame theory (RFT). That is an interesting and important step that gives the FAP clinician a powerful additional set of concepts to apply. It puts a fresh face on the use of contingent social reinforcement as part of the therapeutic agenda.

This book also vigorously embraces the "awareness, courage, and love" model that links more abstract functional analysis and clinically relevant behaviors (CRBs) to domains defined by common sets of functional analyses. Not all will approve of this step, but I know the line clinician will because it immediately makes FAP more vital and focused. And that, in turn, makes FAP simpler: simpler to understand, simpler to teach, and simpler to deploy.

The latter part of this elegant book casts a clear light on areas of growth and difficulty. It shows how to use this model in a creative and practical way. Some issues it covers—such as how to end therapy and to explore what was learned—are often missed in other books. These wise sections alone are worth the price of admission.

As researchers and clinicians further unpack this model I expect to see new pathways forward. My suggestion to you as you read this book is to explore this model with the awareness to see opportunity, the courage to explore new territory thoroughly, and the love of humanity to acquire new skills with humility—to bring all of that to the task. If you do, you will be changed by the journey, as will the lives of those you serve.

—Steven C. Hayes
Foundation Professor and Director of Clinical Training
University of Nevada, Reno

Introduction

Neither love without knowledge, nor knowledge without love can produce a good life.

—Bertrand Russell

You arrive at your office, and you bring yourself with you. But what else do you bring?

Perhaps you bring a bad night's sleep or the stress of Monday morning. You might bring good coffee and a commitment to do good. Are you at a high or low point in your career? Are you learning a new method, or consulting with fantastic colleagues? Or are you wondering what you'll do next because too many weeks have felt "blah" lately? Are you struggling to like some of the people you will see this week?

What joy have you brought with you? What fears? What hopes? What vulnerabilities?

What shame have you brought with you? Are you still stinging a bit from a painful session on Friday? Are you feeling disconnected from a friend because of something that happened over the weekend? Are you dreading something?

As you start your day, how firmly do you hold on to what you stand for as a therapist? How are you holding back? Are you truly looking at your weaknesses as a therapist? How are you trying too hard?

What are you avoiding facing in your life right now? Where are you vulnerable?

And how will all of the variables above affect how you perform as a therapist today? How will they affect your clients?

Your client—maybe he is a new client, let's say his name is Tom—also brings himself and his history to the session. Tom wakes up feeling anxious about his appointment with you. His hands shake as he pours his coffee.

He imagines you will be sitting across from him, quietly professional yet full of assessment. He imagines himself squirming. He rehearses what he'll say so he can sound at least semicoherent. He feels panic rising in his chest.

He recalls a string of nameless doctors questioning him. Though well-intentioned, they all set him on edge.

And so you and Tom meet. What happens as your histories and vulnerabilities and perspectives interact? What will he take away from your interaction? How will you encourage him? How will you subtly discourage him? Shame him? How will you invite him to open up? In turn, how will he shame you? Disappoint you? How will you serve him? Or, if you act to preserve your sense of expertise and competence, will you subtly or not so subtly miss *Tom* and overlook key issues that need attention?

Each client is not just a case, and you are not just a therapist. You and your client are two people engaging in a dance of connection (and hopefully healing) with a foundation that involves hundreds of thousands of years of human evolution. That's a lot for a Monday morning!

Functional analytic psychotherapy (FAP), the subject of this book, is about being aware, courageous, and skillful in the moment when interacting with each client. It's about standing at the head of your own history, with awareness, and engaging with a client who stands at the head of her history. As the interaction unfolds, FAP is then about seeing together, with courage and compassion, how this present moment in therapy may contain the very problem for which your client is seeking help—and then taking the opportunity to grow and change right here and right now in a way that is immediate and experiential and relational. When this happens, the interaction is not only compassionate and connected, but it also creates change.

We have two main purposes in this book:

- First, through the lens of contextual behavioral science, we want to help you recognize that what happens in each moment in a therapy session is a behavior that makes sense in the context of each person's learning history, and that behavior is unfolding now in response to the present. Functional analysis (FA) is the assessment process at the heart of this way of seeing each moment in session. It's a way of relating to behavior that is empathic and compassionate and also principled and precise. In FAP we apply FA to understand the client's problems—in particular, how *this* moment in therapy may evoke these problems. FA is how we "aim" the change processes of FAP. It's also how we understand what this moment means for this unique person.

- Second, we show you how to weave FA with honest, courageous, compassionate, and personally involved engagement in the therapeutic process. A real, authentic therapeutic relationship serves FA because that's the natural medium in which human beings can become "known" to each other—through the vulnerable dance of disclosure and response, by finding a common language and perspective.

The intersection of FA and relationship defines FAP. Why should you care?

First, it's widely accepted that the quality of the therapeutic relationship is important to therapy outcomes (Horvath, Del Re, Flückiger, & Symonds, 2011). FAP is based on research and analysis that looks at what creates strong, connected relationships, and it offers concrete guidelines for creating good therapeutic relationships.

Second, FAP provides a framework for thinking about the therapy process in a highly individualized yet precise way. FAP stands firmly inside the growing movement of contextual behavioral science (Hayes, Barnes-Holmes, & Wilson, 2012; Hayes, Levin, Plumb-Vilardaga, Villatte, & Pistorello, 2013) and behavior therapy more generally, and FAP is based on the central practice of behavior therapy, which is defining specific behaviors and then targeting those behaviors through specific change processes in therapy. In turn, the therapist responds to behaviors not based on what they look like but on what they actually mean for the client (that is, how they function) in the context of his or her unfolding life.

To say that FAP is a *behavior therapy* means something quite different than it did several decades ago. The newest wave of behavior therapies (and therapies of other types) has closed the gap between the principled distance of the behavior therapist and the sensitive attunement of the humanistic psychologist. As therapists, we no longer have to choose between a structured, evidence-based assessment framework and being fully human and sensitive in our interactions with clients. FAP and its fellow travelers—acceptance and commitment therapy (ACT; Hayes, Strosahl, & Wilson, 1999), compassion-focused therapy (CFT; Gilbert, 2010), and dialectical behavior therapy (DBT; Linehan, 1993), in particular—integrate these viewpoints. If you have a background in more experiential therapies, FAP can help you improve the precision of your assessments. If you have a background in behavior therapies, FAP can help you improve the experiential flow and immediacy of your work.

In so many ways, therapy *is* a process: a series of events unfolding between two people who influence each other in exquisitely subtle ways. A breath, a sigh, or an averting of the eyes can communicate more than a long stream of words, especially when therapists or clients are most vulnerable or emotional. And because this process of mutual influence is often subtle, fast, automatic, and ephemeral—or so extended over time that it's hard to connect the dots—it's easy to miss what's really happening in the moment. It's easy to miss that therapy happens in the here and now and unfolds in the ongoing sequence of present moments. It's easy to overlook that the struggle happening in the here and now, in session, is often what happens in other situations in a client's life. It's also easy to overlook the tiny, tentative moments of new possibility in which deeper change might take root.

FAP is about slowing down and tuning into this process and realizing that the interaction is about *you* and your client. FAP is about examining the personal and interpersonal through the general principles of learning while acknowledging that no set of principles entirely survives contact with real life. FAP's stance is that doing due diligence in the therapeutic process also requires knowing our blind spots, passing through vulnerability, taking risks, and expressing what we feel—not recklessly, but strategically.

In the course of a session, a FAP therapist might plot a functional analysis on a white board and then evoke the client's honest expression of anger related to a comment she made during the functional analysis. With a different client, a FAP therapist might spend forty minutes working with the client to express vulnerable thoughts and feelings in the moment, and then spend the last ten minutes of the session defining a concrete behavioral homework assignment. In FAP, the tools of behavior therapy and interpersonal process deliberately mingle.

With its emphasis on an intense, engaged, and individualized therapy relationship, FAP reflects the ongoing and evolving scientific consensus that social relationships are key to shaping human well-being and achievement. Psychotherapy is simply one expression of the power of social connection. It isn't magic, a coincidence, or a trick of scientific psychology that a *relationship* (which is what therapy is) can be incredibly therapeutic. Human evolution has proceeded in such a way that close relationships can influence us tremendously. As a result, we humans are exquisitely sensitive instruments of change for one another.

Because of FAP's focus on genuine engagement in the therapy relationship, and because doing therapy from an interpersonal distance is a violation of this principle, it's fair to say that FAP demands a lot from therapists. It requires you to do your own work so you can own your mistakes with clients, be vulnerable, take risks, feel emotion, and so on. We are in the same situation as our clients: we struggle as human beings.

This stance of favoring genuine engagement is not incidental or arbitrary; it's not a matter of personal preference. It is part of a growing worldwide recognition—core to contextual behavioral science (CBS)—that human well-being is nurtured or undermined by the contexts in which we live, and those contexts are overwhelmingly about other people. As prevention scientist and behavior analyst Tony Biglan shows, summarizing more than five decades of behavioral science in the areas of parenting, education, public health, and clinical science, "nurturing environments" profoundly support human health and well-being (2015).

There are several different ways to focus FAP (Bonow, Maragakis, & Follette, 2012). However, because of FAP's important place in the CBS community and the growing evidence base supporting CBS interventions (Hooper & Larsson, 2015), this book draws heavily on the foundational CBS principles concerning the contexts in which human beings flourish. Like CBS, FAP is about creating a compassionate context for change—one that supports flexible, committed action—in the therapeutic relationship.

EVIDENCE FOR FAP

This book is a clinical guide based on behavioral principles rather than a treatment manual with direct empirical claims. The reason for this is simple: the evidence base for specific applications of FAP principles—what is needed to make empirically supported claims—has quite some distance to go.

That said, one of the priorities of FAP since its inception has been to build a treatment approach that is highly flexible and experiential yet grounded in rigorous principles of behavioral science. FAP is grounded in contextual behavioral science (Hayes et al., 2012) and seeks to apply CBS's principles to psychotherapy, with a particular focus on the nature and challenges of creating, maintaining, and improving therapeutic relationships.

While FAP research has some ground to cover, in this section we provide a brief overview of the research that has been done so far. In diagnostic terms, FAP is a *transdiagnostic* approach: FAP emphasizes therapeutic relationship processes that are important to treatment across diagnoses. Early research on FAP pursued this broad stance with a series of case studies, descriptions of FAP, and small pilot studies with clients experiencing a diverse range of problems, including depression, histrionic personality disorder, borderline personality disorder, obsessive-compulsive disorder, conduct disorder, substance abuse, problems in interpersonal relationships, sexual abuse, chronic pain, academic anxiety, agoraphobia, exhibitionism, anorgasmia, nonspecific personality disorder, and nonspecific anxiety disorder (reviewed in Mangabeira, Kanter, & Del Prette, 2012).

A series of more controlled single-case studies on FAP has also been published (Esparza Lizarazo, Muñoz-Martínez, Santos, & Kanter, 2015; Landes, Kanter, Weeks, & Busch, 2013; Kanter et al., 2006). A total of nine clients were involved in these studies, with a range of depressive, anxiety, and personality disorders. These studies are unique and particularly relevant to this book because they demonstrate the individualized approach to functional analysis that's at the heart of FAP, and they also demonstrate large, clinically relevant changes at the level of the individual client rather than a group average.

Other substantial FAP research has been done with depression. In 1996, Bob Kohlenberg received a grant from the National Institute of Mental Health to study whether FAP training would improve the outcomes of cognitive therapy treatment for depression delivered by experts (Kohlenberg, Kanter, Bolling, Parker, & Tsai, 2002). His team reasoned that cognitive therapy, then recognized as the gold-standard empirically validated treatment for depression, was a great approach but could still benefit from key features of FAP: functional analysis, attention to the therapy relationship, and a focus on improvements in social functioning. The expert therapists first completed their typical therapy with sixteen clients. Then they participated in a FAP training protocol, after which they completed therapy with twenty-four clients. The study found that clients in the first group did well, with about 48 percent experiencing clinically significant improvement. The FAP clients, however, did even better, with about 70 percent experiencing improvements. And interestingly, clients in the first group didn't demonstrate any improvements on a well-validated measure of social functioning: relationship satisfaction. FAP clients, however, demonstrated significant improvements in relationship satisfaction.

Recent research has provided more understanding of the mechanisms responsible for the benefits of FAP found in earlier studies. For example, we now have evidence that FAP's strategy of reinforcing improvements in session (which we'll discuss throughout this book) is a key mechanism responsible for clients' improvements in the single-case studies discussed above (Busch et al., 2009; Oshiro, Kanter, & Meyer, 2012), and that FAP processes were uniquely responsible for the improvements in the cognitive therapy study just described (Kanter, Schildcrout, & Kohlenberg, 2005).

Most recently, and most notably, Daniel Maitland and colleagues (in press) produced the first randomized controlled trial of a FAP treatment for interpersonal difficulties. FAP produced superior outcomes for social connection, anxiety, and avoidance compared to a minimal active control condition (watchful waiting) in a sample of anxious clients presenting with interpersonal problems. In an alternating-treatments design, Maitland & Gaynor (2016) previously demonstrated the superiority of FAP compared to supportive listening for improving interpersonal functioning. In both of these studies, the ratings of therapeutic alliance were also superior for the FAP treatments.

More research is needed. We hope this book might further inspire researchers.

HOW TO USE THIS BOOK

This is an experiential, practice-based book. While we use technical language and rely more generally on your knowledge of psychotherapy, our words are only signposts meant to lead you toward particular experiences and behaviors. We hope you'll fully participate and own those experiences so that you can find your own way of working with FAP. So throughout, please pause and practice what we ask you to practice. As you're probably well aware, training with primarily intellectual content does little to change actual skills (see Beidas & Kendall, 2010). A music arises when you fully practice FAP, and you won't hear it if you only read the words.

We offer exercises that are both practical and interesting and address the full range of FAP principles in order to facilitate your practice of FAP. You can practice these exercises in your day-to-day personal life, in your psychotherapy practice, or both. As you can see, we will address you not just as a therapist but as a whole person. We have several reasons for asking you to engage in a personal practice of the FAP principles.

You are not outside the process of psychotherapy. Indeed, you are at the center of the process. This includes the words you speak, the expressions you show, where you push forward and where you pull back in the dance of therapy, and everything else that contributes to how you appear in therapy. All of this is shaped by your history—not just your professional training, but also your personal history of love and connection, of belonging and loneliness, of suffering and striving, as well as your current life circumstances. You may not always have to reveal yourself, and there may be parts of yourself that you never reveal in therapy. But given that the process of therapy is an exquisitely nuanced dance of influence between two people, even your most subtle dispositions and vulnerabilities may sometimes matter.

As FAP therapists, we don't ask clients to practice or do what we do not do. To be a sensitive instrument and to guide clients well, therapists must be familiar with the path. Empathy is usually informed by personal experience. That said, you must also have enough awareness about the particular ways you've traveled on your own path to discriminate it from the paths of others.

Therapy is demanding and requires self-awareness. Therapists need to engage in ongoing practices of self-care and compassionate self-reflection. You will react to your clients. And sometimes those reactions will be influenced more by your own history than by clients themselves, so you must be able to identify which of your reactions are mostly about you and your history and therefore don't yield broadly useful information about the client involved.

The points above outline the stance we ask you to take as a FAP therapist. A slightly different set of points defines the stance we invite you to take as you go about learning FAP by reading this book. Here are a few specific suggestions about how to get the most out of this book.

Find practice partners. Given FAP's focus on interpersonal interactions, it probably won't come as a surprise that some of the exercises in this book involve interacting with other people. Many can be done with clients, but it will be useful to do certain exercises with people who are not clients. Here and now, at the outset, try to identify a few people who might be willing to engage in some deeply heartfelt conversations with you or play some fun, experiential psychology games. These people could be colleagues, but they might also be friends or family members.

Drop perfectionism and embrace discomfort. Expect to feel uncomfortable while engaging in many of the exercises in this book, as well as while learning functional analysis (if it's new to you) and while practicing FAP in general. It's okay to feel clumsy and anxious. You're practicing something new. Even with all of our experience, the authors of this book continue to feel anxious at times while practicing FAP or training therapists in FAP. You may find it helpful to think of your discomfort this way: it actually represents your attunement and sensitivity to the dance of opening up to another person, and thus your ability to relate to clients from a foundation of shared humanity rather than disconnected expertise. We discuss this idea in depth later in the book. For now, simply focus on accepting the discomfort and reminding yourself that it's a sign that you're on the right track.

Trust your own expertise. Bear in mind that psychotherapy is strong medicine and can do as much harm as good if it isn't managed effectively. That means managing it locally by using the years you've devoted to training to develop the capacity to practice competently. Since we cannot know the particulars of the situations you and your clients face, please don't take anything in this book as an absolute recommendation. If something doesn't feel right to you, trust your gut and follow your expertise—or seek expert consultation. We will ask you to take calculated risks throughout this book, but please don't be reckless or trust us blindly.

Reach out if you need help. If you have questions or concerns about FAP, don't assume it's because you're somehow inadequate as a therapist. Hold us accountable to teach FAP effectively, and give us the opportunity to do so by letting us know what you need. We care deeply about this work, and we remain humble about doing it. If you reach out to the FAP community, you will get answers. You can access the FAP community by e-mailing one of us (for contact information, visit http://www.functionalanalyticpsychotherapy.com/find-a-fap-supervisor). If you're on Facebook, you can ask to be added to the private FAP Facebook group, or if you know someone who is already a member, you can ask that person to add you.

Participate in formal training or consultation. If you want to intensify your practice of FAP principles, if you find that parts of FAP remain difficult to put into practice, or if you simply want a powerful experience of FAP in action, consider joining an in-person or online training or signing up for consultation with one of the growing number of FAP trainers worldwide. Check out http://www.faptherapy.com for a listing of upcoming trainings and available consultants and trainers. Although this book offers important ideas you can leisurely ponder and exercises and processes that you can engage in at your own pace, workshops, online trainings, and individual consultation will provide in-depth, experiential learning about FAP in ways that go beyond the scope of what's possible within a book.

ORGANIZATION OF THE BOOK

This book is organized in two parts. Part 1 (chapters 1 through 5) covers the essential principles of FAP, and part 2 (chapters 6 through 13) addresses clinical practice. Chapter 1 introduces a contextual behavioral view of social connection and describes, from this perspective, how social functioning influences psychological problems and how therapeutic relationships work. Chapter 2 goes deeper into the contextual behavioral perspective at the root of FAP. Chapter 3 introduces the core principles of functional analysis as applied in FAP. Chapter 4 describes the awareness, courage, and love model—a framework for the functional analysis of social connections that can be applied to therapeutic relationships, as well as other social contexts. Chapter 5 ties all of the previous threads together to describe the therapeutic process at the center of FAP as encapsulated in the five rules of FAP.

Part 2 has a slightly different feel than part 1 for a simple reason: although theory is the backbone of FAP, having a grasp of theory isn't sufficient to be an effective FAP clinician. A particular set of skills—personal, interpersonal, and clinical—is required to put the theory to use. We'll begin a bit more broadly in chapter 6 with a presentation of some exercises therapists can do to develop self-awareness and the interpersonal flexibility that supports FAP skills. Chapter 7 presents the elements of FAP at play in the beginning of therapy and sets forth how to strengthen the foundation for FAP work at this early stage. Chapter 8 delves further into the process of evoking and exploring what is happening in session between you and the client. Chapter 9 discusses the next important part of in-session process: how to respond to a client's improvements in reinforcing ways. Chapter 10 reviews all five FAP rules again and discusses a framework for using them in a single interaction: the logical interaction. It also discusses how the actual practice of FAP might deviate from the logical and linear. Chapter 11 covers case conceptualization in FAP. Chapter 12 addresses homework and experiential exercises and how these are used in FAP. Chapter 13 discusses the end of therapy, a topic of special attention in FAP.

PART I

The Ideas

CHAPTER I

Social Connection and the Therapeutic Relationship as Contexts for Change

There is no such thing as a "self-made" [person]. We are made up of thousands of others. Everyone who has ever done a kind deed for us, or spoken one word of encouragement to us, has entered into the make-up of our character and of our thoughts, as well as our success.

—George Matthews Adams

Think for a moment about the most important interactions and relationships you've had in your life. Think about the ones that were the most connected, joyful, and inspiring.

Also think about the interactions that were the most painful and heartbreaking, ending in betrayal or disappointment.

How did all of these experiences shape you? What lessons did you carry forward? What words from another person will you never forget? What habits, shaped in the past, do you repeat today?

Consider Tom, the client mentioned in the introduction, who grew up in a family that felt distant yet also stifling at times. His mother—an executive who worked long hours—taught him that emotions were to be mastered, problems to be solved. He felt anxiety about his emotions. He felt ashamed about his ongoing inability to succeed the way she had. In middle school, a teacher encouraged his writing ability, giving him an experience of pride. From that time forward he prized his literary skill, but he also struggled because his mother doubted its value. A small group of friends in college solidified for him a vision of how society—especially the business world—is oppressive and unethical. He felt close to them, and he felt a righteous indignation about much of the world. Tom, like all people, is a sum of his relationships and experiences. Both affect how he sees himself, others, and the world, as well as how he feels about these things.

Take five to ten minutes to write some things down. What have you experienced and learned from relationships?

Functional analytic psychotherapy (FAP) is about creating therapeutic relationships in which you skillfully and strategically relate to clients in order to create a context for change. While many relationships change lives, therapeutic relationships aim to change lives therapeutically.

Before we get into the specifics of FAP and its approach to therapeutic change, let's start at the beginning, with the perspective that informs each moment of FAP. FAP is grounded in a view of psychology and social influence that integrates contextual behavioral science (CBS) with the growing science of social connection, including how social connections affect psychological functioning. This foundation shapes FAP's conceptualization of the therapeutic relationship and the therapist's stance in each moment with clients. In this first chapter, as a way of building toward the more experiential and applied clinical aspects of FAP, we lay out this foundation.

SOCIAL CONNECTIONS MATTER

Human beings need social connection to thrive, and problems with social connection may create profound suffering. This statement is based on a well-established set of scientific findings that speaks to the fundamental importance of social connection. Here are a few of these findings:

- Having poor or extremely limited social relationships has an effect on mortality comparable to smoking and double the effect of obesity (Holt-Lunstad, Smith, & Layton, 2010). In other words, social connections keep people healthy and help them live longer. Researchers have estimated that the negative health impacts of having poor or limited social relationships is equivalent to smoking fifteen cigarettes a day (Holt-Lunstad & Smith, 2012).

- Both poor relationships (characterized by conflict) and limited social relationships (loneliness) negatively impact stress hormones, immune functioning, and cardiovascular functioning, among many other factors (Kiecolt-Glaser et al., 2005; Cacioppo et al., 2002). In fact, social support is a key influence on outcomes for a range of health problems, from cardiovascular disease to tuberculosis to schizophrenia (House, Landis, & Umberson, 1988).

- Humans have considerable neural real estate dedicated to processing social signals, and this attunement to social signals emerges in the first moments following birth, as babies orient toward faces and mimic facial expressions (Meltzoff & Moore, 1977).

- Social relationships are one of the primary mechanisms that drove evolution of the complex human brain, and they're deeply interconnected with biological systems that regulate human physiology and emotion (Cacioppo & Patrick, 2008; Porges, 2001).

Surveying all these findings, evolutionary science tells us that social functioning has been fundamental to our species' survival and has shaped who we are—genetically, physiologically, and behaviorally. We are the ancestors of the humans who related effectively to others, not just in terms of social mechanisms with obvious evolutionary significance, such as sexual interactions and parenting, but in terms of a host of prosocial relational behaviors that function at the level of groups and promote group well-being, such as friendship, altruism, and cooperative learning and problem solving (Bugental, 2000; Sober & Wilson, 1998). We spread to cover the globe not because of our physical strength or individual smarts, but because collectively our abilities to connect and cooperate make us mighty. (For captivating reviews of this perspective, see Harari, 2015, and Henrich, 2016).

There are four ideas that are central to understanding how evolution has shaped us and the social challenges we face today:

1. We evolved to attune to and operate in small groups.

2. We also evolved to compete with other groups.

3. In any relationship we work to find a balance between close and far.

4. The world today—perhaps unlike the one we experienced in our evolutionary history—involves navigating between and across lots of "in groups" and "out groups," close and far. The world today requires that we become skilled at forming and sustaining relationships across change and at balancing our own needs against the needs of the various groups to which we belong.

We evolved to attune to and operate in small groups. Although today we function in a broad array of social groups—from families to communities (virtual and otherwise) to larger units, such as cities, states, and nations—the key groups in which we evolved and flourished for tens of thousands of years tended to be small. At the large end of size spectrum, they typically reached the famous Dunbar number of 150 (Dunbar, 2010). Even in a world of seven billion people, groups at or below the Dunbar number tend to be the ones that shape us the most. As the science of attachment shows, this shaping starts early, with our primary caregivers (Cassidy & Shaver, 1999). It continues through childhood with adolescent friends and classrooms and into adulthood with roommates and romantic partners. Our emotions, behaviors, and sense of self and purpose are fine-tuned to the subtleties of the relationships and bonding that develop within these relatively small groups.

Our ability to coordinate our actions with others depends on a robust capacity for making sense of the minds of others. The flexible connectedness model (Levin et al., 2016; Vilardaga, Estévez, Levin, & Hayes, 2012)—a CBS framework that is gathering empirical support—argues that our ability to connect with others depends on three distinct capacities: perspective taking (the ability to understand the perspective of another), empathy (the ability to feel what it feels like to be in that perspective), and acceptance (the willingness to experience the feelings that come from being in that perspective). These capacities are the psychological mechanisms of connection. We are so immersed in the water of connection that it's easy to forget that our ability to understand others is a marvelously complex psychological task.

In turn, effective engagement in relationships supports optimal well-being. Across the thousands of research studies on this topic (in addition to the findings cited above), three main themes arise. The first is that close relationships and intimacy are highly beneficial (here, "intimacy" means sharing thoughts and feelings that you don't share with just anyone). Even when we have just one or two close relationships, we tend to be happier and healthier, both physically and mentally. The second theme is that perceived social support matters. Again, it isn't how many friends we have, it's whether we feel that there are people who will support us when we need it. The third theme involves social participation—feeling that we're part of a larger community. This could be an extended family, a group of friends, a network of colleagues, a church or other religious group, a club or sports team, or a volunteer organization. What seems to matter is that we feel like we belong to a group—one that's larger than ourselves and our one-on-one intimate relationships.

We evolved to compete with other groups. The flip side of bonding closely with others, of course, is our tendency to relate with caution, guardedness, competitiveness, and aggression. This tendency has a clear role in our dealings with those outside our social groups, especially with people in competitive or aggressive relations with our groups. In fact, evolution science argues that we bond within groups because a highly cooperative group can outcompete other individuals and groups. In other words, the formation of powerful groups is a key human competitive advantage (the same is true for other social creatures).

When in competition, we seem to have a capacity to turn off the machinery that supports connection. We can dehumanize and disconnect in order to not feel the pain of those we harm or ignore. This ability underlies prejudice, avoidance (of the problems of others), a capacity for violence, and so on (Levin et al. 2016). We have a capacity to disconnect as well as to connect.

All relationships involve balancing close and far. In general, we bond within our groups and compete with others who belong to out groups, but we're sensitive to harm and exploitation even within our closest relationships and the small groups we belong to. Therefore we constantly balance closeness with distance, connection with disconnection, opening up with keeping boundaries, and giving to others with serving ourselves. Interacting with or being influenced by others is a double-edged sword: it might do us good, or it might do us harm. Being close to another person always leaves us a little bit vulnerable and requires a leap of faith. This is the tension of being a socially attuned human being, one with social needs and social vulnerabilities. We have a host of social emotions that steer us through this tension. Anger when our needs aren't met. Guilt or shame when we've violated the needs of another, or the group as a whole. Love and gratitude when another meets our needs. Sadness and grief when another betrays us.

The story of our social relationships is, in many ways, one of finding balance between closeness and distance—between getting our needs met and shielding ourselves from harm and vulnerability. As such, it's the story of how we've been hurt and nurtured and, as a result, how we've learned to relate to others. We all carry this tension, because evolution required groups to struggle with this balancing act in order to function. For survival, we needed to weave delicate threads of connection, yet we also needed to be able to sever them when the cost of keeping them became too high. In fact, sometimes it seems that the very ability to step back and disconnect—so that we can come back and reconnect when the time is right—is part of what makes relationships resilient and flexible.

The world today is different. Not only do we all experience this double-edged sword of human connection, we also live in a world that is quite different from the world of our ancestors, the one that shaped and optimized our mechanisms for social connection. That world was often small and relatively stable with a reasonably well-defined worldview and set of social rules. For example, a child born into a hunter-gatherer tribe in south-central Africa in the 1940s lived a life very similar to a child born in the 1840s or 1540s or even AD 40. This child mainly interacted with the same twenty to thirty people over the course of his or her life. This sort of (from the perspective of 2016) stable social arrangement was the norm rather than the exception for most of human history.

The social scale of the world today is much larger. Many groups—defined by differences, for instance, in religious beliefs, politics, career focus, cultural practices, hobbies, as well as school or sports affiliations—intermingle and live together, and this places many more demands on our ability to adapt and cooperate socially. For example, we experience social transition after social transition, in which we enter new groups, build new alliances, and decide whom to trust and ally with. These transitions might continue across our life span, and we may never settle down in a stable community. Our worldview might differ so markedly from that of our own parents that we have difficulty relating to them. At the same time, we are also the children of parents who faced similar disruptions to their social fabric, similar conflicts and negotiations. Today we face challenges that strain our ability to socially adapt as a normal part of life.

SOCIAL CONTEXT MATTERS

The legacy of this evolutionary history is reflected deeply in our psychology. It's not just that we're sensitive and feel better or worse depending on how people interact with us; in all of our human interactions we are working to balance closeness and distance, learning the lessons of our relationships, and carrying the scars and the victories. Because navigating the social world is so important to our species, social relationships *shape* us. They leave lasting marks, influencing our behavior and well-being.

The links between difficulties with social connection and psychological problems are profound and exist across almost all major psychiatric disorders (Barnett & Gotlib, 1988; Beck, 2010; Horowitz, 2004; Leach & Kranzler, 2013; McEvoy, Burgess, Page, Nathan, & Fursland, 2013; Pettit & Joiner, 2006; Pincus, 2005). The causal arrow probably goes in both directions: social stressors cause psychological stress, and psychological stress, in turn, creates social stress. As a result, many clients who seek psychotherapy aren't just struggling with themselves, they're struggling in relation to others and often have a long and painful history of doing so.

Consider Mark, a client who descended into depression after losing his job eight months ago and is now almost entirely isolated. Although he might seem self-absorbed and cut off, his isolation is actually intensely interpersonal. He grew up in a household in which he was typically ignored or criticized, and given this context, he developed an abiding sense that something was wrong with him. He experiences low-level anxiety and reticence that settle into his body whenever he's around people whom he fears will evaluate him negatively. He has coped with his sense of inadequacy by becoming very oriented toward pleasing others, and most people find him to be a nice guy. Yet, just as if he were asked to speak a language he'd never learned, he has few words for expressing his own needs or feelings; he just knows that he feels "bad." As his depression deepened, he became increasingly overwhelmed by phone calls and e-mails from friends and family members. For him, it was easier to avoid their outreach than to experience the pain of speaking to them. Now he's frozen in excruciating isolation, alternating between various aversive states: harsh self-criticism and despair; guilt about his continued withdrawal, which he knows worries his family profoundly; and numb detachment revolving around sleep, television, and pornography, which only reinforce his belief that he's worthless.

Or consider Joan, who suffers with chronic pain related to a work injury that occurred several years ago. While the more obvious cause of her pain is the injury itself, Joan's suffering in the current context involves many other people. She feels guilty for being a burden to her husband, who is not only carrying the family financially but also handling all of the household chores. Driven by guilt, she periodically overexerts herself at home, exacerbating her pain. When her physical therapist prescribed exercises that were too difficult, she was too ashamed to let him know and instead canceled several sessions in a row. In general, she avoids reaching out to friends or former coworkers because she's embarrassed and frustrated and doesn't want people to see her "like this." Occasionally, she expresses her frustration through hostile comments to her children or husband. Over several months, she came to meet the criteria for depression.

In both of these cases, while it might be possible to imagine a version of the person's problem occurring outside the social context, we can only appreciate the full story of suffering—and the challenges involved in changing—by looking at the social contexts in which Mark and Joan live. Similarly, it may be possible to provide therapeutic relief to Mark or Joan by focusing on a narrower band of psychological functioning, such as activity scheduling or acceptance of pain and other feelings. But these apparently intrapersonal processes necessarily play out across interpersonal contexts, starting with the interpersonal context of accepting help from a therapist.

The point is so important, we repeat it: social context has an ongoing and pervasive impact not only on satisfaction with relationships but on functioning in general—mood; stress levels; general well-being; pursuit of goals; health-related behaviors such as exercise and nutrition; sense of safety; and sense of self, meaning, and purpose. In the language of CBS, social interactions are a major context in which all of these other aspects of our psychology are shaped, both developmentally and in the present. Even how we relate to ourselves is shaped by interpersonal contexts, such as how our parents and others have related to us, how they treat us now, and, in turn, how we relate to them. (Of course, there are myriad other nonsocial causes of pain and suffering, such as genetics, cognitive factors, and all sorts of nonsocial traumas and stressors. We are not suggesting replacing the full biopsychosocial model of suffering with a solely social model; rather, we seek to understand the importance of the social piece of the puzzle and to devote adequate attention to it.)

This relationship between social context and overall satisfaction and functioning makes it interesting to look more closely at the metaphor of connection, as in social connection. We often describe our most influential relationships using metaphorical terms like "close" or "deep." In fact, one of the most popular methods for measuring the closeness of relationships asks people to describe, visually, how much their own self overlaps with others—how much of the other's self is, metaphorically, included in one's own self (Aron, Aron, & Smollan, 1992). These metaphors about the closeness or depth of connection reveal a simple truth: that closer or more intimate relationships involve higher degrees of psychological contact. In these intimate relationships we reveal more of ourselves and open up more of ourselves to influence. We are able to give and receive influence and—ideally—this influence is supportive and beneficial. At the same time, if this influence has been painful, or if we've not been taught how to accept and benefit from connection with others, our suffering may be compounded. A painful history of relationships shapes how we exist in our current network of social relations. And psychological suffering in the present tends to impact how we relate as well.

The challenge of the interpersonal process of therapy is amplified, then, when clients' problems interfere with their effective participation in the process of interpersonal influence that lies at the heart of psychotherapy. For example, when Mark avoids giving his therapist the feedback that their sessions feel too abstract because he is afraid of disappointing the therapist (and the therapist doesn't pick up on this misalignment), or when Joan avoids sharing the extent of her distress with her therapist because she is ashamed, the progress of therapy is likely impaired. And it often seems that this kind of challenge is the rule, not the exception, when working with clients who have substantial or long-standing suffering. As therapists, we encounter the whole person through the social interaction of therapy—and of course they bring their social history to that interaction.

SOCIAL LEARNING

Now, from a contextual behavioral science (CBS) standpoint, let's consider a little more closely *how* social interactions shape behavior. The CBS perspective makes up the foundation of the therapeutic stance in FAP, and there are some general CBS principles that apply to our social relationships. Here we'll only introduce some basic concepts. We'll go deeper in the next chapter—again, not for the sake of theory per se, but because the CBS perspective is a key element in FAP's practical clinical tools.

All Behavior Is Learned

The general perspective of CBS practitioners is that the behaviors we work with in psychotherapy are learned. In other words, behaviors have been shaped into their current form by experiences in the world. If you do something, there is a reason why you do it: you learned to behave that way in previous situations.

This general perspective leads to a very accepting stance: behavior always makes sense in its context. Just as we don't fault the billiard ball for going where physics dictates, we don't fault clients for how their behaviors unfold. (This does not mean that behaviors can't be changed, because we are always able to evolve—that is what learning is about. Nor does it mean that behavior is always optimal. *Making sense* is not the same as being optimal.)

For instance, if a client describes feeling dread when you tell her that you're going on vacation, you might discover that she has a history of painful things happening when others leave her alone. Her feelings reflect that history, as do her efforts to convince you to stay in contact. Likewise, a client reporting daily panic attacks probably learned to fear the signs of fear in his own body, even though this fear of fear paradoxically leads to exactly the experience he doesn't want. As you have no doubt experienced, clients can find it illuminating to gain such perspectives on how experience has shaped their behaviors.

The Profound Influence of Social Interactions in Shaping Behavior

Social interactions have such a profound impact on us for two major reasons: other people constantly deliver experiences that shape our behavior, and, as human beings, we come into this world prepared to be deeply shaped by our social experiences. As we move through the social world, the path we're on is largely a result of our history of interactions with others, which shape a whole range of behaviors related to our psychological well-being, including how we express emotions, express our needs, find safety and security, make important decisions, and solve problems. Momentum from the past carries us forward, and we're nudged in one direction or another by our present interactions with others. Each of us is also nudging others in the process; the influence is reciprocal.

Over time, the effects of this shaping can be positive, resulting in the capacity to effectively seek support from others, process emotions, solve problems, and build shared identity and meaning. If this is the case, we can be thankful that our efforts to connect with others have generally met with enough success that we've continued to reach out and increase our skills for doing so. We can be grateful for the reasonably nurturing social environment that we have drawn upon to process painful experiences; make big life decisions; cope with change; or simply enjoy a quiet, connected time with someone.

Unfortunately, the influence of others over time can also be negative, leading to limitations in our ability to engage socially and benefit from social connections in the ways just mentioned (processing emotions, making decisions, and so on). Specifically, we might end up with patterns of relating to others that are constrained by the past. These patterns may help us feel some degree of comfort or invulnerability in the short term, but they usually have long-term costs. As you've probably seen with some of your deeply suffering clients, these patterns can result in a vicious cycle in which suffering becomes a barrier to connecting with others, and lack of connection with others perpetuates suffering.

Of course, these are broad generalizations for the purpose of illustrating how social interactions influence behavior. The reality isn't so black-and-white. For many of us, it might be more accurate to say that we have ways of relating that more or less work well, and that some of our ways of relating have downsides and bear improvement. And when we're under stress or feeling vulnerable, these limitations may be more costly and may be linked directly to our suffering.

USING THE THERAPEUTIC RELATIONSHIP AS THE CONTEXT FOR CHANGE

Understanding the relationship between social connection and psychological problems, and how improved social connection can lead to improved well-being, leads to a very particular conceptualization of the function and significance of the therapeutic relationship. The therapeutic relationship is a source of influence on the client's behavior—an influence exerted in the here and now. When clients seek therapy, and especially when their psychological problems involve difficulties relating to other people, the therapeutic relationship presents both an opportunity and a liability.

Imagine that Tom, from earlier in this chapter, has come to see you. His responses to you seem stilted. He struggles to articulate his thoughts. He can't seem to find a path forward through life's difficulties. If you become anxious about his uncertainty, or too eager to help, you might bite the same hook his mother bit: completing his sentences, offering solutions, rushing to solve problems. With the best of intentions, you risk perpetuating an insidious interaction in which Tom receives the message that he is deficient and less capable than others. He may comply and yet remain demoralized.

Let us put it more explicitly: in the therapy relationship there is the liability that you may recreate and reinforce the interpersonal problems that are causing your client's suffering. Here are a few other examples:

- A client who tends to criticize others harshly does so with the therapist. The therapist withdraws or responds defensively. The client in turn ramps up his criticism and eventually stops coming to therapy.

- A client typically avoids asking for what she needs. The therapist doesn't know how to help her and makes suggestions that aren't helpful. The client doesn't follow through on these unhelpful suggestions, so the therapist deems her lazy or unmotivated. Consequently, the client feels shame and is even less likely to ask for what she needs, creating a cycle that persists for weeks.

- A client has an internal process of endless rumination and tends to talk with other people in a similar way, moving through tedious, complaining loops. The therapist feels competing urges to listen attentively and recognize the client's pain and to interrupt in impatient frustration. When the therapist finally does make an effort to focus on behavior change, the client perceives the therapist's judgment and feels even more anxious.

This liability, however, is also an opportunity. In essence, the therapeutic relationship gives the therapist an opportunity to be an agent for disrupting dysfunctional social patterns and nurturing more effective ones. You have an opportunity to clearly see the interpersonal issues that clients bring to therapy. You can choose to engage with these issues therapeutically, rather than merely recapitulating what clients experience with others outside of session. The result can be a virtuous circle in which clients improve their relationship with you and thus their relationships with others, contributing to improved overall well-being.

For instance, with Tom you might recognize that his social history has shaped his reticence and anxiety about pleasing others. You might then gently and persistently present opportunities for Tom to voice his own needs and find his own way forward. You might challenge Tom to take those opportunities.

Let's look at a few other ways to create a virtuous cycle using the previous examples:

- You might point out to the client, compassionately, that his criticisms are painful and gently link your experience to the experience of other people the client has pushed away. You might challenge the client to collaborate with you to find other ways to voice his needs.

- You might notice the client's passivity and shame and work closely with her to notice moments when she pulls back, suggesting that she instead find the language to articulate what she wants in therapy and in life.

- You might explain to the client the tension you feel between a wish to listen attentively and a concern that the client's storytelling is not the most efficient use of time in session. Then you could come up with a balanced solution that meets the needs of the client in order to make progress in therapy.

The two fundamental pillars of FAP—functional analysis and genuine connection—balance each other and help you pursue the opportunity to create a relationship that is uniquely therapeutic for each client.

Genuine, Authentic Therapeutic Relationships Are Essential

To experience a different way of relating is a more potent vehicle for shaping relational behavior than merely talking about it. Again, this is a statement about how people learn; we often learn more effectively through experience, also called *experiential learning*, than through passively receiving information. This is not to say that talking is not important—much of our relating consists of talking—but instead that experiencing a challenge and practicing a different behavior can be a potent context for change.

Let's again consider Tom. He may only come to fully appreciate his experiences with his mother, the effects of his history, and the degree to which he is oriented toward pleasing other people through his experience of relating to you and the challenges you offer. More importantly, with you he might begin to find the courage to step through the sense of anxiety that has prevented him from making clear requests and statements of need to others.

Experiential learning in a therapy relationship is a type of work that requires us, as therapists, to be open and direct about what is happening in the relationship, which is a level of genuineness or self-disclosure that many therapists find challenging. This directness might simply manifest as an observation about how the client engages in therapy; for example, "I notice that I find myself uncertain about what exactly you want to achieve here." Or, "I notice that you tend to acquiesce to whatever I suggest we put on the agenda." Or, "I notice you seem quite skeptical about many of the things I say."

Experiential learning might also mean disclosing more vulnerable aspects of ourselves or our reactions to clients. For instance, we might express our frustration to a client who is persistently late, knowing that he tends to avoid contact with the negative consequences of his actions. We might ask him to make contact with our reaction. We might invite him to notice what emotions or sensations come up for him as a result.

Because such interactions are complex, nuanced, and individual, it's important that they are genuine, meaning the therapist is operating in the context of his or her actual experiences and reactions to the situation. Why? First, because any or all of the reactions brought to bear may be relevant to therapy, a therapeutic relationship shouldn't be simpler than a real relationship. Second, human beings are equipped with a fine capacity to detect lack of genuineness—that is, when others are withholding responses or reactions. When lack of genuineness is detected, it is not a neutral fact. Though it may not trigger a primordial sense of threat, it will at least trigger caution, and this can undermine the quality of the therapy relationship. This reaction is especially likely for clients who have been harmed or betrayed by others.

Functional Analysis Keeps Us on Track

Because genuine, authentic relationships are complex, we use functional analysis (FA) to stay on track regarding therapeutic goals. FA is an assessment process in which we use learning principles to understand what a particular behavior represents for the client in the context of his or her own history and life situation.

To that end, we consider questions along these lines:

How was this behavior shaped in the past?

How did it function in the past?

How does it function now?

What costs are associated with it?

In this way, we get a handle on which behaviors represent problems in the client's life, and which—despite seeming clumsy or imperfect—actually represent important steps toward growth. (A third class of behaviors includes those that might grab our attention—for example, a client who is a conspicuous name-dropper—but do not represent any clinically significant issue. It's important to discriminate these behaviors from the other two classes so that we don't try to "treat" what doesn't need to be treated.)

In turn, FA helps ensure that we respond strategically and therapeutically to clients in the moment based on our understanding of their problems and the growth or behavior change they need. For instance, with Tom, we might notice that some clumsy assertions of his needs are actually an important step toward assertiveness.

You might notice that there is a potential contradiction in this process: What if FA dictates that we should see a given behavior as growth (for example, Tom should be more assertive), yet we genuinely find the growth behavior unpleasant (for example, we experience Tom as demanding in ways we are reluctant to support)? Should we suppress our personal reaction in order to nurture Tom's growth?

Luckily, this contradiction rarely arises in reality. First, when we take the time to really understand a client, whether through FA or other means, our responses to the client tend to naturally line up with FA: we feel satisfaction and happiness about the client's steps toward growth because we understand the meaning and the struggle behind those steps. Similarly, we feel some level of genuine frustration or disappointment (balanced of course with compassion and understanding) when we see clients stuck in self-defeating patterns. Second, if you can't naturally respond positively to the client's growth, then this behavior is likely something important to address. For instance, you might say to Tom, "Something is coming up for me. You know I'm supportive of you being more assertive. And I notice there's a way that you're erring on the side of being blunt, even harsh. Have you noticed that too?"

Because authentic relationships involve two people, in the process of FAP our own reactions and perceptions are as important as those of the client. Accordingly, we also continuously aim FA at ourselves, refining our self-knowledge as therapists, asking how we're contributing to the therapeutic moment, and ensuring that our approach serves clients and not our own ends. The assumption is that therapists are also human and therefore susceptible to the influence of clients, just as they are susceptible to ours. When we relate to clients in their suffering, especially if things are happening quickly or with a great deal of emotion, complexity, or struggle, we can lose our footing. Again, FA helps keep us on target.

In the next chapter, we'll lay out the essential, practical principles of the contextual behavioral science perspective that lies at the heart of FAP and similar treatments (most notably, acceptance and commitment therapy).

SUMMARY

- Poor social connection poses as much mortality risk as smoking cigarettes.

- From a CBS perspective, social relationships are a key context for shaping psychological functioning—mood, motivation, emotion, and achievement—and therefore well-being across one's life span.

- Psychotherapy involves processes of social connection and influence, through the therapeutic relationship, that can shape change in the client's psychological and social functioning.

- FAP asks you to balance a genuine, authentic way of relating to your client with understanding based on functional analysis—a way of assessing the function of what is happening in the therapy relationship for each individual client. By doing so, you can ensure that your response to the client is therapeutic and does not perpetuate the client's problems in relationships.

CHAPTER 2

Take a Contextual Behavioral Perspective

To understand all is to forgive all.

—Anne Louise Germaine de Staël

Carl Rogers rose to fame in the United States and worldwide by expressing clearly and passionately that what matters most in the process of psychotherapy is not the expert knowledge of therapists, but rather their personal qualities and how they bring those qualities to their relationships with clients. His work promoted a sea change in the helping professions and influenced the way clinicians are trained to this day. The treatment approach he developed remains the benchmark against which many others are compared. Of particular note, Rogers stood against efforts to control or change clients; he was the voice of nurturance and unwavering support, in opposition to those who advocated manipulation and control.

What is less well-known is that Rogers was also interested in the scientific study of the process of therapy. To that end, he allowed a number of researchers to have access to recordings of his psychotherapy sessions. One resulting study is particularly relevant to FAP. In 1966, Charles Truax published his findings regarding Rogers's responses to clients. His expressions of warmth and regard for his clients were not, in fact, unconditional; his responsiveness was not the same regardless of a client's behavior. Rogers responded more warmly or with more encouragement to some kinds of remarks, particularly those that represented client growth, and responded in a more reserved way to others. The result of this pattern was that, over the course of therapy, the client remarks that Rogers responded to in a nurturing way increased in frequency, whereas the other types of remarks decreased in frequency.

How could it be that the man who preached unconditional support was actually responding conditionally? The answer is simple: in keeping with the science and principles reviewed in chapter 1, the therapeutic relationship (or any relationship, with intimate relationships often being more influential) may exert more or less subtle influence on the client and therefore function as a process for behavior change. This influence happens quite naturally in a social connection that feels completely accepting and supportive.

Today, such processes are deliberately harnessed—and linked to other established processes of behavior change—in a range of evidence-based therapies, including motivational interviewing, acceptance and commitment therapy, and dialectical behavior therapy. FAP focuses directly on shaping interpersonal behaviors that affect social functioning and psychological well-being and on cultivating caring therapeutic relationships that deliberately and authentically shape these behaviors. This stance represents an alignment of the perspective of behavioral science, Rogers's perspective, and caring relationships and principles of learning. A key aspect of this alignment is thinking about therapy relationships in terms of qualities (such as warmth and genuineness) as well as processes of behavior, learning, and influence.

Contextual behavioral science (CBS) is the contemporary field of study that best represents FAP's perspective on learning principles and how to put them to use clinically in a therapeutic relationship. In this chapter we introduce you to that theoretical perspective. Our stance is that using CBS clinically doesn't require a massive investment in the study of its theory or philosophy. Instead it requires understanding a relatively small set of core principles or assumptions. Think of this approach as the 80–20 rule for clinical CBS: 20 percent of the CBS principles and assumptions account for 80 percent of the approach's clinical utility. If you want to spend time reading about and exploring the other 80 percent, you can do that. (We enthusiastically recommend *The ABCs of Human Behavior*, by Jonas Ramnero and Niklas Törneke for this purpose.)

In outline form, here is the 20 percent that you need to know:

- Everything people do is behavior.

- Behaviors are events.

- All behavior happens in the moment.

- Behaviors are steered by consequences.

- Learning by consequences sometimes creates less than optimal results.

- You can't understand all the ways behavior is influenced, but partial, iterative understanding can lead to useful results.

- These ways of understanding people and behavior are fundamentally empathic and compassionate.

We discuss each point in greater detail below.

EVERYTHING PEOPLE DO IS BEHAVIOR

Let's start with the term at the center of this discussion: "behavior." Behavior is what we study, understand, and influence. Behavior is what people do; it's action. It's how we move through the world, transition from one situation to the next, and exert influence.

Many of us are used to making a distinction between thinking and behavior, in which behavior means outwardly observable actions like walking or talking. But in CBS we include in the same bundle everything that people do: speaking, thinking, imagining, hearing, perceiving, feeling, doubting, knowing, believing, intuiting, hearing, and on and on. If a live person can do it, it's behavior. Right now as you read this, that's behavior. Right now as you think about whether what you're reading makes sense, that's behavior too. And right now as you notice yourself thinking, that's behavior too. Being aware of your behavior is behavior. It's all part of the same stream of behavior, interacting with the world, within itself, and with the behavior of others.

Bundling all actions together in this way becomes useful, as we will explain.

By the way, when you speak with clients, you don't have to use the clunky term "behavior." You can use whatever word makes sense in the context: action, thinking, choosing, movement of spirit, or whatever. It doesn't matter, as long as you keep track of the concept at the center of this word cloud: there are many things people do that can be looked at through the principles of learning.

BEHAVIORS ARE EVENTS

A key characteristic of a behavior is that it is an event, occurring at a particular time and place with a particular person. Think for a moment about how many behaviors have occurred for you so far today. Think of all the overt actions you have made—those we could see if we were watching you via a camera. Think as well of all the covert psychological behaviors that have happened: each thought, each sensation, each decision, and so on. Think of the discrete fleeting behaviors that make up a moment. Think as well of the extended, complex behaviors that make up the meaning of our days and our lives—reading this book, getting a graduate degree, and so on.

Watch the flow of behavior inside you in this moment:

Now I am thinking this…

Now I am feeling this…

Now I am going here…

And thinking this…

As you might expect, there's no shortage of behaviors to work with. Behavior is a continuous, complex stream that moves through each of the seven billion people on the planet (sleep is a behavior too). In fact, so much behavior is occurring in any given moment that there's simply no way any of us can maintain conscious awareness of all of our behaviors, let alone all of the influences on our behavior. The result is a kind of chaos—not in the sense of disorder, but in the sense of complexity to such a degree that it often defies mechanistic understanding. This is the medium of psychology.

ALL BEHAVIOR HAPPENS IN THE MOMENT

A feature of behavior is how often we slip away from contact with or awareness of the behavior that is happening in the moment.

Here's an example that will be familiar to most psychotherapists: you ask a client what he's feeling, meaning what's happening in his body right now, and he simply says "bad," or "I feel like I can't get anything right." These are, of course, conventional, sensible responses. Yet notice that they put the client at a distance from what's actually happening: that his body is feeling a certain way, that he isn't breathing very much, that he isn't noticing the tension in his shoulders or the way he's clasped his hands around his knees. In particular, he isn't noticing that he's having the thought *I can't get anything right* or *I feel bad*, which is quite distinct from the sensations he is actually experiencing. He might live much of his life in this way, wrapped up in generalized thoughts about what is happening, yet rarely in contact with the momentary play of events flowing through him and how this behavior is shaped and shapes itself.

In a similar way, as therapists we might talk about clients having a personality disorder, being resistant, having a transference reaction, being psychopathic, being depressed, or having a certain attachment style. Yet if we stop at such terms or labels, it's difficult if not impossible to locate, in time and space, the concrete behaviors we're referring to. Unless we provide more information, we're obligating others to guess what we mean or, worse, to make blind assumptions that they know exactly what we mean. If another therapist tells you, clinician to clinician, that a client she's referring to you is depressed, you might have some general ideas about what's happening, and you might know what sorts of questions to ask to get more specific information about the client, but you don't know any of the specifics. This person might be an insomniac who obsesses about suicide but has no notable feelings of sadness, only a ringing emptiness. Or this person might spend eighteen hours a day in bed consumed by grief and bouts of crying. At best, the other therapist's description orients you toward what sorts of questions could be helpful to ask the client. That's very useful indeed, but it's only the beginning of an assessment.

Of course general labels aren't inert. They shape how we relate to the person we're labeling. The client who labels himself a failure stays at a distance from himself and treats himself unkindly. We react with distrust or disgust to the client labeled a psychopath. Labels form a basis for judgments and discriminations. And insidiously, these labels can steer our behavior even when we aren't deliberately being pernicious or judgmental.

Because the flow of behavior is the medium of psychology, and because we often lose track of that flow in ways that distance us from ourselves and what matters, the first and most basic step in the CBS perspective is to orient ourselves to seeing behavior as the flow of events it really is. Relating to the flow of events in this way is about humane, connected, and empathetic understanding—staying close to the story of what is actually happening rather than our stories and labels about those events. It's about getting in touch with what is actually happening here and now—and whatever we wish to change.

Here are some of the fundamental behaviors we orient ourselves to in psychotherapy:

- Actions

- Thoughts

- Utterances

- Images

- Urges

- Sensations

- Feelings

- Questions

BEHAVIORS ARE STEERED BY CONSEQUENCES

The experiential foundation of CBS is noticing what's happening in the moment. We aim to notice, with some level of precision and mindfulness, how judgments may cloud our view of what's happening. In turn, that in-the-moment awareness allows us to begin to notice how our behavior is shaped—steered this way or that way—by the consequences it creates. In other words, the CBS perspective is about making sense of the flow of experience in terms of some basic principles of learning.

Again, there are really only a few principles that are especially useful to understand:

- Some behavior functions to increase contact with certain things.

- Some behavior functions to reduce contact with certain things.

- When a behavior functions to get a payoff, a person will be more likely to repeat that behavior in the context where he or she received that payoff.

- When a behavior doesn't get a payoff, or it incurs a cost, a person will be less likely to repeat that behavior in the context where he or she didn't receive that payoff or incurred a cost.

In the sections that follow, we'll take a closer look at each of these ideas.

Some Behaviors Function to Move Us Toward Things

There are certain things or states or situations in the world that we tend to move toward. When we are thirsty, we drink water. When we are lonely, we seek social contact. Often we move toward things that feel good or meet some biological need or give meaning. The things that we move toward are referred to as *appetitive*.

It's important to not assume that the thing itself is intrinsically appetitive, because what is appetitive for us depends on the situation we are in (for example, whether we are thirsty or lonely) and, to some greater or lesser extent, who we are and our particular history. Many people like donuts and will move toward them, but after a few donuts, the donuts are no longer appetitive. In turn, in any large crowd of people, there will be a variety of different purposes, sets of values, tastes, and so on—in other words, different things that are appetitive.

The flow of behavior tends to move us toward what we find appetitive. What were the things your behavior functioned to move you toward today? As you read this book, what does your behavior move you toward?

Some Behaviors Function to Move Us Away

Conversely, sometimes the function of our behavior is to reduce contact with or move away from something. Things that we move away from are referred to as *aversive*. The first three donuts were appetitive. The fourth donut—the one that makes us sick—becomes aversive. We push away certain thoughts or feelings because they are painful. We react against certain statements from others.

The Payoffs of a Behavior Can Reinforce That Behavior

Sometimes behavior gets a payoff: it moves us toward an appetitive thing that we enjoy or away from an aversive thing that causes us harm or distress. When we have these experiences, learning happens:

> When our behavior successfully moves us toward an appetitive thing or moves us away from an aversive thing, we become more likely to repeat the behavior in the same or similar situations in the future. This is called *reinforcement*, the process by which the probability of behavior in a given setting increases.

The Costs of a Behavior Can Decrease That Behavior

At other times, behaviors have costs: they take us farther away from the appetitive thing or bring us closer to the aversive thing. When this happens, another type of learning, called *punishment*, occurs: those behaviors become less likely to recur in similar circumstances in the future.

As with aversive and appetitive stimuli, whether a given consequence will actually be reinforcing or punishing can't be determined in advance. You have to wait and see how the consequences affect the behavior.

When you stand back and observe the flow of behavior, you can begin to see more clearly the different ways that consequences influence behaviors. For example:

- When there is a strong payoff coming, or you have a strong sense of the payoff for a behavior in the moment, it is easier to endure the aversive things that might happen along the way.

- When there is no sense of payoff, it is more difficult to persist in the face of aversive things.

- One of the most desperate places to get stuck is when you know that a behavior is important because of its long-term consequences, yet you constantly get derailed while pursuing it because of the pain involved, or because numerous other appetitive "shiny gold objects" draw you away.

Function Is Active

CBS doesn't take the view that humans are passive agents or automatons who are pushed around by the world and are at the mercy of their environment. Central to the principles we've just outlined—about how behavior functions—is the notion that humans are actively operating on the environment around them. Every aspect of human behavior is an active, ongoing, mutual interaction with the world. The CBS perspective considers how behavior is shaped by context *and* the ways behaviors create or perpetuate context and the situations people find themselves in.

This interdependent relationship is the central meaning of the word "function." How does this behavior produce consequences in the world? What consequences has the behavior produced in the past that have shaped it, making the behavior worth repeating now?

PROBLEMS WITH LEARNING

The behavior we engage in now, in this situation, reflects the history of consequences we received in similar situations in the past. Because we are always bringing past experience to the present moment (that's what learning is), the past is always present.

At the same time, what worked and was reinforced in the past does not always work well in the present. Said another way, the influence of historic consequences doesn't always steer us well in the long run.

One form of this breakdown involves limited contact with the future. We could call it the problem of "consequences now matter more than consequences later." For instance, when people are addicted to cigarettes, they are excessively under the influence of the immediate results of smoking (for example, relief from tension and withdrawal symptoms), despite the fact that the long-term consequences can be deadly. Or consider how this dynamic plays out for Mark, whom we mentioned earlier. He learned to avoid expressing his needs to the important people in his life because, due to early life experiences, it makes him anxious to do so. In the short term, he avoids the anxiety of making requests, but in the long term he stands a good chance of feeling more disappointed or resentful because his needs aren't met.

In these kinds of situations, behavior is too heavily constrained by its short-term results, despite the fact that being constrained in this way doesn't work well in the long run. This pattern happens in interpersonal contexts all the time. We avoid raising a difficult issue in the moment because we don't want to feel uncomfortable in the short term. Yet that avoidance leads to ongoing dissatisfaction and a bigger problem later. Or we gossip, complain, or attack because it feels satisfying in the moment, even though a few hours later we feel ashamed, and in the long run we undermine trust and closeness.

Another form of the breakdown of learning involves the past. In this case, behavior that functioned well in the past can persist into the present even though it no longer functions very well. We could call it the problem of "past learning is out of touch with the present." Consider Gillian, who avoids expressing her wishes because she was consistently punished for doing so as a child. She may persist in this behavior even though her current partner is eager to understand her and respond compassionately toward her. Behavior that's been met with such painful consequences in the past can be especially problematic because the person now avoids the situation or behavior that prompted the pain, as is the case for Gillian. In fact, she may feel fear simply at the thought of expressing her wishes. When people avoid such situations, they deprive themselves of opportunities for new learning. As a result, Gillian loses the chance to learn that expressing her wishes will actually produce positive consequences. Because of her avoidance, she remains under the influence of old learning and is less effective in her current context. This kind of avoidance can persist for decades.

If psychological problems occur when past learning excessively controls our behavior, more effective behavior often occurs when people balance being guided by the past with being responsive to what seems to be working best in the present. In other words, we benefit from past learning but remain able to flexibly adapt our behavior to the present moment. Similarly, if problems occur when short-term consequences excessively control our behavior, such that we cause long-term problems, more effective behavior typically occurs when we build a capacity to tolerate whatever short-term consequences are necessary to achieve our long-term aims; more effective behavior also occurs when we are able to find a clearer sense of the long-term value of our actions here and now in the present. Or in other words, when we have a vivid sense of the purpose or goal behind our actions, we become much more able to tolerate frustrations and discomforts and forgo easy distractions in favor of persevering toward what matters to us. CBS terms these capacities, taken together, as *psychological flexibility.*

In turn, taking the CBS stance—being able to see our behavior clearly and see the ways that it gets stuck—tends to help us become more psychologically flexible.

LANGUAGE: A VERY SPECIAL KIND OF BEHAVIOR

Notice how much of the CBS stance is about learning to "see," that is, observe and label behaviors and how behaviors function. All of this involves language—and language, like everything else people do, is behavior. Not surprisingly, then, language plays a very special role in the CBS framework. In humans, language is an important behavior that allows us to operate in and be shaped by social interactions. By and large, therapy is a process of language. On the flip side, sometimes language can powerfully curtail our flexibility, such as when people decide, based on past experience, that they know exactly what's going on and, as a result, miss what's really happening.

In our treatment of language in this book, we're guided by relational frame theory (RFT; Hayes, Barnes-Holmes, & Roche, 2001), an empirically established CBS account of language and cognition. Briefly, RFT posits that the behavior at the core of language is the behavior of relating. For instance, we relate objects and words to one another, such as when we relate the verbal label "tree" to an actual tree. Similarly, we can relate words to each other; for example, we say, "Blue is a color." We can relate things in many ways. For instance, "blue is a color" is a relation of hierarchy, given that color is a category that contains several things, one of which is blue. Another type of relation is that of opposition: day is not night. These are very fundamental relations. The analysis of RFT has allowed us to break the operation of language down into these fundamental pieces of behavior. These relations, in turn, influence how we respond to the things we're relating to. For example, "This apple is good" or "This apple is bad" steers our behavior.

As for language operating naturally in a mature human being, that's what happens when you take these very simple relations, multiply them by a trillion, then put them in a blender, along with other people and massive chunks of the world, and run that blender at high speed for several decades. The result is a very complex soup of relations and influences and an ability to engage in the present-moment behavior of relating a whole bunch of things that aren't in the here and now to whatever is present. Again, these relations influence how we respond to the things to which we're relating. Remember when we warned in chapter 1 that labels are not neutral? For instance, if you relate your child's teacher and "stupid," thinking to yourself *That teacher is stupid*, you'll respond to him differently than if you relate other words to him. Similarly, some clients may come to therapy with all sorts of thoughts about how they should interact with you—without having any prior experience with you, or perhaps with therapists in general.

Part of what we do carefully in therapy, then, through the process of functional analysis and our therapeutic relationship, is influence how people relate to themselves and their behavior and the world around them. From the CBS perspective, this is no doubt a "common factor" across any form of therapy. If you're interested in learning more about RFT and this common factor, we encourage you to check out *Learning RFT* (Törneke, 2010) or *Mastering the Clinical Conversation* (Villatte, Villatte, & Hayes, 2015). In this book, our presentation of FAP is strongly influenced by RFT; however, we won't invoke RFT directly beyond this point.

THE CLIENT IS RIGHT: DON'T ASSUME, ASSESS

If you're having the thought that learning is incredibly complex, you're right. When we study behavior, we're studying something of marvelous complexity. As therapists, we must witness the ongoing flow of this complexity and bring great humility and appreciation to our attempts to influence it. This is of course what we all know as clinicians. CBS echoes this wisdom. As Skinner said, "Behavior is a difficult subject matter, not because it is inaccessible, but because it is extremely complex. Since it is a process, rather than a thing, it cannot easily be held still for observation. It is changing, fluid, and evanescent, and for this reason it makes great technical demands upon the ingenuity and energy of the scientist" (1953, 15). Of course, for mental health therapists, we typically have only one hour per week with a given client, so this difficulty is greatly compounded: it's like trying to watch a parade through a pinhole.

This complexity and inaccessibility of behavior has direct implications for how we must venture to understand it from a CBS perspective. Beware of any tendency to dismiss or distort clients and their experience in service of preserving a case conceptualization or other theory about how things should be. Instead, listen and watch and see what works. An anecdote from the early science of behaviorism illustrates this concept: A famous scientist reached the end of some grueling and fastidious experiments with rats and found that one of his well-considered hypotheses didn't seem to hold up to reality. But he accepted this, saying, "The rat is always right." In other words, clients might not behave as we think they should, but they are nevertheless behaving exactly as they ought to.

The good news is that we don't need to know everything in order to be helpful. The goal is not to be right; it's to be helpful. We can take a pragmatic approach and focus on knowledge that works. A large component of the art of behavior therapy is knowing how much factual information and specificity is necessary in order to focus treatment without making it unnecessarily complicated or inflexible. We don't need to find the "best" way or the "right" way. After all, there are numerous ways to describe clinical phenomena and a variety of paths to behavior change. Our task as clinicians is to find one path that works.

WHY IT'S IMPORTANT TO UNDERSTAND LEARNING AND FOCUS ON FUNCTION

Hopefully everything you've read in this chapter has underscored that CBS is an intrinsically compassionate way of understanding and working with clients. At its core, CBS is about seeing behavior and seeing the influences of learning in the present so we can become more flexible and effective in the present.

Everyone has a history that makes up the meaning of this moment. And yet that history is invisible to us, as observers. So it is so easy to misunderstand people, to miss the meaning of their actions. In psychotherapy especially, in which our job is to create change in behaviors, we need ways to see that invisible context of learning and function.

Social psychology research on what's called the *fundamental attribution error* (Jones & Harris, 1967; Gilbert, 2002) has nicely captured our view on this point. On the one hand, we tend to explain our own mistakes and failings through an appeal to context; for example, "I wasn't lazy. I had a lot on my plate this week. I was stressed and needed to rest." We can make these kinds of generous interpretations of our own behavior because, in part, we have access to the contexts that shaped us. Furthermore, we tend to provide similarly generous interpretations for the behavior of those we care about.

On the other hand, we aren't as generous with strangers, as we can't see beyond their appearance and their history is invisible to us. The same is true of people whom, for whatever reason, we dislike. We're much more likely to judge them based on their supposed intrinsic qualities as people. The attribution error we make in these cases is that we blame people's attributes for their behavior, rather than imagining that, within their context, their behaviors make sense, as we do for ourselves.

Another way to say this is that we tend to see people's behavior in its context when we're at our most compassionate. In a sense, seeing someone's behavior in context is simply another way of describing empathy and understanding. And likewise, we are much more likely to feel understood by someone who takes a generous view of our actions and more likely to be open to that person's influence. CBS is about developing that generous stance of seeing action in context. In fact, CBS researchers (Hooper, Erdogan, Keen, Lawton, & McHugh, 2015) recently showed that training in perspective taking decreases the chance that people will commit the fundamental attribution error.

Not surprisingly, for many people seeking psychotherapy, one way they've gotten stuck is by failing to see their own actions in context. They've become bogged down in negative and generalized self-attributions: "I'm a loser," "I'm unlovable," and so on. By helping them see their behavior in context, we can help them achieve a more self-compassionate stance. And as we said in the previous chapter, when you deeply understand someone and care for her, then what's good for her—her growth—will naturally become appetitive for you, so you'll tend to nurture or reinforce more of that. Perhaps this is what a skilled listener does, even without noticing it. And given how central social connection is to well-being for humans, as discussed in chapter 1, it should come as no surprise that a close relationship can be such a subtle and sensitive instrument for behavior change.

CBS helps us get below appearances in order to investigate the deeper functions of behavior and to build a deeper kind of empathy and understanding and, therefore, influence. In turn, we seek to see a client's problematic behaviors as they happen, respond in ways that evoke new and more effective behaviors, and reinforce those behaviors so they take root, not only in the client's relationship with us but in other contexts as well.

In the next chapter, we turn to more concrete ways in which we put the CBS perspective to work in the therapy relationship using functional analysis.

SUMMARY

- The psychological perspective at the root of FAP is contextual behavioral science (CBS).

- The CBS perspective involves a small set of basic assumptions, including

  - everything people do is behavior, including thinking, feeling, sensing, and so on;

  - behaviors are events happening in time and space; and

  - behavior is steered by its consequences. Some consequences cause the behavior to increase in frequency; other consequences cause the behavior to decrease in frequency. "Function" is what a behavior achieves in terms of these consequences.

- There are problems that result from learning through consequences. Behavior can become too constrained by past experiences and therefore be out of touch with the present. It can also become too influenced by short-term consequences, even if it leads to long-term costs.

- The influences on behavior are complex. You won't be able to gain a definitive understanding of them, but you can attain a good enough understanding to exert influence.

- Understanding function and learning history is a road to empathic, compassionate understanding—to making sense of the contexts and experiences that lead people to behave as they do.

CHAPTER 3

Stay Grounded in Functional Analysis

A little reflection will show that there is beyond question a body of very important but unorganized knowledge which cannot possibly be called scientific in the sense of knowledge of general rules: the knowledge of the particular circumstances of time and place.

—F. A. Hayek

Toward the end of the session, Tom seems to freeze. He had been engaging well, talking about his progress with writing this week. You ask him what obstacles might come up inside of him as he continues his writing and job search next week.

"I still struggle with…am I likable?" He pauses. "Sometimes I wonder… It's silly, but—what do you really think about me?"

You stumble for a moment, remembering a supervisor's old rule: don't answer the question directly. But that doesn't seem quite right in the moment, so instead you decide to offer honesty. "I want you to know, first of all, that I'm honest with you about how I feel about you. I have so much respect for the work you're doing here. I look forward to our sessions every week."

"I appreciate you saying that," Tom says. "I guess there's part of me that thinks you're just being nice."

You see him freezing up for the next few minutes. He averts his eyes, and his breathing is high in his chest. You're not sure what else to say, so you wrap up the session.

A few hours later you receive an email: "I'm so sorry I screwed up. I froze. I could see the look on your face when I said you were just being nice. I always mess up like that. I hope you will forgive me."

What was happening for Tom in that moment in session? And for you?

Functional analysis (FA) is the assessment framework that guides the process in FAP. It stands on top of the basic contextual behavioral foundation described in chapter 2. Moving beyond the general stance of CBS involves building a highly individualized and specific grasp of a particular client's behaviors and their functions—including the "particular circumstances of time and place" that have shaped and continue to shape this client's actions.

FA can be a daunting, technical process. Like building skill at chess, or painting, or business negotiation, it can take years to master. This is because using FA to understand a unique situation requires not just understanding FA principles but also developing the capacity for pattern recognition when applying those principles (How does this particular situation make sense? Have I seen this pattern before?). Pattern recognition facilitates making sense of complex information, and it is born from years of experience. We cannot promise to make you an expert at FA in one chapter. Instead, as in the previous chapter, we aim to present the key principles that represent the core clinical value of FA, and in this way we aim to get you started on the road to mastery. It will be up to you to practice.

Doing a functional analysis suggests a discrete procedure, with distinct rules and a beginning, middle, and end. In clinical practice, FA might take this form at times, but more often—as with many forms of assessment—the process is more diffuse, iterative, and flexible. In fact, flexibility is a strength of FA. You can use it as much or as little as is effective. To start, we suggest the following reframing: rather than thinking of FA as a procedure, we invite you to practice "thinking functionally." Just as a chess player thinks about positions, a painter about light, or a negotiator about opening statements, a successful practitioner of FAP thinks about function.

Thinking functionally is a process of building your understanding of how a behavior functions in the contexts that have shaped it. It revolves around three key questions:

What is the behavior?

In what contexts does it or did it occur?

What is or was its function in those contexts?

FAP especially focuses on functional thinking to work with a client's problem behaviors that show up in the therapy process. The aim in FAP is to create a highly individualized, assessment-based approach to each therapy relationship. As you participate in the therapy process, functional thinking is a touchstone to return to again and again—a reminder to notice function, to not let avoidance of important issues take root in the process, and to work the process in a way that's effective for the client. The process is what matters. FA is a tool for being focused and strategic in the process, not a replacement for the process.

In this chapter, we'll start with a broad application of thinking functionally and gradually narrow the focus to thinking about the therapy process. In the sections that follow, we lay out some basic steps involved in thinking functionally in FAP, starting with the questions above.

STEP 1: ORIENT TO BEHAVIORS AND CONTEXTS

In the case of Tom, whom we've been following from chapter 1, Tom came to therapy stating that his problem is "feeling so unworthy all the time. I need to feel more confident." This is a typical presenting problem that we encounter in therapy. It is focused on a pervasive negative feeling and an inability to shake that feeling. To boot, it comes with an idea about what is needed instead: to feel confident. As you have no doubt experienced as a clinician, however, while the original presenting problem often describes exactly what the client most longs to fix, only sometimes does the presenting problem describe in a useful way what needs to change in order to produce that shift. We have to look deeper to find that useful understanding.

The situation is similar any time we're working with a complex system, and behavior is certainly a complex system. If you go to a physical therapist because your lower back hurts, it might turn out that the source of the problem lies in the placement of your computer monitor or a problem in your feet. Similarly, when a person feels depressed, the proximal source of the low mood might lie in a frustrating work environment, a divorce, a medical condition, and so on. Chronic irritability might originate in a sense of shame. Anxiety and a feeling of being out of control might arise out of rigid efforts to control. And so on. Clients may or may not be aware of the links between their problems and the sources of these problems. (And of course there may be multiple "sources" interacting in complex ways.)

In turn, the pathway that leads from source to problem might involve a number of steps. The placement of the computer monitor causes lower back pain because neck position causes discomfort, which causes postural changes that cause tension in other areas and, down the line, the result is back pain. The work situation punishes assertiveness, which gives rise to resentment and a sense of shame at home, and because the client lacks the skill for seeking support, hopelessness sets in.

From a CBS perspective, then—mirroring the task of "seeing behavior" described in the previous chapter—our initial task is to see and understand the behaviors involved in the client's issues.

To see that ongoing stream of behavior clearly, we ask questions—lots of questions—that build empathy and understanding and allow us to describe the client's experience like a screenwriter or novelist. We might ask the following questions:

What was happening when you started to feel that way?

What were you doing?

What were you thinking?

What were you feeling?

Where were you when that happened?

What happened before that?

What factors do you think contributed to that?

When you felt that way, what did you do?

What happened next?

What did you do next?

Then how did you feel?

How did others respond?

How did you respond?

What happened after that?

What else happened?

These questions are all about understanding the sequence of events: everything that falls under the umbrella term "behavior"—thoughts, feelings, urges, and actions—as well as the responses of other people and the events in the world to which the client was responding.

Notice that none of these questions include the word "why." As a rule, we avoid why questions at this stage because why questions lead to reasons that may not be connected to the actual flow of events; for example, "I don't know why—I guess I'm just weak." Or, "I don't know, you tell me."

At the same time, bear in mind that you aren't interested in the flow of events for its own sake. You are tracking the flow of behaviors and contexts relevant to a given client's presenting problem. You are aiming to eventually zero in on what seem to be the key behaviors that lead to the presenting problem, as identified by either you or the client.

Imagine you have a client, Susan, who says she feels burned-out at work. Here is some sample dialogue; it illustrates this process of tracking behaviors that lead to the presenting problem and zeroing in on the key behaviors that seem relevant.

Therapist: So you feel burned-out.

Client: Yeah, I just really don't want to be there. It's agony to get out of bed on Monday morning.

Therapist: Sounds really challenging. Tell me more about what it's like to be at work. Actually, let's review last week. When you arrived at work on Monday, what were you looking at?

Client: Well, it starts even before that. I was already late on a project. I volunteered for it, stupidly, two weeks ago, even though I knew I wouldn't have time for it. Then I procrastinated all day Saturday and most of Sunday, and then finally had to put in about six hours on Sunday evening. I was miserable.

Therapist: Ugh. What was going on that you accepted a project even though you didn't have time?

Client:	Oh, man. I do that a lot.
Therapist:	Do you say yes first and then think through the costs later?
Client:	Exactly. I'm a yes person.
Therapist:	Are you aware that saying yes *might* be a bad idea when you say it?
Client:	Well…yes, recently I have been having a little sense of dread when I sign up for new work. But the thought of saying no…that's just not what you do.
Therapist:	That's not what *you* do. I say no all the time.
Client:	Ha! At my work, not many people say no. I don't say no. You get judged if you say no.

Immediately with the inquiry—"When you arrived at work on Monday, what were you looking at?"—the client described a series of events that, based on the therapist's understanding of burnout, seem likely to have contributed to the client's presenting problem. Further questioning seemed to confirm this hunch. Imagine that more similar questions reveal a few key patterns that recur again and again:

- She's severely overcommitted, often sacrificing her evenings and weekends to work on projects that she doesn't enjoy but has promised to complete.

- She tends to quickly agree to doing more work and feels regret afterward.

- She tends to avoid saying no or otherwise expressing her reservations about a task when speaking with supervisors.

- She tends to get into arguments with coworkers about what she perceives as their inefficiencies that negatively impact her own work; she enters these conflicts in a confrontational, judgmental way.

In this relatively simple demonstration, Susan discovered that she already knew what many of the relevant patterns were but had not yet put together the whole picture in such a way that she could understand her experience. Toward the end of the discussion, then, you might step back and summarize what you have learned:

I think you're feeling burned-out for good reasons. You're in a situation where your needs are constantly sacrificed in favor of work. You're carrying a near-constant state of stress about deadlines. You don't feel able or hopeful about changing this situation. And you don't have much support at work. In fact, your relationships with coworkers are often another source of stress.

When there are multiple possible factors bearing upon a presenting problem, it can also be useful to ask a clarifying question to get at which factor is most important. You might ask Susan,

"Which of these issues, if we fixed it, would have the biggest effect on your burnout?" Susan, for instance, might discover that even if she had less conflict with coworkers, she would still be stressed-out. After some discussion, you might discover that limiting her acceptance of new work will have the biggest impact; not only will it free up her weekends so she can take care of her relationships and do other rewarding things, but if she is less stressed overall she will be less likely to become upset with her coworkers' foibles.

STEP 2: CLARIFY FUNCTIONS

As you zero in on the behaviors that seem to create the problem, you may begin to get a sense of how the behaviors function. Recall from chapter 2 that there are two very general classes of function:

- Some behaviors function to move us toward something appetitive.

- Some behaviors function to move us away from something aversive.

Grasping the function more specifically usually involves digging into—with more psychological depth—the situations in which the problem behavior happens. This often means looking at the client's experience—emotions, thoughts, images, sensations, and so forth—more closely. Consider the following exchange with Susan.

Therapist: I'd like us to understand better what was going on for you in that moment when your supervisor asked for volunteers for a project, and out of everyone in the room, you were the one who immediately stepped forward. What was going on inside of you in that moment?

Client: What do you mean? I think I just ha ve to say yes.

Therapist: I get it. Let's see if we can put that moment in slow motion. Let me ask a few questions to help focus the lens. First, in the meeting last week, before there was a request for volunteers for the project, what were you feeling as you sat in the meeting?

Client: Pretty good. I had just finished a report. Was kind of riding the high from that.

Therapist: And what else?

Client: Slightly annoyed, because I knew the POS group was going to sit on the report for a week and then make some annoying objections.

Therapist: Okay. Hmm. Let me think. If you hadn't been riding high, would you have been more or less likely to volunteer for the work?

Client: Less likely. I would hesitate. That time I just dove right in.

Therapist: Right, without connecting that the timelines were really not workable. Okay. So moving forward, one thing we might work on is ensuring there is a "waiting period" before any yes; that way you can check out the plan more carefully. [Here the therapist hypothesizes that the appetitive thing Susan moves toward, especially when feeling confident, is contribution. This is only a problem because she does it without regard of the workability of the commitment. In other words, Susan's initiative does not work well in this context. She might need to learn the skill of the soft commitment: "I would be willing to do it, but can I have an hour to just confirm that this will be workable?"]

Therapist: Okay, now let's go back to the POS group. When you say yes, what does it get you with respect to them?

Client: Oh, simple. It shows them that I am going to keep moving no matter what. I'm the achiever. I look good.

Therapist: Does it say the same thing to your supervisor?

Client: Yes. Though…good lord! Who knows if that's really true. She knows I'm burned-out as well.

Therapist: And…imagine this. If you had slowed down and considered that this timeline was actually not a good fit for you, what would have happened if you didn't raise your hand to volunteer?

Client: Oh. Well, it would have felt uncomfortable. I'd sit there awkwardly waiting… I'd think, "Is anyone else going to step up? What a bunch of slackers."

Therapist: Would you think about what they're thinking of you?

Client: Of course. I always step up, so they'd be thinking, "Where's Susan?"

Therapist: So is it fair to say your impulsive volunteering is partially about an unwillingness to sit in that discomfort and risk your coworkers thinking you're not showing up? And you are also wanting to show the POS group and the supervisors that you are on the ball, even though you don't know if that's really the effect you are having on them? And those little nudges are enough to propel you to unwise yes after unwise yes?

Client: Yes, that's fair.

For Susan, in the situation where she impulsively says yes, the therapist has identified a couple of functions of that behavior: She is moving toward the appetitive stimuli of being accomplished at work and looking good to her colleagues and supervisor. She is also moving away from the aversive stimulus of their questioning her willingness. At this point, the three main questions of functional analysis have been addressed: What is the behavior? In what contexts does it or did it occur? What is or was its function in those contexts? And look how far the therapist has come from Susan's presenting problem of "I feel burned-out at work."

Again, in terms of general heuristics, you are looking for only a few basic functional patterns:

- The client's behavior functions to avoid something unpleasant (real or imagined).

- The client's behavior functions to approach something appetitive (real or imagined).

Your search for function has gone far enough when there is a sense of coherence—as in yes, that makes sense—and a sense that there is an adequate explanation of the presenting problem.

Let's look at a couple of more subtle points related to this process of clarifying function.

Zeroing In on the Functional Consequence

A common pitfall in functional thinking is making the assumption that a seemingly aversive response has the function of punishing a problem behavior, and then being puzzled at why the behavior persists. For example, let's say a woman gives her husband the cold shoulder and he gets angry and yells at her. Why would she persist then in stonewalling him? Or consider Susan: If saying yes consistently lands her in hot water, why does she persist?

The reality is, if the behavior is happening, there is some form of payoff—either now, in the past, or intermittently.

For example, for the woman who is stonewalling, it's possible that shutting down—even though her husband yells at her—feels safer and more powerful than trying to speak when she is upset and hurt. In other words, the consequence of getting yelled at is not the functional consequence—the consequence that actually influences her. The consequence that influences her is the relative sense of control she gets. For Susan, the situation is similar. The functional consequence is the immediate sense of looking good and not looking bad. The negative consequence of burnout doesn't actually have enough influence over her in that moment to lead to a different choice.

This counterintuitive assessment also applies to seemingly appetitive consequences. "I know I should just fill out my time card, but I just don't want to do it…so I procrastinate all day." Some people might think of turning in their work hours as moving toward something appetitive because it leads to being paid; however, let's look more closely at the actual function of the behavior in this example. It's possible that avoiding the time card all day allows a continuous escape from the aversive experience of facing the fact that hours are short this week, so it will be difficult to pay the bills.

Inquiring About Avoidance

One important thing to note about avoidance is that sometimes we've avoided some situation—perhaps a painful experience from the past—so thoroughly and for so long that it is no longer clear what we are avoiding or whether the thing we fear would actually occur in the present. Susan's volunteering, for example, helps her avoid the (imaginary) situation in which others think poorly of her. However, by facing that fear, she might discover that in fact nobody judges her when she hangs back. For this reason, it can be useful to put the client in touch with what he or she might contact by no longer avoiding a situation. Try starting the exploration with this question: What would you have to face (or do or feel or respond to) if you didn't do this behavior?

Going into History

As suggested in the passage above, to understand why a behavior happens in the present, it's often useful to get into the history of the behavior. In relation to avoidance, the thing that a behavior functions to avoid (for Susan, being judged) might not actually be present in the present. But if we look into the history, we will find it.

Therapist: Do you remember experiencing the fear that others would judge you—that they'll think you're not going to show up—earlier in your life?

Client: [pauses] Well… Oh, yeah. I was going to say no, but…that's the whole story of me and my mom. Especially after her divorce, it felt like she was constantly hounding me to be there. I hated that.

What emerges in this conversation is that Susan has a long history of people reacting negatively to her "not showing up"—that is, their perception of her not being there. She learned that "not showing up" incurs judgment, which is painful to her, and so she works to avoid that aversive situation. However, working to avoid that aversive outcome by *constantly showing up* is now having a negative effect on her life. What she doesn't realize is that, in general, others are much less likely to judge her than she fears. Getting clarity about how the past is different from the present can help people become more flexible.

Going into the Future

Finally, when clarifying the function of a behavior, it can be useful to go into the future.

For example, we might balance out the "consequences now matter more than consequences later" problem by getting in closer contact with the future consequences of a problem behavior. With Susan, we might spend some time discussing the likely consequences if she continues to work at her current level of burnout.

Therapist: What will happen if you keep living this way—say, for another twenty years?

Client: That's hard to think about. Who knows what would happen to my health. Could I physically keep going that long? My son…he wouldn't know me. That's horrible to think about.

Even though examining consequences is often painful, it can help increase the motivation to change the behavior because doing so makes the aversive consequences of maintaining the problem pattern more salient and more painful.

The flip side of this pain is to get in contact with what might be gained—what purpose, what meaning, what goals, what freedom—if one were to let go of the constricted problem behavior.

STEP 3: LOOK FOR FUNCTIONAL CLASSES

Once you have collected a set of problem behaviors and identified their functions, you will start to notice basic patterns in the function of the problematic behaviors that are somewhat unique to the individual. For instance, Susan is very sensitive to looking bad to others, and she will work hard to look good even when the costs are high (burnout, conflict, and so on).

We can then start looking for other situations in which Susan similarly avoids (something like) "looking bad." In other words, we now have a hypothesis about how Susan might struggle in other parts of her life.

Therapist: Are there other places in your life where you try to avoid looking bad? Does it ever happen with your husband?

Client: Yeah. I hate it when he is critical of me. Or sometimes even an innocent question— for some reason I take it as an attack. Then I can be really bitchy with him.

We might then ask if she has experienced a related dynamic with friends. Susan discloses that she lost one of her best friends due to complex circumstances: Susan had to cancel attending her wedding, letting her friend down, and since then Susan has been unable to feel connected to her friend due to feelings of deep shame.

As different as these behaviors may appear on the surface—volunteering for more work, speaking crossly to her husband, and withdrawing from her friend—they all have a common function: helping Susan avoid feeling ashamed or deficient or "not looking good." Behaviors are functionally similar when they serve similar core functions: for instance, avoiding some specific feared outcome or seeking some desired appetitive outcome.

In turn, once you can see the common function, there is an opportunity to focus more flexibly on the root problem—facing shame, in Susan's case. Sets of behaviors defined by a core common function in this way are known as *functional classes*. You can look clearly at the cost of the whole class. You can muster reasons to overcome this struggle. And you can look for instances of the functional class occurring in the therapy process. More on this key element of FAP in step 5 below.

STEP 4: DEFINE IMPROVEMENTS

Up to this point, we've focused on problem behaviors. The next step in functional analysis—and an extremely important one—is identifying and testing behaviors that will help alleviate a client's problems. With Susan's problem of overcommitting by saying yes impulsively, we might improve her skill at saying no, which could help her say no in ways that are more likely to garner people's understanding and support rather than their judgment.

Once you have a hypothesis about which behavior would be more effective at a crucial moment for the client, you can help the client put that behavior in place. Then you can evaluate whether or not the behavior helps. With enough practice, does the behavior help change the whole stream of behavior such that the presenting problem is somewhat ameliorated?

STEP 5: NOTICING CLINICALLY RELEVANT BEHAVIOR

Now we'll look at a very important focus of functional thinking in FAP: seeing the client's problem behaviors (and improvements) when they occur in the session and in the therapy relationship.

Noticing clinically relevant behavior in the moment is key in FAP because of the opportunity and the liability described in chapter 1: if we don't see these behaviors clearly, we risk reinforcing problem behaviors or punishing the tentative steps toward improvement or change. If we see the behaviors clearly and understand what they mean—that is, how they function for this person— then we can make sure we respond therapeutically. What do we mean? Instead of reinforcing problem behavior, we evoke and reinforce needed improvements in a way that is authentic and compassionate. This process is the focus of the remainder of the book.

Why is functional thinking useful for this process? For starters, function is not typically visible, so delving deeper into the function of a behavior in order to understand it is very useful. Also, once you can see a client's behavior in functional terms (as functional classes, for instance), it becomes easier to notice moments in which the behavior arises, even if what happens in session is, on the surface, quite different from what happens outside—in the client's life.

Here's an example of functional thinking: Imagine a client tells you—as one of her presenting problems—that she's having trouble initiating sex with her partner. FAP would *not* call for you to look for situations in which the client might want to initiate sex with you so she can improve her skills in this area.

Instead, your functional analysis might lead to the discovery that the behavior of initiating sex is part of a broader functional class of behaviors: this client generally finds it difficult to reach out sensitively but directly to someone else to get her needs met, and one place this deficit shows up is with her partner in the bedroom. If the client buys that this is a valuable area to work on, you can attend to situations in the therapy relationship that invoke this behavior, from mundane situations, such as needing to reschedule a session, to those that make the client feel more vulnerable. For example, perhaps she finds herself wondering one day if you really care about her, and she wishes to appropriately seek reassurance about that.

Here's another example: Susan is critical and defensive with her husband, overly compliant with her supervisors at work, and overly polite and nondemanding in session with you—even though she occasionally appears irritated by something you've done. All of these behavioral examples are instances of a general functional class of behaviors that function to avoid the vulnerability she feels when she is assertive about her needs.

The common structure in all of these examples is that the problem behaviors both inside and outside of the therapy relationship are part of the same functional class. Being able to see the function parallels between in-session and out-of-session events helps build a momentum and coherence in the effort to change behavior—"In here we're going to work on the same things you're working on in your life."

CRBS: CLINICALLY RELEVANT BEHAVIORS

In FAP, we refer to behaviors that show up in the therapy room that are related to the client's clinical problems as *clinically relevant behaviors* (CRBs). CRBs are divided into two categories: an example of problematic behavior is referred to as CRB1, and an example of improvement relative to this behavior is referred to as CRB2. With clients, we commonly drop the CRB prefix and just use the generic abbreviations "1" and "2" to refer to problems and improvements. These abbreviations become useful shorthand language, as in, "Did you just do a 1?" "Was that a 1 or a 2?" And so forth.

A major strength of this terminology is its simplicity. Asking "Is this a 1 or a 2?" focuses the conversation on functional analysis. The question is easy to remember in the moment during therapy, yet it encapsulates a great deal. It represents the ongoing focus on the process of assessment and brings that focus to bear on the present moment.

This CRB terminology allows us to state the aims of FAP quite simply. Clinically, we seek to reduce the frequency of CRB1 and increase the frequency of CRB2. Using functional analysis to define CRB1 and CRB2 is, therefore, the key aim of the functional analytic process in FAP. The terminology is also the foundation for case conceptualization in FAP.

Key Features of CRB1 and CRB2

1. CRB1 and CRB2 are only CRBs because they are functionally related to the client's presenting problems.

2. CRB1s and CRB2s should always be behaviors that clients have some control over and therefore can work on changing with deliberate effort. For instance, fear may be a problematic response to showing vulnerability, but it's hard to choose to change fear. A better focus—one in which the client would have more choice—might be the behaviors the client engages in when afraid. For example, the CRB1 might be to hold back and avoid disclosing something to someone who is in fact trustworthy, and the CRB2 might be to disclose despite the fear.

3. Label CRB1 and CRB2 in ways that are empathic, validating, and motivating. Use the client's own language when possible. Steer away from terminology that's overly clinical

or judgmental. It's fine to use metaphors to describe functional classes of CRB. For instance, the behavior of avoiding self-disclosure could quite reasonably be called "keeping your guard up" or "having your wall up," and the behavior of disclosing too much too soon might be called "spilling." Ensure sufficient precision by checking that you and your client are on the same page regarding how you use these terms.

4. Remember that CRB1 isn't inherently bad, and CRB2 isn't inherently good. In fact, it's often important to relate to CRB1 with as much acceptance and compassion as you would to CRB2.

Discriminating CRB1 and CRB2

In this section we offer some practice in thinking functionally—specifically in discriminating 1s and 2s.

Here's a warm-up. Imagine a client asks you to call her physician to request a prescription refill. What's the function of this behavior for the client? If you're like about 50 percent of people we've asked during trainings over the past couple of decades, you have an immediate sense that the behavior is problematic. Perhaps you think the client seems overly demanding or dependent, which is definitely a possible assessment. The client may have a habit of making excessive, unreasonable demands. In contrast, the client may also have a very good reason for asking you. Perhaps she is working hard to be more assertive because failing to do so in the past has caused her a lot of problems.

Notice that the implications of these different functional interpretations of the request would steer your response in different directions. If the request is an example of CRB1, you might decline the request and ask the client to make the phone call herself. If it's an example of CRB2, you might agree to make the call, perhaps also expressing that it's not typical for you to agree to such requests, but in this situation you see how it could really help.

EXERCISE: EXPLORING POTENTIAL FUNCTIONS OF CRB

Read each scenario below, and then, on a separate piece of paper, write your ideas about what the functions of the behavior might be and whether the behavior is likely to be CRB1 or CRB2. Given the scant context we're providing, there will be several functional possibilities in each case. The challenge is to write a few different interpretations for each scenario, including at least one in which the behavior is CRB1 and another in which it's CRB2. Go through all four scenarios in this way before reading our sample interpretations.

- **Scenario 1:** A client arrives for his session. When you ask him what he'd like to focus on in this session, he says, "I don't know."

- **Scenario 2:** You greet a client in the waiting room and mistakenly call her by the wrong name. She appears irritated for a brief moment and is silent as you enter your office.

- **Scenario 3:** At the end of a session, a client says, "I've been meaning to ask you something. I think you're a pretty cool person. I wonder, when therapy is over, is there any chance you'd like to get a beer sometime?"

- **Scenario 4:** You're helping a client cope better with memories of trauma. One day in session she says, "Is it okay if we talk about something else today? There's something I'd kind of like to talk about."

Here are our sample functional interpretations for these scenarios. As always, such interpretations are only hypotheses to be evaluated through assessment with a given client.

- **Scenario 1:** A client arrives for his session. When you ask him what he'd like to focus on in this session, he says, "I don't know."

  Possible interpretation 1: This is CRB1 for the client. His avoidance of identifying and expressing his needs leads to problems in many areas of his life.

  Possible interpretation 2: This is CRB2 for the client. He tends to excessively control himself, is perfectionistic, and avoids asking for help when he doesn't know what to do. Saying "I don't know" represents a step toward identifying a situation in which he needs help and engaging in a meaningful dialogue about that situation with the therapist.

- **Scenario 2:** You greet a client in the waiting room and mistakenly call her by the wrong name. She appears irritated for a brief moment and is silent as you enter your office.

  Possible interpretation 1: This is CRB1. The client avoids expressing her irritation or disappointment with others and tends to gradually disconnect from them as her resentment grows.

  Possible interpretation 2: This is CRB2. The client usually overreacts to minor slights, which causes difficulties in her relationships. In this instance she's been successful in not overreacting.

- **Scenario 3:** At the end of a session, a client says, "I've been meaning to ask you something. I think you're a pretty cool person. I wonder, when therapy is over, is there any chance you'd like to get a beer sometime?"

  Possible interpretation 1: This is CRB1. The client tends to be oblivious to social limits (such as the difference between a therapeutic relationship and a friendship), and this insensitivity creates conflict and suffering for him.

  Possible interpretation 2: This is CRB2. The client pervasively avoids asking for what he wants, and he's working on being more assertive, regardless of the possibility of being declined or rejected.

- **Scenario 4:** You're helping a client cope better with memories of trauma. One day in session, she says, "Is it okay if we talk about something else today? There's something I'd kind of like to talk about."

  Possible interpretation 1: This is CRB1. The client consistently tries to avoid her trauma memories and primarily uses distraction to cope with those memories and the emotions they bring up.

  Possible interpretation 2: This is CRB2. The client tends to be so preoccupied with her trauma that she neglects other important aspects of her life.

The Functional Idiographic Assessment Template

When starting functional analysis with a client, you can begin with a blank slate, creating a way of talking about the client's problems that is completely tailored to her. That said, sometimes it's helpful to review existing lists of common CRBs or, more broadly, functional classes of interpersonal behavior relevant to FAP with your client. Rather than making a description from scratch, these lists provide language you and the client can choose from to describe what might be happening.

Glenn Callaghan (2006) developed the functional idiographic assessment template (FIAT), a tool for identifying functional classes of behavior when performing FAP. Callaghan analyzed the typical FAP treatment targets among his own clients and his students' clients and came up with a set of five key functional classes of interpersonal behavior. He organized these functional classes into a questionnaire with numerous specific behaviors set forth for each class. You may find the full FIAT useful in identifying CRB1s and CRB2s, especially as you're getting familiar with the FAP approach. It can be found at http://www.functionalanalyticpsychotherapy.com/fiat.pdf.

For the purposes of this chapter, we've streamlined the items on the FIAT, presenting them as descriptions rather than questions. Keeping in mind the five classes of behavior can help you be alert to specific in-session behaviors that may indicate a possible CRB1. The worksheet only lists CRB1s, but deriving corresponding CRB2s is straightforward. And doing so can stimulate your thinking when you work on case conceptualization. You may also find it useful to show the form to clients and to work together collaboratively to identify the behaviors that are relevant for the client.

Read through the following descriptions of various types of CRB1 and check off any that arise frequently, either in session or outside of session. Take special note of any categories for which many items are checked. They could represent classes of behavior that are particularly problematic or where improvements would be most useful.

CLASS A—ASSERTION OF NEEDS (IDENTIFICATION AND EXPRESSION)

Class A behaviors include anything people want or value or "need," including the need to state opinions, ideas, convictions, passions, longings, desires, dreams, and—basically—who they are. "Assertion of needs" also includes making requests for social support or other needs that are more practical.

Possible Class A CRB1s

_____ Difficulty identifying needs or the type of help or support wished for from the therapist or others

_____ Difficulty expressing needs

_____ Difficulty getting needs met by the therapist or others

_____ Expressing needs too subtly or indirectly

_____ Pushing the therapist or others away with neediness

_____ Giving much more than is received in return

_____ Being extremely independent and feeling too vulnerable when receiving help

_____ Being too demanding when asking for needs to be met

_____ Being unable to tolerate the therapist or others saying no to requests

_____ Other: _____

CLASS B—BIDIRECTIONAL COMMUNICATION (IMPACTS AND FEEDBACK)

Class B behaviors involve how people affect others and how they give and respond to feedback. The term "feedback" refers to how others respond and react to the person's behavior. Feedback can be verbal or nonverbal and in the form of facial expressions, body language, and so on.

Possible Class B CRB1s

_____ Difficulty receiving positive feedback, such as appreciation or compliments

_____ Difficulty receiving negative feedback, such as criticism

_____ Difficulty giving positive feedback

_____ Difficulty giving negative feedback, including constructive criticism

_____ Having unreasonable self-expectations, which may show up as perfectionism or a pervasive sense of failure

_____ Having unreasonable expectations of the therapist or others

_____ Being hypersensitive to or overly aware of his or her impact on the therapist or others

_____ Not having much awareness of his or her impact on the therapist or others

_____ Inaccurately assessing his or her impact on the therapist or others

_____ Being hard to track or follow in conversation

_____ Talking too much or for too long without checking impact

_____ Making too much eye contact

_____ Making too little eye contact

_____ Other: _____

CLASS C—CONFLICT

Aggressive or hostile class C behavior is just one of many potentially problematic behaviors that can come up with conflict. Unworkable responses to disagreement or uncomfortable interactions can also include many behaviors that are more passive or avoidant.

Possible Class C CRB1s

_____ Difficulty tolerating conflict or disagreement

_____ Difficulty expressing negative feelings

_____ Avoiding conflict

_____ Expressing anger indirectly, such as by being passive-aggressive

_____ Expressing too much anger

_____ Not being willing to compromise

_____ Being ineffective at resolving conflict

_____ Apologizing too much

_____ Assuming everything is his or her fault

_____ Blaming the therapist or others for problems

_____ Creating unnecessary conflict

_____ Using conflict as way to avoid closeness

_____ Being unwilling to forgive the therapist or others

_____ Other: _____

CLASS D—DISCLOSURE AND INTERPERSONAL CLOSENESS

Class D behaviors relate to "interpersonal closeness," which refers to behaviors that lead to feeling connected to or close with another person.

Possible Class D CRB1s

_____ Difficulty conversing

_____ Difficulty expressing closeness and caring

_____ Difficulty receiving closeness and caring

_____ Being fearful of closeness or attachment

_____ Being reluctant to take emotional risks

_____ Being reluctant to self-disclose

_____ Being reluctant to let his or her true self be seen or heard

_____ Downplaying the importance of what he or she shares

_____ Talking about himself or herself too much

_____ Not listening well

_____ Being self-absorbed or asking for too much support

_____ Being secretive

_____ Being too intrusive when asking about the personal experiences of the therapist or others

_____ Not being aware of the needs of the therapist or others (for example, going overtime in session or not giving the therapist openings to talk)

_____ Talking too much and too tangentially

_____ Not trusting others

_____ Trusting others too easily or too soon

_____ Other: _____

CLASS E—EMOTIONAL EXPERIENCE AND EXPRESSION

Class E behaviors, related to emotional experience and expression, refer to all types of emotions, from sadness and anxiety to love and pride.

Possible Class E CRB1s

_____ Difficulty identifying emotions

_____ Being unaware of emotions as they're happening

_____ Intentionally hiding emotions

_____ Being flat or distant in emotional expression

_____ Difficulty with crying

_____ Difficulty feeling or expressing sorrow, sadness, or grief

_____ Difficulty feeling or expressing anxiety or fear

_____ Difficulty feeling or expressing joy

_____ Difficulty feeling or expressing pride

_____ Difficulty feeling or expressing humor

_____ Engaging in negative self-talk when feeling emotions

_____ Expressing emotions in an overly intense manner

_____ Unable to control his or her expression of emotions

_____ Talking about emotions too much

_____ Having overly labile or intense emotions

_____ Unable to have perspective on his or her emotions; feeling overwhelmed by emotions and unable to detach from them

_____ Expressing emotions in a way that annoys or alienates the therapist or others

_____ Avoiding or suppressing certain emotions

_____ Other: _____

Flexibility: A 1 or a 2?

As you think about the preceding examples or reflect on your own clients or yourself, you might notice something important: sometimes it isn't at all clear whether a particular behavior is CRB1 or CRB2. In fact, a particular behavior may seem to include both problematic aspects and improvement. Let's return to the example of the client who asks you to call her physician for a prescription refill. The request itself might in some ways be CRB2: it represents assertiveness, and the client's life will be better if she's more assertive. At the same time, the particular way in which she's assertive (perhaps she doesn't validate enough or her tone of voice is too harsh) causes her some trouble, so there's an element of CRB1, as well. How does FAP deal with such situations?

Although it can be useful to cleanly discriminate between CRB1 and CRB2, doing so shouldn't be forced. Multiple functions, including problematic behavior and improvement, can and often do mingle in the same behavior. Recognizing that multiple functions are present allows us to move beyond the simpler question of whether a given behavior is CRB1 or CRB2 and instead ask, "How is this behavior an improvement, and how is it a problem?" From there we can nurture the threads of CRB2 and weed out the threads of CRB1, or we can shape CRB1 into more effective behavior.

The ACT Matrix: A Very Useful Tool

Another invaluable tool for functional thinking and discriminating 1s and 2s is the ACT matrix (Polk & Schoendorff, 2014; Polk, Schoendorff, Webster, & Olaz, 2016). We highly recommend *The Essential Guide to the ACT Matrix*, which discusses the use of the matrix tool in the context of ACT and FAP-based treatment.

Seriously, it is hard to overstate how useful the matrix is as a clinical tool!

Clinically Relevant Therapist Behavior

So far we've focused on client behaviors. But, as we stated in the introduction of this book, your behaviors as the therapist are an equally important part of the process of therapy. Anything and everything you do in therapy has a function for you and will have a function for your clients: your behavior will affect the clients in some way, and the effects can either support the therapeutic process or interfere with it. As part of your functional analysis of the in-session process and the therapy relationship, therefore, FAP asks you to pay attention to your own behaviors as well as those of clients. More broadly, we invite you to develop a broader awareness of your patterns of behavior across cases: How do you tend to get into trouble or undermine progress as a therapist? When are you at your best? A therapist's personal history and personal relationships are often involved in these patterns. We'll address this topic of "personal" more directly in chapter 6.

For example, with Susan you might grow impatient with her confusion about identifying her own needs more clearly or her anxiety about reducing behaviors that are clearly (to you) self-defeating, and your impatience might lead you to focus excessively on behavior change rather than building motivation, clarifying purpose, or finding emotional acceptance. You might see this pattern of impatience about behavior change show up commonly with anxious, highly controlled clients.

Paralleling the terminology for client behaviors, therapist behaviors that interfere with the therapy process are known as T1s, and those that support therapy process are T2s. Like CRBs, T1s and T2s are defined based on how they function for you and your clients in therapy: Do they serve to facilitate or detract from therapy progress? You may, of course, have different T1s and T2s with different clients. Here are some examples:

Examples of T1

- Being too controlling or directive

- Avoiding clients' expressions of emotion

- Focusing excessively on problem solving (as opposed to validation, acceptance, and present-moment experience)

- Allowing clients to direct the focus of sessions in ineffective ways

- Failing to define case conceptualizations or homework activities precisely enough

Examples of T2

- Allowing clients to collaborate in planning sessions

- Allowing or inviting clients' expressions of emotion

- Providing validation, expressing acceptance, and attending to present-moment experience

- Directing the focus of the session effectively

- Focusing attention on the problem solving needed to define precise treatment plans or homework assignments

STEP 6: THE PROCESS OF FUNCTIONAL ANALYSIS— HYPOTHESIS TESTING

Finally, let's return to the notion of functional thinking—or functional analysis—as a process. We labeled this section "step 6," but it's not really a discrete step. If it were a step, it would be looping back through all the previous steps as you learn more about the client and what works in therapy to help him move forward. In other words: functional thinking is an iterative, hypothesis-testing process. It is a process of questioning, investigating, testing, revising, and clarifying.

The most important—possibly the only—criterion by which a functional analysis is judged is this:

Has this analysis helped us achieve the desired therapy outcomes?

If not, no matter how coherent or elegant or right the analysis feels to you, it must be revised or discarded.

A spirit of hypothesis testing and iteration is important, as well, because the phenomenon we are seeking to understand is inherently complex. We have to puzzle our way through it. To illustrate, we'll explore the example of the client who asks you to call her physician for a prescription refill. If you follow our guidelines in this chapter, your first step would probably be to consider the client's stated clinical goals. Let's say she has ongoing difficulty expressing her needs. Perhaps she has an overbearing husband and an extremely demanding boss, and she's mostly focused on being obedient and staying quiet, at the cost of feeling disconnected and miserable. In this context, you might notice that asserting her needs in this way is something new, even if it seems clumsy. Therefore, it would be extremely important to recognize this in your response.

If you continue to explore, however, you might discover other aspects of the behavior or context that might temper your response. For example, perhaps when she does, on rare occasion, assert her needs, she tends to make rather rigid and inconvenient requests, alienating others or leaving them unhappy with her. As a result, they typically refuse her requests or comply only begrudgingly. Ultimately, she walks away from these interactions thinking that requesting things of people doesn't work very well. And because she's blind to the way her requests come across as rigid and inconsiderate, she's decided that it's only worthwhile to inconvenience others if a request is extremely important. How might these considerations shape how you respond to her?

Now we'll make this situation even more realistic—and realistically complex. Imagine that the client makes her request at a time when you're feeling especially harried in life. Perhaps the session is already running overtime. Maybe you're thinking about your next client, who's one of the most challenging clients you've ever had. Perhaps you're experiencing health problems or feel you don't have enough time for yourself. For whatever reason, when you hear this request to do yet another thing, you immediately feel tension in your body. How would all of this impact how you respond to her?

Now imagine that this client is very attuned to your emotional response. She accurately perceives your response as stress or irritation, and she interprets your response to mean "My therapist is angry at me and I made a mistake." If you're attuned to her as well and sense this reaction—and how it fits in with her presenting problem—how would those aspects of context shape your response? In contrast, if she doesn't tune in to your emotional response to her request, how would this shape your response?

Ideally, your functional thinking becomes responsive to all aspects of context. After all, these kinds of complex, evolving contexts are the arena in which clients' behaviors are functioning and in which they must find their way.

Finally, thinking functionally is a process because behavior is a complex system. As we help clients change one aspect of their behavior, often new challenges emerge, and thus new assessment—new analysis—is needed. The client who stops drinking alcohol, for instance, now has to deal with lots of difficult emotions. Once Susan has learned to be more assertive, she now has to contend with her dissatisfaction with her job and her husband. Functional thinking is an adaptive process that serves the process of therapy.

A Basic Functional Analysis "Script"

Functional analysis can take a variety of forms. It can happen in a more structured assessment, or it can happen more casually, spread out over many sessions. It can be incredibly technical and detailed, or it can be quite loose and seemingly conversational.

Over the years we have found that a few core common questions define many functional analysis conversations, and these questions can often be organized into a kind of natural flow. Here is a version of that flow.

To build your skill with functional thinking, you might practice this flow with a partner. Ask your partner to pick a real-life problem situation, and then ask the following questions. Listen supportively to the answers. Don't attempt to problem solve. Follow the flow of questions. Feel free to modify the questions slightly to fit the conversation you are having, but don't deviate too much. Trust the questions. Observe the results.

What is the problem situation that you want to talk about?

What happens in that situation? What do you do? What does the other person do? Describe the interaction.

What is the key thing you do in that situation that contributes to the problem? Be specific.

Does that behavior ever show up in other situations in your life?

Does that behavior ever show up between you and me?

What is the immediate payoff for you doing that behavior? What do you "get"?

What is the cost of that behavior in the short term?

What will happen if this behavior continues long term?

If you didn't do that behavior, what would happen? What would be difficult? What would you have to face or feel or accept?

For what purpose would you be willing to feel or face or accept that?

Considering all of this, what is the key thing for you to work on?

Once you have completed the flow, see if you can step back and summarize what you learned about the situation, the behavior, how the other person is stuck, and what that person needs to do to move forward. Ask for feedback about whether your summary is on track and whether the other person feels understood by you.

Finally, exchange feedback about the process. For example: Which questions were especially useful? Which questions were less useful? Which questions were you uncomfortable asking but actually proved insightful? What insights were discovered?

SUMMARY

- Functional analysis is the central assessment method of FAP, standing upon the foundation of the CBS perspective.

- Functional analysis is a complex method. Expertise is built, in part, on pattern recognition and lots of experience. Start to master functional analysis by practicing functional thinking, which is centered on this question: "What is the function of this behavior?"

- Functional analysis involves a few basic steps:

  - Orient to the behaviors involved in the presenting problems.

  - Assess function.

  - Notice functional classes (sets of behavior defined by a common core function).

  - Define improvements.

- FAP adds a unique step to functional analysis: to notice how the problem behavior may show up in the therapy relationship. A CRB1 is an example of a client behavior related to problems occurring in the therapy session. A CRB2 is an example of an improvement occurring here and now. One aim of FAP therapy is to increase the frequency of CRB2 and decrease the frequency of CRB1.

- Iterate the above process as needed until positive therapy results are achieved.

CHAPTER 4

The Stance of Awareness, Courage, and Love

How do I know you're one of the good guys?
You don't. You'll have to take a shot.

—Cormac McCarthy

Remember a time when you took a massive risk to move toward someone—massive enough that your hands were shaking or you stuttered your words. Recall how vulnerable you felt in that moment. *I can't believe I'm actually going to say this…* But, for whatever reason, you decided that the message or the truth was important enough to leap off this cliff.

Whatever you imagined was going to happen next, it's more than likely that underneath the thoughts there was a visceral sense of vulnerability. The world faded into the background. Your own sensations came to the fore. And you became acutely focused on what the other person was saying or communicating through an expression or posture.

Was there a smile of reassurance saying to keep going?

Was there an impatient shifting in the seat and a glance toward the door?

And then—if you were so lucky—remember the relief you felt when the other person sighed generously and said, "I'm so glad you're telling me this. I completely get where you're coming from."

In this chapter, we introduce another framework for functional analysis: awareness, courage, and love (ACL; Kanter, Holman, & Wilson, 2014; Tsai, Callaghan, & Kohlenberg, 2013). We developed this framework to help clinicians orient their assessment of social connection toward a few key functional classes of behavior—identified by scientific findings—involved in the development of close relationships. Specifically, there's one key pattern that happens over and over again in healthy intimate relationships: one person engages in vulnerable self-disclosure (for example, courage), and the other responds with understanding, caring, or validation (for example, love). Decades of research establish this pattern (Reis, 2007; Reis, Collins, & Berscheid, 2000). In our own research laboratory, we showed that the responsiveness (that is, love) of the person hearing the vulnerable disclosure is a crucial ingredient in the generation of closeness: students vulnerably disclosing personal experiences to each other only reported increased social connection when their partner responded with signs of understanding and validation (Haworth et al., 2015). Given all of the existing evidence, including our own experience, if your client's presenting problem involves difficulty with intimacy, we venture that ACL may be worth assessing.

In the ACL framework, "courage" refers to sharing openly with another person despite feeling something aversive, such as fear, shame, caution, or uncertainty. Mark Twain described courage in a similar way: "Courage is resistance to fear, mastery of fear—not absence of fear" (1894, p. 155). Our definition of courage goes beyond what is said to include other moves toward another person: gestures, body language, acts of service, gifts, or even holding one's tongue or simply remaining present with another. In FAP, courage is defined by this common functional thread of moving toward someone despite aversion.

In a similar vein, love in the ACL framework corresponds to responsiveness, particularly responding to another person in a way that reinforces that person's courage. "Love" is also defined broadly, beyond what we say, and includes all the other ways we might welcome another person's courage, such as agreeing to a request, listening respectfully, and sometimes even saying no—in a way that makes the person feel understood, accepted, and respected for behaving courageously.

Sense of connection tends to arise when two people, reciprocally and over time, make courageous moves toward each other and respond in loving ways to each other's courageous moves. This link between courage and love can be readily understood in behavioral terms: one person moves (courageously) toward the other with self-disclosure, opening herself up to influence as a result. When the other provides responsiveness (love) as a consequence, the first person's move is reinforced, such that over time moves of various forms toward another increase in frequency. On the flip side, we tend to stop opening up to those who aren't responsive.

This process is pervasive in social life. It happens in small ways: for example, when two strangers meet and get to know each other, perhaps during their first day together at work or school, with one revealing something about himself (such as where he was raised) and the other showing responsiveness (such as by sharing a memory linked to that place or talking about where she was raised). It also happens in really big ways, such as a marriage proposal—a huge moment of vulnerability for the asker in which the other person's responsiveness (or lack thereof) has massive implications. And, of course, it happens in countless ways that lie between these extremes, such as when a couple comes home from two respectively long days at work and one partner wants to vent about her day (disclosure), and the other listens with love (responsiveness) rather than tuning her out because he's tired.

This courage-love process also happens in psychotherapy. Clients engage in vulnerable disclosure (which in other contexts may be met with some kind of aversive response), and the therapist aims to be responsive, reinforcing disclosure in a way that serves therapy. If this process isn't happening, there's often a fundamental problem. A therapeutic relationship requires vulnerability and responsiveness; without them, the therapist won't have access to the client's vulnerable psychological processes, much less have any influence over those processes.

To this basic courage-love chain, FAP adds "awareness": the capacity to know when and how to make a courageous move toward someone or to offer a loving response in a way that fits the immediate context. We recognize that the terms "courage" and "love" might evoke expectations that these behaviors will look a certain way. And all three terms (awareness, courage, and love) were indeed chosen for their vividness. However, it's critical to see these terms as functional classes. And as such, behavior carrying these functions can take a lot of different forms. Courage might include anything from a tearful disclosure to a polite request to simply staying in the room with someone who's furious with you. Love might include anything from soft eye contact to an impassioned soliloquy.

As with the language in the FIAT, these functional classes are only starting points for functional analysis, and any or all of them may not necessarily be involved in a given client's situation. It's your job, through assessment, to sort out whether and how the ACL conceptualization might be useful or valid in a particular case.

In addition to serving as a framework for functional thinking, the discussion in this chapter should also offer insight about how social connection works as well as an opportunity for self-reflection. Despite the importance of social connection to human well-being and its involvement with psychological suffering, it has been our experience that many clinicians don't understand how social connection works in great depth, let alone from a contextual behavioral science perspective. In turn, given the overlap between social connection and the therapeutic relationship, the awareness, courage, and love framework also provides a useful way of thinking about your therapy relationships.

In the sections that follow, we'll discuss awareness, courage, and love separately and in greater depth. Then, we'll offer suggestions regarding functional analysis. Toward the end of the chapter, we'll take another look at how awareness, courage, and love fit together. We'll also describe how ACL informs the therapist's interpersonal stance in FAP.

AWARENESS

"Awareness" broadly refers to being awake and alive to what's happening in the present moment in a social situation. This means being aware of yourself, the other person, and what's happening between the two of you. In contrast, lack of awareness results in one being on autopilot, disconnected from the present moment and more engaged with the mind than being fully flexible and present in the moment. A key function at the center of awareness is the ability to notice and act upon opportunities to engage in courage or love behaviors toward others. Another is to track whether these moves increase connection, and then make adjustments as necessary.

When working with clients who need help with social connection, imagine yourself in their shoes. What kinds of things would you tend to pay attention to when interacting with others? What kinds of things would you tend to think about? If clients are having problems with social connection, the ACL framework suggests that a primary issue might be awareness: they aren't paying attention to the right things. In this case, a big part of the solution is probably for these clients to develop a better awareness of social interactions, which could include thinking about specific ways to maximize the success of an interaction. As a therapist, your task might therefore be to assess your clients' self-awareness and awareness of others in the following three key areas.

Present-moment bodily sensations, thoughts, and feelings: This first, and perhaps foundational, aspect of awareness is comparable to mindfulness: bringing accepting, nonjudgmental awareness to what one is feeling and experiencing as it happens, and having a flexible perspective on one's thoughts and reactions as they happen.

Values, needs, goals, and identity: Developing closer social connections requires being aware of prosocial values, needs, and goals in interactions. This involves being able to answer questions like "Why am I engaging in the interaction?" "What is my goal?" "Who am I and who do I yearn to be?" and "What is my best self?" It's often useful to have some kind of living, present-moment awareness of these things as interactions occur. It can also help to remember the longer-term costs of more limiting ways of relating.

Others: People also need to be aware of the other person when interacting. This can be difficult for the obvious reason that no one has access to other people's private thoughts and emotions. The ingredients of this form of awareness are perspective taking, empathy, noticing nuances in body language, and asking questions to increase awareness—sometimes something as simple as "What are you feeling right now?" Shaping awareness of how one is impacting others in the moment can also be accomplished by asking for feedback, another type of relational skill; for example, asking "How are you responding to what I'm saying?"

These forms of awareness must generally be balanced. Some people seem to be overly focused on others at the expense of themselves. Others are overly focused on themselves. Assessing the impact of these imbalances can be an important part of the functional analysis.

The ultimate goal of awareness is to make it more likely that people do something functional: engage in effective courage and love behaviors, for instance, or engage in behaviors that move them toward goals or values rather than away. When working with clients, one helpful way of framing the task of awareness may be to talk about awareness of opportunities for courage or love or other CRB2s.

In behavioral terms, awareness may be seen as a behavior that transforms function. For example, through awareness, situations that in the past evoked avoidance can take on new functions that are more adaptive. Consider a client with a history of trauma who avoids any interpersonal interaction that makes her feel anxious, which is causing difficulty in her relationship with her partner. Eventually, through therapy, she may notice that in certain interpersonal situations she feels her heart beating faster and can identify her emotions as "anxious." She may also develop the capacity to notice that these situations share similarities with her trauma experiences. And she may notice too how her partner's demeanor in the moment communicates safety and support, not threat. She may then remind herself of her values about connecting with her partner rather than withdrawing. In this way, the process of awareness can increase her chances of engaging in interactions in a meaningful way, rather than avoiding.

COURAGE

As a reminder, in FAP, "courage" refers to vulnerable disclosure, which can take many different forms in different relationships and at different moments. Across all these contexts, courageous behavior may involve several key functional categories. The first is that there is some vulnerability, risk, or uncertainty about the outcome of the behavior; the person isn't completely sure that what he's doing will be received well or accepted by the other. The second is that the person is revealing or expressing something about himself—self-disclosure. The third is that the person is asking for what he needs. We'll look at each of these three categories individually in the sections that follow, but first we'll put them all together to define "courage" as being able to, despite vulnerability, express oneself appropriately, meaningfully, fully, and effectively in social situations.

Choosing to Experience Vulnerability

Emotional vulnerability is fundamental to the specific kind of social interaction that builds closeness and intimacy. Vulnerability is comparable to the concept of willingness in acceptance and commitment therapy. It involves allowing oneself to experience vulnerability and emotion in an interpersonal context, rather than suppressing, denying, or otherwise avoiding doing so. This aspect of courage doesn't require that people say anything; they only have to show up fully, with awareness of what they're feeling. Even if they don't express their experience verbally, others can often see or feel the difference.

Offering Self-Disclosure

In essence, "self-disclosure" means describing to others what one is aware of in the moment, including feelings, thoughts, memories, values, and sense of identity. With clients, you could refer to it as "speaking your truth" or "speaking from your heart." This is different from expressing oneself with a more particular goal or request in mind (covered in the next section); it's expressing oneself simply to be understood, seen, heard, or validated. This behavior could be as simple as saying "I'm tired," or it could be as complex as sharing one's history of sexual trauma or coming out of the closet to family members.

Asking for a Need to Be Met

Asking for what one needs is a huge category of courage because there are all sorts of things people need to be able to ask for in relationships. Here are a few of the most important subcategories:

Closeness involves seeking a deeper connection or expressing a desire to get closer to someone: "I'd like to feel more connected to you." "I'd like to tell you more about what I'm struggling with, because I greatly value your perspective on these things."

Boundaries and assertiveness involve setting limits or otherwise giving negative feedback and requesting that others behave differently: "It's difficult for me when you cancel our meetings at the last minute. Can we find a way to prevent this from happening in the future?"

Support involves asking others for help. A common hang-up for people is that they have difficulty accepting that they're worthwhile and deserving of help and entitled to make requests: "I'd like to ask you a big favor. Would you be willing to help me move this week? It would mean a lot to me."

Feedback involves asking others to give their opinion, whether positive or critical: "Can you tell me what you think I'm doing well in my job, and what you think I could do better?"

Of course, sometimes people express their needs in the form of statements that aren't direct requests but nevertheless function in that way. These too can run the gamut, from something as basic as "We're out of milk" to "Wow, I'm really feeling financially stretched"—said by a client the same week your bill arrives.

Note that asking for what one needs is functionally different from self-disclosure. With self-disclosure, responsiveness is pretty simple (though not necessarily easy): what matters is that the response communicates understanding and validation—acknowledgment that what the person is experiencing is real and makes sense. With specific requests, understanding and validation aren't enough. The person wants whatever has been requested—or at least a response that acknowledges the request: "I understand what you want, but I can't give it to you."

LOVE

As discussed earlier, "love" is about how we respond when others interact with us in ways that are courageous. First, are we even aware that the other person is doing something courageous by choosing to experience vulnerability and emotion, offering self-disclosure, or asking for a need to be met? Then, are we able to respond lovingly, or at least in a way that doesn't cause the person to regret reaching out? Ultimately, love involves acting for the good of the other person. In the ACL framework, love that responds effectively to another person's courage is of special interest because of the role this responsiveness plays in creating social connection. This kind of response requires awareness of what the other person needs—an awareness that often hinges on empathy and perspective taking.

Within this general framework, it can be useful to discriminate a few natural functional pairings between the categories of courage outlined above and specific forms of love that match them.

Providing safety and acceptance—paired with choosing to experience vulnerability and emotion: When others choose to be vulnerable and express their emotional experience, what they need in response, at a very basic level, is safety and acceptance. We'll discuss this further in chapter 5. For now, we just want to emphasize how important safety and acceptance are. It's much easier for people to be vulnerable when they're met with clearly articulated acceptance, which creates a sense of safety.

Expressing understanding, validation, and empathy—paired with offering self-disclosure: The idea of expressing understanding, validation, and empathy is basic for most therapists; we're trained to reflect and summarize what clients say to us. Within the ACL framework, these responses are considered to be especially functional, particularly when people have engaged in self-disclosure that makes them feel vulnerable. People need to feel understood and validated, especially when they're vulnerable. Sometimes a simple expression of understanding is enough: "I hear you," or "I understand what you're saying." At other times a more elaborate expression of understanding may be needed, such as reflecting back what you understood the person to say.

Giving what is needed—paired with asking for a need to be met: When someone asks for something specific, the response should be specific as well. This calls for awareness, which is required to accurately and sensitively identify what's needed, even if the person's communication is indirect or disguised. Here are several categories of responses. As you'll see, most have a bearing on the list of courage behaviors above, under "Asking for a Need to Be Met."

- **Providing closeness:** This starts with nonverbal behavior: providing attentive posture, making eye contact, and displaying other signs of engagement. Providing closeness verbally can take myriad forms, and most call for courage. Stepping up in this way continues the courage-love cycle and deepens connection.

- **Respecting boundaries and being open to feedback:** When someone engages in courageous behavior related to setting boundaries or giving negative constructive feedback, a response characterized by love demonstrates respect for those boundaries or openness to the feedback.

- **Apologizing:** When someone engages in courageous behavior related to giving negative feedback, a response characterized by love usually calls for a sincere apology at an appropriate level.

- **Promising:** This is an important skill for responding to others in a loving way, yet it can be challenging and even scary to do well. It's important for people to consider what they can genuinely commit to and follow through on. In other words, promises shouldn't be overly expansive or optimistic. A realistic promise builds more trust: "I want you to know that I will always try to take you seriously. I can't promise that I'll always be able to give you exactly what you want, but I can promise that I'll seek to understand your requests and do the best I can."

- **Expressing appreciation:** This can involve describing the qualities we admire or appreciate in others or describing how they did something that was helpful. It's unfortunately rare for people to hear details about their positive qualities from someone else, so being specific is usually welcome. As with many of these forms of love, expressing genuine emotion enhances connection.

- **Reciprocal disclosure:** Recognizing the vulnerability of others and responding with matching vulnerability is important because this reciprocity is a natural aspect of close relationships. Of course, this kind of reciprocity isn't always appropriate in therapy, but some self-disclosure by the therapist can be important, as long as it's functional, balanced, and well-timed.

Of course, we aren't advocating that anyone comply with requests unconditionally. That's impossible, and not all requests are reasonable. In addition, learning to cope with other people's refusal to comply with requests is a critical skill—one that people can only learn when their requests aren't fulfilled. Yet even in refusing a request, we can bring love to our response.

SELF-LOVE

There's another variant of love that we have found to be useful to delineate. *Self-love* is about responding to oneself in caring, accepting, compassionate, loving, reinforcing ways. It can be especially important when people have engaged in courageous behavior and haven't received a loving response, or when they're in a situation characterized by poor responsiveness in general. It's also crucial for people working in environments that don't offer much nurturance, including therapists working with clients who resist vulnerability and instead offer a lot of resistance or aggression. FAP focuses on three key aspects of self-love.

Self-acceptance: This simply means bringing acceptance to whatever one becomes aware of in oneself. This topic has been explored at length in the acceptance and commitment therapy and mindfulness literature. In FAP, we view self-acceptance as crucial when working on intimacy and social relationships.

Accepting love from others: It may seem odd that we include accepting love from others in the category of "self-love." However, rejecting or dismissing others' attempts to provide help, support, or love is often a form of self-denial, perhaps wrapped up in beliefs such as "I'm not worthwhile" or "I don't deserve to be helped." Therefore, we view accepting love from others as functionally an act of self-love.

Self-care: This refers to activities that soothe, calm, rejuvenate, or recharge people or bring them pleasure. One function of such activities is that they allow people to continue to act effectively in other contexts. In the ACL framework, we focus on self-care that helps people respond to difficulties in their relationships. Self-care is crucial when people are trying their best and it isn't working, when they're so scared that they don't know what to do, or when they're simply exhausted from stressful interactions.

ACL AS THE INTERPERSONAL STANCE OF FAP THERAPISTS

At its heart, FAP involves working within the therapeutic relationship in a way that embodies the processes of social connection, with guidance from functional analysis. Therefore, awareness, courage, and love are every bit as applicable to the therapist's stance as they are to client behaviors. And by bringing into the therapy room the behaviors that demonstrate awareness, courage, and love, you can also model these behaviors for clients. To that end, here are some key questions to ask yourself throughout your interactions with clients.

Awareness: Are you aware of what's happening in the moment, in yourself and, to the extent detectable, in your client? Are you aware of the functions of what's happening in the here and now? In particular, are you aware of opportunities for you to engage in courage or love behaviors? And are you aware of your client's awareness of such opportunities?

Courage: Are you strategically, effectively, and compassionately disrupting your client's normal patterns of relating ineffectively, including through avoidance? Are you willing to be with your client in feeling the discomfort or uncertainty of stepping outside his comfort zone?

Love: Are you creating an accepting, understanding, and responsive environment in which your client feels welcomed to courageously and vulnerably disclose what he's experiencing and what's happening in the moment, even in relation to you? In particular, are you responding to any improvements in the moment, as they happen, in a way that will reinforce them?

Self-love: When a client doesn't respond well to your efforts in therapy and you feel discouraged or uncertain, are you able to take care of yourself in ways that fuel your motivation to persist in being a positive disruptive force for this person?

Bear in mind that these touchstones of the therapeutic stance in FAP are functionally defined. We aren't asking you to take deep breaths and say risky, dramatic things in every session, and we aren't asking you to cry and express how moved you are by your client's courage—though you may, of course, do so if these moves are genuine for you and work for your client. Courage and love can take many forms: subtle, humble, careful, funny, proud, celebratory, aggressive, gentle, profound, reverent, irreverent, and more. Follow the function, not the form.

FUNCTIONAL ANALYSIS BASED ON ACL

Functional analysis based on ACL involves making sense of a client's specific behaviors (or absence of behaviors, such as not taking courageous risks) or your own behaviors in the therapeutic relationship in terms of the broad functional classes of awareness, courage, and love.

If clients have difficulties with social connection, one simple way to proceed is to consider whether they have deficits in the domains of awareness, courage, or love. If so, you can address those deficits by shaping awareness, courage, or love behaviors that work for clients in their interpersonal contexts. When working with clients on their social connection, you need not even use the terms "awareness," "courage," or "love" if they aren't functional for the client. The terms are just labels for the functions. You could instead talk about noticing, paying attention, having empathy, taking risks, being willing, caring, supporting, respecting, and so on.

More specifically, you can look for CRB1 within these functional classes. For awareness, a client's CRB1s might include not attending to goals in social situations, not taking the perspective of others into account, or making unfounded assumptions about others. For courage, a client's CRB1s might show up as avoiding courageous moves altogether or being courageous in ways that don't function to create connection, such as being too vulnerable too soon or being overly demanding. And CRB1s related to love might include not being responsive to others or being responsive in ways that don't function well for others.

Bringing the focus to in-session processes, you might find deficits in a client's awareness, courage, or love repertoires in interactions with you, and through functional analysis you might link these deficits to problems outside of session. Similarly, you might notice issues related to your own awareness, courage, or love repertoires with clients in general or with particular clients. As a reminder, courage for therapists isn't primarily about emotionally vulnerable self-disclosure—though that might be important at times. More often, it's involved in giving certain types of feedback or making requests that put rapport or your expertise on the line.

PUTTING IT ALL TOGETHER

Awareness, courage, and love are often best assessed within their mutual context according to how they functionally relate to each other for a particular person in particular contexts. This is clearly salient to courage and love, given the reciprocal link between them outlined at the beginning of this chapter. You can inquire about this link using questions along these lines:

Are you aware of opportunities for courageous or loving behaviors on your part?

Are you aware of others engaging in courageous or loving actions toward you?

Are you courageous in offering loving responses?

Are you loving enough when offering courageous responses?

Of course, all three aspects of ACL work together in these ways. Awareness without courage may result in knowing one is stuck but having a feeling of not being able to do anything different, and awareness without the ability to show or receive love may be experienced as a feeling of emptiness or loss. Courage in the absence of awareness can result in taking risks that range from thoughtless to dangerous, and courage without love can result in reckless reactions that have painful consequences for others. Finally, love without courage or awareness can become a somewhat impotent kindness or caring in which the person never risks anything too bold or disruptive, or he misses connecting accurately with the experience of the other person.

These examples illustrate the kinds of problems clients may have in the realms of awareness, courage, and love, and the balance between them. They also illustrate how the ACL framework supports individualized assessment.

QUICKLY ASSESSING ACL

We'll end this chapter with a set of questions that you can use to quickly assess ACL processes. We have one question for each aspect of awareness, courage, and love set forth earlier in this chapter, so hopefully this assessment tool will also help you remember and keep track of the entire ACL model. Ask clients the following questions, and consider how different contexts—for example, different relationships—affect the patterns of behavior:

Awareness

Do you notice what you're thinking and feeling?

Do you know what you need or value and have a sense of your goals and identity?

Are you aware of other people's feelings and needs?

Courage

Are you able to be openly vulnerable and emotional?

Do you authentically share what you feel and think?

Do you ask for what you need?

Love

Do you help others feel safe and secure?

Do you express empathy and understanding and provide validation?

Do you give others what they need?

Do you accept love from others?

SUMMARY

- ACL (awareness, courage, and love) is a framework for the functional analysis of behaviors that research shows are involved in social connection and therapeutic relationships.

- Awareness involves paying attention to yourself—your present-moment experience as well as your values and goals over time—and others, especially in order to notice opportunities to engage in courageous or loving (or other effective) behaviors.

- Courage involves moving toward another person despite potential vulnerability or aversion. Courageous behaviors include emotional vulnerability, self-disclosure, and making requests.

- Love involves responding to others' acts of vulnerability or courage in responsive, accepting, empathic ways.

- The ACL framework defines important aspects of the therapeutic-relationship stance promoted in FAP.

CHAPTER 5

Shape Process with the Five Rules of FAP

It's easy to think it's about *them*, about him or her, but it's about *you*. And me. Connecting. Right now, in this conversation. Not that one. *This* one.

—Susan Scott

"Every time my wife criticizes my behavior, of course, I get defensive."

You pause as the dots connect. "Is it possible that this—criticism, getting defensive—occurred between us earlier in session?"

There's a flickering frown. "No, it's pretty different here. Why would you ask that?"

"Well, I asked because it seemed like you were a little defensive then. And...you seem a little defensive now. Do you see what I mean?"

She shrugs, irritated. "Okay, well now that you point it out, yes."

"What could you try right now that would appear less defensive?"

"I guess..." She stops and appears to stare off into the distance. "I feel like when I receive criticism, my mood changes very quickly and I feel as though my self-esteem has deflated. And my guard goes up." Suddenly, she seems on the verge of being tearful.

You are surprised at the change in her tone. "You know. It's amazing how different that sounds. How different it feels. What is it like for you?"

"Vulnerable. I'm anxious." She purses her lips and looks away. "Anyway..."

"Is it okay if we just pause in this?" You pause a few beats. "I know we've talked about it before...it just strikes me how that bit of pause, that bit of vulnerability—even about the fact that you feel guarded, it makes all the difference. I know she wants you to give her this as well. And give it to yourself. It means so much."

"It's so hard for me..." She *is* tearful this time.

"I know. What does it mean for you?"

"Just that I could relax and be...trust her. I'm like a feral cat so much of the time." She weeps softly.

"I want that for you too. To be able to take that pause and be seen...to let yourself be. Let her see you. What if you could do this with her?"

When a client brings her interpersonal struggle—bound up with her psychological struggle—to the therapy relationship, when you see the very issue that is causing strife in her relationships occurring here and now, in therapy, you have a liability and an opportunity. Your relationship, here and now, will leave a mark. The liability rests in replicating what experience has shown her: that vulnerability is dangerous; that it's better to remain distanced and defended.

If, however, you have done the work to know her interpersonally—to see, for instance, how resistance to asking for what she needs, in part, maintains her depression and leaves her feeling voiceless—then you may see the behavior for what it is: something learned and once adaptive but now maladaptive; a costly and avoidant behavior that is both comfortable and uncomfortable at the same time. If you have done the work to know her empathically, so you can know what this moment feels like for her on the inside, you will be able to pause sensitively. You will be able to disrupt what normally happens in order to create something different. This is your opportunity, in which you will be able to walk with her into the novelty and anxiety of change.

FAP is about these moments in the therapy relationship, when a compassionate (and functional) understanding of the other person allows you to see and evoke and reinforce a different way of relating. In the first half of this book, we have mainly focused on the first part of this formula: seeing behavior from a contextual behavioral science, or functional, perspective. While this seeing is foundational to FAP, the heart of the FAP process lies in how you use that seeing to create change.

The process of change in FAP is essentially the process of influencing CRBs, as they happen in the therapy process, in such a way that you decrease the frequency of CRB1 and increase the frequency of CRB2. In this chapter, we present five rules (originally published in Kohlenberg & Tsai, 1991) to guide you in the process. Note that we use the term "rule" in a specific sense, meaning "Try it; you'll probably like it because good things will happen." This is in opposition to a more rigid prescription: "The rules are something you must do or something bad will happen."

The five rules are a learning tool to help you get your head around the FAP process. This chapter is primarily devoted to discussing each rule. For each, we've included questions for self-reflection or consultation. In part 2 of the book, we'll detail how to practice with these rules.

Here, then, are the rules:

Rule 1: Notice CRB.

Rule 2: Evoke CRB.

Rule 3: Reinforce CRB2.

Rule 4: Notice your effect.

Rule 5: Support generalization.

RULE 1: NOTICE CRB

Over the years, Bob Kohlenberg has often said that rule 1 is the most important rule in FAP. The reason is captured somewhat in our discussion of Carl Rogers in chapter 2: when you understand which behaviors serve a client and represent growth and flexibility and which represent being stuck and don't serve the client, you'll naturally tend to respond in ways that nurture and support the more effective behaviors. Broadly, then, rule 1 is about awareness: understanding what is evoked in the client during the work of therapy and how that behavior relates to the clinical problem. It also involves empathy, as what's needed in the moment is an exquisite sensitivity to the client's experience, who she ideally wants to be, and how close she is to that ideal in each moment.

Because this awareness is structured by functional analysis, rule 1 encompasses much of FAP and is the foundation for all the other rules. More technically, noticing CRB is about discriminating which behaviors are CRB1 and which are CRB2, as well as how these are being evoked and shaped in the moment. As discussed in chapter 3, on functional analysis, this requires appreciating the larger context in which the client lives and understanding the emotions and other internal experiences she may be experiencing.

This process of seeing various contexts and functions in the stream of behavior—and all of the associated judgments about what's effective and what isn't—is ongoing, collaborative, and complex. We'll address the specifics of how to put this rule into practice in part 2 of the book. For now, we'll offer a few examples of noticing CRB in the moment. As you'll see, these observations only take on a definite meaning in the context of a broader functional analysis:

- A client seems overly accommodating when it comes to scheduling, and despite this being convenient for you, you also know that she struggles with asserting her needs.

- A client seems to close up in a big way, with body language indicating shame, when you touch upon a particular topic.

- A client whose relationships are characterized by a lot of avoidance and conflict seems underengaged in session, and it seems the therapy isn't meeting his needs.

- A client who struggles to express emotion in her daily life cries in one session, and at the next she seems withdrawn.

- Despite appearing to be quite honest and direct in his disclosures, a client confuses you by seeming to shift between radically different views of himself and the world, and he also complains that nobody understands him or wants to get close to him.

Questions for Self-Reflection or Consultation: Rule 1

- What are the client's patterns in interpersonal relationships in daily life? Which patterns are problematic?

- What are the patterns in the client's process with you?

- Are there any points of functional similarity between outside-of-session relationships and in-session processes?

- What are the client's specific behaviors related to these patterns?

- Which of your behaviors contribute to these patterns?

- Are there any noteworthy patterns in the therapy relationship that are difficult to conceptualize, such as the client being confusing, annoying, or unsettling?

- Do you have any blind spots, areas of confusion, or vulnerabilities, perhaps related to your life history, that affect your ability to see the client's CRBs clearly?

RULE 2: EVOKE CRB

Once you attune with exquisite sensitivity to the client in the moment and can see the functions of what's happening in the here and now, you can be more strategic and explicit about creating a context in which CRBs are evoked. In other words, you can talk directly about what's happening in the therapy relationship, how it relates to clinical problems, and how different, more effective responses can be practiced. Rule 2 is about being strategically and deliberately evocative in this way.

Said another way, once you clearly see the contexts in which a client struggles most and therefore has the most to gain by improving her behavior, you have an opportunity. Beyond passively noticing CRBs when they happen naturally, in keeping with rule 1, you can invite the client to notice these moments as they happen and directly encourage a different response. This is where becoming a positive disruptive force for clients becomes a more deliberate, strategic, and collaborative act of courage and compassion.

It's crucial that creating this kind of deliberate, evocative context doesn't result in a more artificial, manipulative-feeling interaction, as this would undermine the foundation of social connection on which everything else stands. The spirit of rule 2 is to attend to what happens naturally in the therapeutic process and approach what's happening boldly, flexibly, and compassionately. In this way, rule 2 often requires courage from the therapist because evoking in order to prompt something new, outside the comfort zone, can disrupt behaviors that are the status quo path of least resistance for client and therapist alike. Yet if you avoid being evocative, you risk allowing dysfunctional patterns to continue and may even reinforce those patterns.

Evoking has functions beyond prompting CRB. An evocative interaction also elicits a range of emotions, thoughts, and other reactions from both client and therapist. Often these reactions play a large role in why the desired CRB2 is so difficult. For instance, the prospect of asking for what one needs can be bundled with intense shame or anxiety, or sharing the experience of sadness with someone may be accompanied by a deep fear of humiliation. When you evoke CRB and begin to shape CRB2 (rule 3), you aren't just asking clients to respond to what you're presenting in the moment; you're also inviting them to respond with acceptance and compassion to whatever they're feeling in that moment. Therefore, when you evoke CRB, your responsibility is to be attuned and responsive to the entire moment and to support clients as much as you're challenging them.

Here are a few examples of evoking CRB in the moment:

- If you know a client who struggles with asserting her needs, you can invite her to begin each session with a clear statement of her needs.

- If a client fears intimacy, you could courageously ask him to practice sharing what he wants to avoid discussing and encourage him to ask personal questions of you that could build connection in the therapy relationship.

- If you know a client has difficulty accepting love from others, you might ask her to notice your warm expression as she enters the room.

- If a client has asked you for help in being more responsive to the emotions of his family members about a death in the family, you could spend a few minutes talking to him about your own mother's death, providing him the opportunity to respond to your emotions (taking care to ensure that the interaction remains focused on the client's goals).

Questions for Self-Reflection or Consultation: Rule 2

- Which situations in therapy or behaviors from you evoke CRB from the client?

- What do you avoid doing because the client's CRB is aversive to you? Are there any topics you're avoiding, in regard to either the therapy relationship or the therapeutic process? Is that avoidance effective in therapy?

- Have you brought up the issues you've identified in session? And have you owned your part in the cycles unfolding between you and the client?

- When evoking CRB2, are you sensitive to the balance of courage and love the client needs? Are you courageous enough when evoking CRB? Are you loving enough?

- If you were to describe the client's struggle in the most clear, bold, and compassionate way, what would you say? Would it work to present this statement to the client? If yes, why? If not, why not?

- How does your history affect the way you challenge the client or evoke CRB?

RULE 3: REINFORCE CRB2

After noticing and evoking CRB, the next step in FAP is to shape CRB2 so it persists. From the contextual behavioral viewpoint, what matters most in accomplishing this is consequences: how you respond to CRB in the moment as it happens. Once you observe a more effective behavior (via rule 1) or directly evoke it (via rule 2), provide attention and respond in a way that will hopefully be reinforcing.

FAP focuses on reinforcing CRB2 because aligning with the positive function of supportive social connection is a more potent and effective way to shape behavior than punishing CRB1. After all, think about how it feels to be in a relationship in which your steps toward growth are invited, praised, and supported, versus one in which your missteps are scrutinized and criticized. The former creates a more nurturing context for growth and well-being.

In this way, responsiveness to CRB2 (corresponding to love) is functionally equivalent to rule 3. In many ways, rule 3 lies at the heart of FAP because it instantiates a specific mechanism of change: reinforcement of CRB2. One could argue that the other rules only provide a supportive context for applying rule 3. The big challenge with rule 3 lies in determining which of your responses will actually function as reinforcing for a particular client in a particular context. The following sections provide some general guidelines in this regard.

Respond in a way that's socially natural but intense. Your responses need to make sense to the client and come across as relevant to the world outside of therapy, so it's important to be socially natural. This is different from being socially typical or appropriate, as these kinds of responses often aren't strong enough. Therefore, you would ideally identify your natural response and then amplify it beyond what social norms would dictate. This way, your response will be explicit and command attention and reflection. The most influential responses are likely to break the bounds of convention or propriety in this way, which is part of what makes them memorable and beneficially disruptive. To be clear, these responses break social conventions because they're unusually strong or loud, not because they're weird or hard to make sense of. They typically channel and express what other people might feel but not say.

Emphasize safety and acceptance. When seen from an eagle's-eye view, high above and with good perspective, therapy is centered around working with a client who's experiencing vulnerability and emotion in the context of a social interaction. What that client needs from you at a very basic level is safety and acceptance. It's all too easy for therapists to get caught up in problem solving or wanting to "fix" clients and forget this basic vulnerability. Express to clients that they're fully safe and accepted by you. Do this explicitly, with authenticity.

Speak with conviction. Like everyone, clients have doubts, especially in the moments of vulnerability surrounding their CRB2s. So when you respond to CRB2, your voice should be clear, strong, and authentic. The best responses are bold and crystal clear, especially in terms of being 100 percent accepting of clients, no matter how emotional they get. This is especially important when clients are very emotional, because at these times they may latch onto ambiguities or silences and view them as indicators of judgments or lack of safety. Find a way to clearly and compassionately state your acceptance: "I want you to know that as you're sharing this with me, I'm feeling 100 percent accepting and loving toward you, and I feel really confident that you're safe with me."

Learn what works for a given client. For some people, intense, emotional outbursts of appreciation can be aversive, causing shame or raising fears that the person must now reciprocate or live up to a new standard. For others, highly emotional appreciation is extremely validating. As always, the function of the response is what matters—not the form. This makes it important to attend to individual clients and discover what works for each.

Be authentic. Most of all, don't be phony. Humans are very skilled bullshit detectors, especially those who have been harmed by others in the past. Inauthenticity prevents or destroys connection and influence. Responsiveness is most effective when you bring your unique voice and emotion to it, rather than following a script, talking like a professional, or offering typical therapist responses such as "I'm so proud of you" or "You're so courageous." Conveying genuineness through tone of voice, eye contact, and facial expressions is also extremely important—sometimes more important than your words.

Here are few examples of reinforcing CRB2 in the moment:

- Acknowledging a request for more session time by granting it.

- Sharing a heartfelt response to the client's life history, such as expressing how inspired and moved you are by her courage and persistence, and why you feel that way.

- Saying something like "This is an awesome 2 for you!" while offering your hand for a high five.

- Telling a client that his CRB2 has renewed your enthusiasm for your work.

- Joining a client in her vulnerability after she describes something she feels ashamed about by sharing that you've had a similar experience.

Questions for Self-Reflection or Consultation: Rule 3

- Can you see the client's moments of improvement? Do you feel engaged in the client's process of change?

- Is the client aware of your responses to her vulnerability, improvements, and growth?

- Do you respond to the client in openhearted ways that feel genuine to you?

- Do you hold back your authentic emotional responses or conceal them within a lot of other information, such as disclaimers, psychoeducation, or case formulation?

- What do you value and cherish about the client? How has this client affected you? Have you let the client know these things?

RULE 4: NOTICE YOUR EFFECT

Remember that reinforcement doesn't exert its effects immediately. Rather, it's a process in which behavior increases in frequency as a result of its consequences over time. Therefore, to ensure that you're effectively reinforcing your clients' CRB2s and helping them move toward their therapy goals, you need to attend not only to how you respond in the moment but also to how their behavior evolves over time. In fact, what happens over time is much more important than the events comprising any single moment. (And given that mistakes are inevitable in therapy, thank goodness for this fact.)

The only way we can know the impact of any single moment of interaction is by noticing how the process of therapy unfolds over time. When CRB2s are increasing in strength and frequency and CRB1s are decreasing, then therapy is working. Of course, if this isn't happening, you want to know that too. Therapy is always a work in progress.

Here are a few examples of ways in which you can determine the effect of your actions in the therapeutic interaction:

- After an intense exchange in which a client expressed a lot of emotion and you reciprocated in a heartfelt way, you might inquire about how she experienced the interaction.

- If you and the client seem to keep repeating a similar pattern, such as a session that's more intensely emotional followed by a session that's more withdrawn, you could ask the client whether he has the same impression and what that pattern might represent.

- After you've tried to provide safety in response to a client's vulnerability, you can directly ask whether she feels safer.

- When a client is going through a stuck period in therapy, you could ask him whether he thinks anything you're doing isn't helpful.

- At the end of each session, you might ask the client, "How was I in responding to you today?"

- You can also use various monitoring tools or standardized measures, such as asking clients to use a diary card to record the frequency of their CRB1s and CRB2s in daily life.

Questions for Self-Reflection or Consultation: Rule 4

- Is the client changing within the therapeutic relationship over time? Are you seeing more CRB2 and less CRB1?

- Are the two of you repeating the same cycles and patterns?

- Are you talking with the client about how things are evolving in the therapeutic relationship and in the therapy?

- Do you and the client discuss the effects you have on each other?

- Do you acknowledge and discuss the changes you're seeing in the moment?

- Are you working with any issues or limitations of your own that could impede the client's progress?

RULE 5: SUPPORT GENERALIZATION

Of course, the point of therapy is not just to change client behaviors in the therapy room; the goal is behavior change outside of therapy that's sufficiently sustained and durable so that therapy can eventually end. *Generalization* is a behavioral term for the process by which behavior in one context transfers to other contexts. Thus, rule 5 calls for attending to and supporting the transfer of improvements from the context of therapy to all of the relevant contexts outside of therapy. In FAP, this generalization is achieved in two ways: by discussing functional analyses and case formulations, and by assigning home practice of CRB2.

Discussing Functional Analyses and Case Formulations with Clients

In FAP, therapists discuss their functional analyses and case formulation with clients and include them in developing the formulation as much as possible. This helps clients to start seeing how various functions show up in life outside of session. When clients are aware of the parallels between their in-session and outside-of-session behaviors and can notice their CRBs in the moment, they can see the progress they're making in therapy and how it can be meaningful and useful in other contexts.

To this end, we recommend that you reflect on chapters 2 and 3, about seeing function and doing functional analysis, and think about how you can share those principles with clients: How can they collaborate with you in developing a functional analysis? Then take this approach whenever it makes sense, especially after you've reinforced CRB2. That's the key moment when verbal learning will promote generalization of the new behavior to other contexts. Talk about what just happened so the client can see the connections between what she did as CRB2 and what you did in response, and how all of this matters and applies to her life.

We have a term for this kind of debriefing: *in-to-out parallels*. This refers to taking what just happened in session and making a parallel with a situation the client cares about outside of session. Here are a few examples of in-to-out parallels:

- When you show vulnerability to me in here, you see how I can be really open and safe for you. It actually gives me space and motivates me to be there for you. I think your partner wants this from you too. What do you think?

- When you ask me for what you need, I'll always try to give it to you—like right now. So guess what? I think this is true for your friends too. Maybe not every one of them, but from what I've heard from you, Mary really wants to support you, no?

- I bet your mom would have the exact same look on her face as I do right now if you tried this with her.

Assigning Home Practice of CRB2

The second way to implement rule 5 is by assigning homework—typically working to practice new CRB2s, developed in session, with others. Take another look at those examples of in-to-out parallels we just provided. Can you see how each could lead to a specific homework assignment?

The best assignments flow directly and immediately from powerful in-session interactions. For example, consider a client who has difficulty forming close relationships and makes minimal eye contact with you when she's struggling with expressing feelings. After identifying minimal eye contact as CRB1, you can establish increased eye contact as the relevant CRB2 and make this an explicit in-session target. After an instance of reinforcing this CRB2 in the here and now, you could then ask the client to try to increase eye contact with others. All of this might be stated in the following way: "When we first started therapy, you tended to avoid expressing your feelings and to reduce our connection by diverting your eyes. That created distance between us. After you became aware of this issue and were more willing to have eye contact with me and express your feelings, our relationship became closer. I'm going to suggest that you try to do the same thing with your friend Carol and see what happens to the closeness in your relationship with her." You could then schedule a very specific homework assignment for the client to do this with Carol in a certain context. You might also discuss how this might feel risky, given that we can't guarantee how others will respond, and why it might be important for the client to take the risk anyway.

Here are a few examples of how you can promote generalization of new CRB2s:

- Collaborate with the client in functional analysis and the identification of CRB1 and CRB2.

- Get the client's feedback about how in-session moments are similar to or different from important out-of-session contexts.

- Point out how what the client did in session with you is relevant to relating to others, and offer some guidance on how to practice the CRB2 with others.

- For a client who has difficulty identifying her needs, after she's successfully done so in session, assign homework that involves getting in touch with her needs each day.

- Help the client schedule particular activities that offer opportunities to practice a new CRB2 immediately after that CRB2 shows up in session.

Questions for Self-Reflection or Consultation: Rule 5

- Does the client agree with your conceptualization of how his in-session CRBs are functionally similar to relevant out-of-session behaviors?

- If not, have you discussed where the two of you disagree?

- Are you discussing the ways in which the client is taking what he's experiencing with you out into his life?

- How well is this transfer of CRB2 into daily life working? What might improve the process of generalization?

EXPERIENCING THE FIVE RULES OF FAP IN CONTEXT

We'll close this chapter, and part 1 of the book, with the same dialogue that opened this chapter, but this time annotated to show the five rules of FAP in action and the CRB the therapist is responding to. Although it's brief, the transcript also conveys the kind of relational focus, flexibility, and individualization that's characteristic of FAP. Note, however, that this is just one example of FAP as it plays out between one particular therapist and one particular client. FAP isn't about a particular style; it's about process. We'll reinforce this important point in part 2 of the book, where we provide numerous dialogues illustrating FAP skills in action—examples that demonstrate a range of therapeutic styles.

"Every time my wife criticizes my behavior, of course, I get defensive." [Description of an out-of-session problem.]

You pause as the dots connect. "Is it possible that this—criticism, getting defensive—occurred between us earlier in session?" [Noticing a potential CRB earlier in session (rule 1) and drawing a parallel.]

There's a flickering frown. "No, it's pretty different here. Why would you ask that?" [CRB1.]

"Well, I asked because it seemed like you were a little defensive then. And...you seem a little defensive now. Do you see what I mean?" [Rules 1 and 2: Noticing and evoking CRB.]

She shrugs, irritated. "Okay, well now that you point it out, yes." [Emerging CRB2.]

"What could you try right now that would appear less defensive?" [Rule 2: Evoking CRB.]

"I guess..." She stops and appears to stare off into the distance. "I feel like when I receive criticism, my mood changes very quickly and I feel as though my self-esteem has deflated. And my guard goes up." Suddenly she is on the verge of being tearful. [CRB2: Vulnerable self-disclosure.]

You are surprised at the change in her tone. "You know. It's amazing how different that sounds. How different it feels. [Rule 3: Reinforcing CRB2.] What is it like for you?" [Rule 4: Checking on the effect of the therapist's response to the client's CRB2.]

"Vulnerable. I'm anxious." [CRB2.] She purses her lips and looks away. "Anyway..." [CRB1.]

"Is it okay if we just pause in this?" You pause a few beats. [Rule 2: Evoking CRB.] "I know we've talked about it before... It just strikes me how that bit of pause, that bit of vulnerability—even about the fact that you feel guarded, it makes all the difference. [Rule 3: Reinforcing CRB2.] I know she wants you to give her this as well. And give it to yourself. It means so much." [Rule 5: Supporting generalization, in this case by describing the function of in-session behavior—that her vulnerability leads to connection.]

"It's so hard for me..." She *is* tearful this time. [CRB2.]

"I know. [Rule 3: Reinforcing CRB2.] What does it mean for you?" [Rule 2: Evoking CRB.]

"Just that I could relax and be...trust her. I'm like a feral cat so much of the time." She weeps softly. [CRB2.]

"I want that for you too. To be able to take that pause and be seen...let yourself be. [Rule 3: Reinforcing CRB2.] Let her see you. What if you could do this with her?" [Rule 5: Supporting generalization by suggesting homework.]

SUMMARY

- The moment-by-moment process of FAP is guided by functional thinking and proceeds through the five rules of FAP.

  - Rule 1: Notice CRB.

  - Rule 2: Evoke CRB.

  - Rule 3: Reinforce CRB2.

  - Rule 4: Notice your effect.

  - Rule 5: Support generalization.

PART 2

The Practice

I am rooted, but I flow.

—Virginia Woolf

When Nick came to therapy he was down a miserable, bitter hole. His voice on the answering machine was clipped: "I've been referred to you for treatment by the inpatient unit. How does this work? Call me back please."

Arriving at the first session, he sat tensely in a heavy peacoat and well-worn Brooks Brothers shirt. His hair and beard were neatly trimmed. His body was tense and heavy, jaw set. His eyes, darting around, betrayed his anxiety but also a quickness of mind. He often seemed on the verge of rolling his eyes, anticipating the next annoying or mundane thing that might be said.

Given the vagueness of the referral and the previous treatment notes, the first few sessions centered on diagnostic assessment and rapport building. What stood out to the therapist was the depth of Nick's despair and the emptiness he felt. He also felt a lot of rage. Hatred, even. They talked about whether there was anything he liked. Sometimes he liked opera or classical music, but these also seemed to make him miserable, just slightly more exalted in his misery.

Then in the third week, Nick took a big risk. He described what it felt like to go to a department event and perceive waves of little slights and insults coming at him from faculty and fellow graduate students; to feel a rising sense of fear, then terror, and then paranoia—*they must all be thinking that I'm a fool.* Such interactions left him with a burning pain inside of his chest. "Is this normal?" he gasped. "I need to know if this is normal. I don't have anywhere else to turn. It's either work with you or I'm done. I will kill myself."

This moment—when he was willing to share an experience that was deeply disturbing, that undermined his willingness to trust everyone—was when the real therapeutic relationship started. He asked a genuine, vulnerable question and relied on the therapist's responsiveness.

Together the therapist and Nick eventually decided that the valid diagnosis was borderline personality disorder. The treatment that followed incorporated elements of dialectical behavior therapy, acceptance and commitment therapy, and FAP. The treatment took several years, and it was successful.

Afterward, recalling what worked, Nick said it had helped that he and the therapist were the same age, that they shared a worldview, and that "he felt like me." They developed a framework for thinking about what had happened to him, and how he was changing in the here and now. The core of what he experienced as being helpful was simple: deep empathy. This took many forms, including seeing the experience together, understanding it, naming it, and then asking for change—inviting change even when it was difficult to change. They responded to victories and hashed out lots of disagreements. They looked at how Nick hid in the moment and how the therapist hid. They put a whole range of emotions onto the table. The therapist had to apologize numerous times, take feedback, and even share longings and aspirations to help paint the picture of what it means to be human.

What occurred between the two of them is a form of the dance that is the therapeutic relationship. Regardless of the theory or framework or principles the therapist brings to therapy, what it feels like to actually go *there*—to do the work of change through a relationship—is another thing entirely. One cannot *do* this kind of relationship from a distance. One is pulled out of theory into amazement, intimacy, and connection again and again. And, at the same time, one returns from the disorientation of the process to theory and principles again and again.

FAP aims to shed light on this process while providing basic principles to help you navigate the therapeutic relationship. FAP will give you solid roots, but it will also allow you to genuinely flow with the other human being whose well-being is the task you both share.

In this part of the book we transition from the ideas of FAP to the actual practice. We ended part 1 with an overview of the five rules, which describe a process for attending to what is happening in the moment of therapy and shaping change in that moment. But how does one put the rules into practice? How does one do FAP?

The answer to these questions takes us back to the beginning of the book. FAP is about capitalizing on the inherent therapeutic functions of a close, courageous relationship and being guided by functional analysis in order to make the impact of the relationship as targeted and therapeutic as possible. Following the 5 rules, then, is not about using a technique or manipulating your client. The rules are instead like signposts that point you toward what matters when you're engaged in the process of therapy. Similarly, functional analysis is a guide that helps you understand what is happening in the therapeutic relationship. Put another way, the process of relating to clients is what is at the center of FAP. It's the place where you must put the rules and the functional analysis into action.

Part 2 is organized by several crucial moments in the therapy process. Each moment requires certain skills and capacities of the FAP therapist. The moments are beginning therapy (chapter 7), evoking clinically relevant behaviors in the moment (chapter 8), and responding to clinically relevant behavior—specifically, reinforcing CRB2 (chapter 9). Finally, chapter 10 puts the whole process together, chapter 11 discusses case conceptualization, chapter 12 covers homework and experiential exercises, and chapter 13 is about ending therapy.

Before discussing these key moments in therapy, however, let's start with what is in many ways the foundation of FAP: your personal capacities as a therapist.

CHAPTER 6

Know Yourself

To fully relate to another, one must first relate to oneself.

—Irvin Yalom

Why did you become a therapist? Let's look at what some therapists participating in the online FAP community have to say.

I knew what it was to suffer. I wanted others not to be alone in that suffering.

To be there when others want to run, when even you want to run.

I fell in love with the science of psychology at a time in my life when I felt a strong need to learn more about myself. Then, after witnessing the great potential psychotherapy had for bettering the lives of people, I decided that practicing it was what I wanted to do with mine.

I wanted to pull one other person out of the hole I had been in.

At the beginning, to help people suffering. Right now, it is a selfish reason; I am a psychotherapist because it makes me a better person.

One of the reasons was to learn how to heal, and to bring that back to my family.

Because helping others helps me, and I wanted to turn what happened to me into something good.

When I was a teenager I experienced some losses and some pain, and in facing them I recognized the importance of having loving, meaningful, and deep connection with others as a way to heal the wounds I have in my heart.

Unquenchable curiosity about the formation and the falling away of knowledge about ourselves and the world around us. Seeing the opportunity to be of service to another person by simply being myself.

First I wanted to save the world. Then I realized I can barely save myself. Now I am content if my clients can just sit with themselves.

I wanted to make sense of repeated existential crises I experienced as a child, which I continue to experience to this day. I wanted to understand and support my own sense of lostness and other vulnerability and extend my support to others around me—ultimately to feel less alone.

I had a wonderful psychotherapist that made an actual difference in my life. I wanted to do the same for other people.

I wanted to understand people, and life.

I was deeply curious about the whys behind life trajectories, the whys behind (my own) suffering—and the big question about the meaning of life—all the ponderings of a soul-searching teenager... Only later on it turned into a wish to help others.

To understand more deeply why I do the things I do, and why others do the things they do, and with that understanding decrease our mutual suffering.

To understand why people (some people) are so miserable.

I wanted to help myself and others feel they had real choices in their lives. To have the life they really yearned for. And to know what that was.

I was taught from a young age that feelings don't matter. I got therapy for major depressive disorder as a young adult and had to reorient my approach to emotions. After what I've been through, I feel so much empathy for people who are suffering emotionally. I wanted to do something to help others feel better.

Curiosity about how people work, how misery works, how triumph works. How families fall apart. A love of story.

It is very reinforcing to perceive that I truly "see" someone. I feel reinforced when someone "sees" me—the good, bad, and ugly.

I spent a long time dangerous and destructive. In doing therapy, I could see a way to be useful. That has meant a lot to me.

Because I genuinely enjoy seeing people "waking up, becoming alive, and starting to live" this life and taking care of themselves. I wouldn't put this into words then, like now, but I have the same look in the eyes when I am witnessing "waking up" as then. I woke up and started to take care of myself at the age of twenty-five, and I am still learning how to live this life.

I wanted to help people and better understand my family. And luckily I found the healing through connection, and now I want to show the same path to my clients.

Self-knowledge has always been a fascinating field for me. Being influenced as an adolescent by Socrates and Scott Peck, I took the decision to dive into the exploration of self-awareness and to encourage others to do this leap as well.

I loved ideas and stories of suffering and redemption but believed I was too awkward and deficient to ever help people. At a certain point, because some key people believed in me, I decided to take on the challenge of becoming what I thought I could not be, and of helping others enter their fear and shame as well.

In a moment of cynicism an armchair critic might say, "Therapists are in it for themselves—they're all just working out their own issues."

This is meant to disparage therapists, but the cynic misunderstands our purpose and goals. Our personal commitment to our work—why we do it—is one of our greatest sources of strength, insight, and empathy. As in any profession that demands intellectual and emotional labor, creativity, persistence through ups and downs, independent thought, and dedicated study, the most compelling whys are always deeply personal. If we are to be effective in our chosen field, it is crucial that we are grounded in a living sense of purpose that makes the struggle meaningful.

Besides purpose, you are present in the therapy you offer in other ways. Most concretely, in any given moment of any given session, you are not outside the process looking in. You are as central to the process as the client; your reactions are the medium of therapy. We're not just talking about your techniques and grasp of theory, but also your emotions, your avoidances, your willingness to feel, and your personal experiences and how they shape what you bring to the therapeutic relationship. Your worldview. Your convictions. This is the landscape of working as a therapist (Alves de Oliveira & Vandenberghe, 2009; Vandenberghe & Silvestre, 2014).

FAP asks you to ground your practice by relating well, to yourself and others, deliberately and effectively across a whole range of social relationships, roles, and situations. FAP shares this focus on personal practice with numerous other therapy approaches:

- Psychoanalytic training involves completing your own analysis.

- Dialectical behavior therapy asks therapists to develop a personal mindfulness and skills practice.

- Acceptance and commitment therapy asks therapists to practice psychological flexibility using the processes in the hexaflex.

- Compassion-focused therapy asks therapists to develop a compassion practice.

Across all of the approaches listed above, therapist self-development is as much about ensuring that therapist issues remain distinct from client issues as it is about inviting the therapist to participate in a more self-disclosing, self-involving way. For example, when a client becomes angry at you and you "feel disrespected," will you remain flexible and therapeutic? Or will you react impulsively? Will you listen beyond your own reaction to hear what the issue is for your client, distinct from what it is for you?

Your ability to notice and modulate your own reactions contributes to what you will tend to evoke (or avoid evoking) and reinforce (or fail to reinforce) in your clients. For example, if you feel angry or ashamed when a client gives you the feedback that she didn't understand what you just explained, you may subtly punish or extinguish such feedback—even if that's the last thing you would want to do. If you are averse to "conflict" or avoid making others "feel bad," you may not address the negative impact a client has on other people—and which you experience firsthand in the therapy relationship—thereby missing a crucial dimension of the client's presenting issues.

Nuanced self-awareness allows you to step back from such patterns. By seeing them clearly and appraising their costs—to you and to your clients—you can instead find opportunities to engage your clients with a flexible balance of courage and compassion. Therapist self-development is an ongoing reflective process, a self-discovery process, as well as a skill-development process. It is well supported by functional thinking.

The therapist self-development process (or struggle) is not just reflected in clinically relevant moments in the therapeutic relationship. Again and again in our consultation with clinicians, we see how the extended process of therapy itself—especially the trial and error and persistence demanded by challenging cases—brings therapists face-to-face with their own vulnerabilities around persistence, faith, trust, control, and so on.

One consultee, for example, described feeling a sense of incompetence and uncertainty when her client did not respond to her initial interventions. In response she felt a great deal of pressure—grounded in a genuine empathy—to help or solve her client's issues. In other words, the function of her empathy was to increase her distress and ineffectiveness! With consultation, she came to realize that her pressure and anxiety led to more of exactly what the client didn't need: an expectation of changing, an urgent need to solve "the problem," and a sense that the problem was intolerable. And this intention came across to the client even with innocuous questions like "What are you feeling right now?"

This urgency to resolve uncertainty and pain had a deep history for the therapist. By practicing acceptance of her own discomfort with uncertainty (and with awareness of how her past had shaped it), she gradually built a more flexible stance from which to empathize with the client's pain, while remaining grounded in her own perspective, as a therapist, of trust and compassion. In turn she was able to more effectively invite her client to let go of "control" and instead find and embrace the choices he did have.

When you master your own fears and vulnerabilities, you don't just solve those particular issues—your struggle with uncertainty, or criticism, or whatever; you learn, in a visceral way, what only genuine, boundary-expanding self-development can teach you. You learn what it means to face what seems impossible or overwhelming and to grow through the process. So often this is what we ask our clients to do, so knowing the territory personally is invaluable.

In this chapter, we will walk you through a series of exercises designed to guide you in your personal practice of self-development:

- The life history exercise asks you to look at your most formative learning experiences—both negative and positive—so you can see clearly where your current vulnerabilities and strengths lie and how your experiences shaped them.

- The client history audit, paralleling the life history, asks you to look at how your experiences with clients—throughout your career—have shaped who you are and where you are vulnerable as a therapist.

- The feedback interview is about stepping beyond self-reflection and looking at your strengths and weaknesses from the perspective of someone you trust.

- Risk-taking is the practice of looking at the important things in your life or therapeutic work that you are avoiding, out of some aversion to discomfort or uncertainty, and deliberately challenging yourself to step forward.

- Finally, the therapeutic purpose statement invites you to define who you are as a therapist, who you want to be for your clients, and what type of therapeutic relationships you wish to provide.

LIFE HISTORY

We are creatures defined by our history. We think of who we are based on what we've done. Our expectations of how others will treat us are largely shaped by our history. We learn what will be painful and what will be safe. Because of this learning we are susceptible to missing the present moment and instead staying within the confines of what is safe.

The life history exercise is about finding insight from your life story: how your history has shaped you, and in what ways it has created vulnerabilities and strengths. The goal of this exercise is to help you be effectively present in the therapeutic relationship. Telling your story is effective for this goal because it allows you to see the meaning of this moment by recognizing the specific episodes that preceded it. Telling your story is not about the details, rather it's about the narrative—how does the history make this moment meaningful? Just as you wouldn't understand *Return of the Jedi* if you haven't seen *Star Wars* and *The Empire Strikes Back*, you can't understand the context of this episode of your life without knowing the past.

Consider the following:

- Why do angry clients make you especially anxious? Did you learn that anger is dangerous in your history?

- How has your history left you unprepared to empathize with those who struggle at school? Did you always find effort relatively effortless?

- How does the fear of making a mistake lead you to avoid certain types of vulnerability? Did you learn that making mistakes means you are incompetent or unlovable?

Seeing clearly your story creates the possibility of understanding other perspectives. For instance, it may allow you to see that anger is not as dangerous as it feels, or that mistakes are a road to learning. Knowing our story well, even the most shameful chapters—and living closely with it and sharing it with those who matter to us—also tends to connect us with a broader sense of common humanity. In his memoir *Telling Secrets* (1991), Frederick Buechner makes this point and several others well:

> I have come to believe that by and large the human family all has the same secrets, which are both very telling and very important to tell. They are telling in the sense that they tell what is perhaps the central paradox of our condition—that what we hunger for perhaps more than anything else is to be known in our full humanness, and yet that is often just what we also fear more than anything else. It is important to tell at least from time to time the secret of who we truly and fully are—even if we tell it only to ourselves—because otherwise we run the risk of losing track of who we truly and fully are and little by little come to accept instead the highly edited version which we put forth in hope that the world will find it more acceptable than the real thing. It is important to tell our secrets too because it makes it easier that way to see where we have been in our lives and where we are going. It also makes it easier for other people to tell us a secret or two of their own, and exchanges like that have a lot to do with what being a family is all about and what being human is all about (p. 2–3).

Step 1

The first step is to make some kind of representation of your story, either visual or narrative.

Option 1: Creating a Visual Timeline

On a piece of paper, draw a vertical line down the middle of the page. Label the top of the line "now" and the bottom "birth." To the right of the line, record positive life events, using the horizontal distance from the line to represent the degree of positivity; in other words, events farther away from the center line are more positive. To the left of the line, record negative life events in the same way. You need not write a detailed description of each event; a brief label is sufficient. Of course, some events may have both negative and positive aspects. In such cases, feel free to record the event on both sides of the line.

Option 2: Writing a Narrative

Write your history in narrative form. This format allows for more in-depth description of the circumstances and impacts of various events, but it can also be overwhelming. We encourage you to write freely in a way that works for you. Take as much or as little time as feels right. Do this exercise in a way that is a 2 for you.

Step 2

Now step back and reflect on your story and how it has shaped you. You can do this immediately after completing step 1, but in our experience this second reflective step is often more productive after a pause of at least twenty-four hours.

When you're ready to reflect, read through the following questions and pick a handful that seem relevant to you. If you can't choose, work through all the questions in order.

Awareness

- Which key events most shaped who you are today?

- What lessons did you learn about yourself from these events?

- What lessons did you learn about others from these events?

- What lessons did you learn about the world?

- What effects have these lessons had in your life? How do they shape how you see specific people in your life?

- How do you relate to these lessons? For example, do you accept them or resist them? Do you mostly keep them out of awareness, or do they often make up part of your mental landscape?

Courage

- As you reflect on your life history, where do you feel discomfort, which may be reflected by emotions such as fear, anxiety, or shame?

- Which parts are the most painful to linger with?

- Where do you feel urges to speed up and move on? If you slowed down, what would you notice?

- What did you learn about taking risks by showing your emotions or vulnerability with others?

Love

- Where do you feel the most love or compassion in your story?

- Can you bring more love or compassion to aspects of your story, perhaps those that are the most difficult to see compassionately?

Step 3

Pick one theme from the preceding reflections on your life history that seems particularly relevant to your life at the moment. Then answer the following questions in the context of that theme.

- What do you do that is counterproductive? What are your 1s?

- In situations in which your 1s happen, what matters most to you?

- Relative to your 1s, what sorts of behaviors might represent improvements? What are your 2s?

- Look ahead to the coming week, or whatever time frame seems relevant, and identify a few situations in which these 1s and 2s might happen. What would your 2s look like in these situations?

Therapist Avoidance Questions

Avoidance often occurs in the most difficult or stuck part of our relationships; avoidance of vulnerability limits our closeness with others and impacts our therapeutic relationships. As a supplement to thinking about your 1s and 2s in general, then, think specifically about the function of avoidance in your life. The questions below explore parallels that may exist between what you avoid in your daily life and what you avoid as a therapist. Write brief responses to each of the following question:

- What do you tend to avoid addressing with your clients? With the clients you have seen or will see this week, what are you avoiding?

- How does this avoidance impact the work you do with these clients?

- What do you tend to avoid dealing with in your life? Be specific, and consider tasks, people, memories, needs, and emotions (including longing, grief, anger, sadness, and fear). What are you avoiding this week? This month? This year?

- How does your avoidance in daily life impact the work you do with your clients?

Once you've identified particular areas of avoidance, you can begin to explore what your 2s would be in those situations. It can be useful to revisit these questions over time because avoidance evolves.

Optional Exercise: Share the Life History with a Partner

One final option for working with the life history exercise is to share your story with others. Sharing your story provides a natural opportunity for vulnerable disclosure and responsiveness from your listener. In FAP trainings, we confine the verbal story to five minutes, not only for the sake of giving everyone time to share but also because brevity compels us to get to the essence of the vulnerability in the story sooner, rather than spending a lot of time on the details of storytelling.

Share in a way that feels vulnerable, by which we mean taking a workable step beyond your normal comfort zone into a place of vulnerability. This can be either a small step or a large step; the choice is yours. Whichever life history method you use, take time to respond vulnerably and compassionately after each person shares his or her story.

CLIENT HISTORY AUDIT

Your history as a therapist also shapes who you are in therapy. On the one hand, many of us remember the client who got away, the client who pushed past all our limits, and the clients with whom we felt powerless. On the other hand, we may also remember the clients who most inspired us or taught us the most about something.

In this exercise, you will make a detailed audit of your clinical history. The aim is to put all your clients on the table and, with clear eyes, reflect on how they've influenced you.

Step 1

Make a list, by year, of all the clients you've seen. Consult old session notes, records, and so forth. If you've been in practice for more than a handful of years, this task may be quite difficult. Do it anyway, perhaps limiting your audit to the clients you can remember; however, if you have the records, by all means make an exhaustive list. You may add supervisors or consultants to this list as well.

Step 2

Survey the list and pick out one client, or a handful, who shaped you the most, then answer the following:

- What did you learn from these clients?

- What did you discover about yourself?

- What did you come to fear?

- What do you tend to avoid now because of your experience with this client?

Repeat this step with as many clients from your audit list as you wish. Notice any themes that develop in the lessons you learned from clients.

Optional Step 3

The final step is an exercise in perspective taking. From the perspective of the clients you most struggled to understand or work effectively with, try to answer the following questions:

- What did I experience and learn as a child?

- How did I learn to cope?

- What is my biggest fear?

FEEDBACK INTERVIEWS

We don't always see ourselves clearly. And sometimes, in important ways, other people see us more clearly than we see ourselves. In this exercise, you will take advantage of this possibility. The feedback interview is intense because you invite others who know you and care about you to offer insights about your behavior—both strengths and weaknesses. You elicit this feedback via a structured interview, during which you suspend your reactions (to the extent possible) and instead focus on drawing out and understanding the perspective of the other person. You may come to see yourself more clearly while expanding your grasp of your 1s and 2s.

Step 1

Pick someone who knows you and has your best interests in mind. You can conduct the interview solely for yourself. Or, if appropriate and both parties agree, you can take turns conducting the interview. Pick someone you trust to give caring feedback; or, if you're up for the challenge, you can certainly choose someone who might be bold or confrontational. Either way, be sure to explicitly invite the other person to be honest and compassionate.

Step 2

Mentally prepare yourself:

- What are you afraid of?

- What might you hear?

- How would you react at your best?

Step 3

Do the interview. We highly recommend using a script to structure the conversation. This can facilitate greater courage, whereas ambiguity or lack of structure can lead to avoidance. Here are some questions you might consider using. Feel free to adapt them as you see fit.

- What do you most appreciate about me?

- What do you wish I would appreciate more about myself?

- What do you see me actively working on in my life?

- What do you see me doing that's self-defeating?

- What do I do that brings others close to me?

- What do I do that can put up barriers between me and others?

- When I'm at my best, what do I do?

- When I'm not at my best, what do I do?

Just listen, and clarify.
Thank the person for his or her insight.

Step 4

Now it's time to debrief:

- Did the feedback fulfill your expectations?

- Did the feedback match up with your existing self-assessment?

- How is the feedback-giver biased?

- How is the feedback giver more accurate than you (perhaps more than you'd like to admit)?

RISK-TAKING

Risk-taking is a central personal practice among members of the FAP community. Tim Ferriss, author of *The Four-Hour Workweek* and winner of *Wired* magazine's self-promotion prize in 2008, writes that "A person's success in life can usually be measured by the number of uncomfortable conversations he or she is willing to have" (2007, p. 47). The FAP version of this idea looks something like this: a FAP therapist's success can *often* be measured by the number of uncomfortable conversations he or she is willing to have. In essence, the practice of taking meaningful personal risks builds skills that translate to the therapy room.

Risk-taking is about courage—a willingness to move forward toward what matters while carrying your vulnerability or pain or uncertainty or the reality of failure or whatever comes. Below we offer some examples of practices you might follow to cultivate your risk-taking in ways that will serve your development as a FAP therapist. Start with option 1 below and then consider options 2 and 3.

Option 1

Step back and take a ten-thousand-foot view of what you are avoiding in life. Consider your professional life, personal relationships, health, finances, home maintenance, family, spirituality, community, creativity—anything and everything that is meaningful to you. For many people, there are a few lingering elephants that have not been squarely looked at for some time. You know what (or who) they are. Take a deep breath and name them. Write them down on a piece of paper or right here:

_____

_____

Now consider these questions and write down your answers:

What is most important for you to begin moving on now? And over the coming year?

_____

_____

What is the internal or external obstacle you must face to begin moving?

_____

_____

Are you willing to move through that obstacle—or figure out how to get around it—in order to move forward?

_____

_____

What do you need to do to get started?

_____

_____

Option 2

Every day, take a risk. Remember, "risk" is not the same as "reckless." It is strategic.

A meaningful daily risk may seem quite pedestrian. For example, be more assertive about how you want your meal prepared when ordering at a restaurant. Commit to send out invoices every week. Slow down, turn off your phone, and spend time with your kids (yes, that can be a risk for some). In contrast, a risk can be life changing. Reach out to your estranged brother and apologize. Send a thank-you note to your high school teacher. Sign up for a triathlon. Track your daily risks in a diary or some other kind of document. Rate the risk in intensity if you wish.

Option 3

Find a colleague or friend or family member who wants to practice deliberate risk-taking and share your risk logs with each other periodically. Meet over coffee or beer or online and give each other feedback about the risks you've taken. Give and let yourself receive appreciation.

Gareth, one of the authors, exchanged risk logs with his close friend Chris Hall for a year. Chris was transitioning from unhappily employed to self-employed to happily employed—a major set of professional risks—and Gareth was moving through some of his own early career developments. Those talks were deeply motivating and satisfying highlights every month for both of them.

THERAPEUTIC PURPOSE STATEMENT

We'll wrap up this chapter with an exercise in getting clear on who you are and what matters to you in your relationships with your clients and in your work as a therapist in general. While here we focus on your values as a therapist, we highly recommend that you commit to ongoing values work and goal setting more broadly. The acceptance and commitment therapy literature is full of great resources for these types of work (in particular, check out Dahl, Plumb-Vilardaga, Stewart, & Lundgren, 2009).

A note before we get started: While "purpose statement" connotes a finished, polished document, please do *not* approach this exercise with that goal in mind. Crafting a purpose statement is a practice that you will start imperfectly and then continue steadily—or sometimes in fits and starts—like shaping and reshaping a sculpture from a block of clay.

Step 1

Reflect on the moments or messages or ideas or people that have been most inspiring to you in the course of your career; for example, the feedback of a specific client or supervisor, a therapeutic relationship you thought was strong, or a type of therapy you found effective. Don't worry yet about making anything coherent. Just assemble all the things that made you light you up in some way. Put them in a list or otherwise lay them out on paper or a screen.

Step 2

What themes or patterns or unifying ideas do you see in the things that are meaningful to you? What tensions do you see that don't need to be resolved because, in fact, you are committed to both sides of the tension? Is there anything you put down because "you should," but in fact you don't really care for that thing? What seems most important to you?

Step 3

Given your reflections above, draft a single statement (or two or three) that captures who you want to be as a clinician today and where you want to focus your intention and energy today and in the coming ninety days. Let go of the need to make something that will last forever and be perfectly right. What feels right today?

Step 4

This step is critical. Put your purpose statement aside for at least forty-eight hours. Then revisit it and ask yourself if it's still right. What would you change to make it more right for today? Rinse and repeat, continuing weekly or monthly or quarterly or annually forever.

A NOTE ON BOLD PERSONAL MISSIONS: DO NOT LET THE FIELD SILENCE YOU

We are professionals. Our first steps into the field begin a process of professionalization, through which we learn to follow the path of what works. We mean this in the sense of what maintains the working of the profession, what obeys the rules and respects the risks that we have not personally experienced—but that our profession has learned to respect. As students and professionals we benefit immensely from that learning. We agree to follow the laws and principles of professional ethics. We agree to serve our client's needs and to act on the basis of what is effective rather than what we idiosyncratically believe.

And yet beyond professionalism, our work is also intensely personal—and difficult, and sometimes lonely—because, in part, of the professional structures (confidentiality, individual therapy) in which we work. There can also be a conservatism in professional contexts that insidiously distances us from our more personal experience and values. For example, academic settings and professional organizations often communicate to clinicians that they should not be open about their own struggles with psychological suffering (and the sense of purpose that can arise from that suffering). Thankfully that trend is changing.

If you hold a personal mission in this field, do not let the absence of that personal thing in the articulation of the professional rules and the professional context alienate you from it. Cling to your mission. It is not wrong. It may not be spoken by those around you. But it is vital and life giving. Hold on to what is vital.

SUMMARY

- Develop self-awareness and practice courage and purpose in order to effectively navigate therapeutic relationships.

- Maintain an ongoing practice of self-reflection and courageous risk-taking to move yourself toward what you care about.

- Assess and shape your own 1s and 2s across diverse contexts.

CHAPTER 7

Lay a Foundation at the Beginning of Therapy

Out beyond ideas of wrongdoing and rightdoing, there is a field.
I'll meet you there.

—Rumi

Henry is late. Three minutes…six minutes. You're about to call him when you hear a confident stride coming down the hall, matching the voice you spoke with on the phone last week.

He enters the room and asks, without urgency, "Am I late?"

"Yes, a few minutes," you reply.

"Just how I like it." He seems to be studying the art on your walls, vaguely distracted, but something says he's making a show of being confident. There's a slight hint of apology behind the breezy acknowledgement, but it would be easy to miss.

"Are you often late?"

"Yeah, unfortunately it's a thing for me." He pauses. "Maybe more than I'd like to admit."

You are slightly surprised by his honesty, given his impassive face. You press further.

"Do you always avoid apologizing for it?" There is no disapproval in your voice, just curiosity.

He in turn is surprised by your directness. "Ha! I don't know. I guess."

As the meeting unfolds, you learn more about Henry. He is a recent college graduate. His parents and step-parents are high achieving. He was also in trouble a fair amount as a kid.

He remains confident, even steely, in his presentation. His eyes are often focused, looking out the window or at the floor. Occasionally he looks at your eyes in a way that seems intent on showing you that he's confident. And yet you don't believe he's confident beneath his exterior.

"What do you want to get from therapy?"

"I don't know. Just someone to talk with. Talk things out."

"Hmm. I don't know what that means exactly. How about this: I want to understand you, help you understand yourself, and help you move toward what matters in your life. Are you up for that?"

"Yes." A long pause. "Well, that's actually what I want."

"One thing I notice about you right off is that you seem hard on the outside, and I can't tell what you're feeling on the inside. I like your charisma and confidence, but how you express it can be slightly off-putting, to tell you the truth. Are you aware of any of this about yourself?"

"Yes." Another pause. "Actually I often feel like an asshole." He says this without vulnerability.

You worry that you might have been a bit too forceful, but the honesty is a relief.

"I was very direct with you just now. Would you mind telling me if I am ever off-putting to you?"

"Sure, but I want that."

"Actually… I can see how your confidence or aloofness would invite directness from others. I can also see how that could lead you to stay invulnerable, guarded in a way. I wonder if that's how you learned to be, or if you're living up to something. Any of what I'm saying resonating for you?"

"I'm not sure. I feel like I'm open. You'll have to figure that out as we go along."

Later in the session, you realize that Henry remains vague about what he wants—not just about therapy, but about what he wants in his life at the moment. He hides his emotions or isn't in contact with them when talking about what would seem to be emotional topics. He can be off-putting with his confidence, but he is also very capable of directness and truth telling. This probably works well for him in some contexts, but there's pain and vulnerability behind his front, and perhaps his confidence and hardness are about avoiding vulnerability. You've learned that he has a lot to live up to after all, and he has a considerable history of being negatively judged for his actions.

He validates this intuition toward the end of the session when, while completing a routine assessment, you ask if he ever thinks about killing himself. He pauses for a moment. And when he speaks, it is with feeling.

"I think about it every day. I wouldn't act on it, but I think about it."

"You don't know me well yet. But what matters most to me is that the work I do is based on reality—the real experiences of my clients. I don't want to do therapy on half-truths. So I'm grateful to you for sharing that part of your truth with me. That's what will make this work well between us. In turn I aim to earn your trust. I will be genuine, and I invite you to be the same. That will allow me to see you—I can't help with what I can't see. And by seeing you clearly I can help more."

The previous story is in many ways quite extreme. It's not a perfect start to therapy, but the therapist and Henry went on to develop a strong relationship. Things unfolded the way they did based on who Henry is, who the therapist is, and the nature of their engagement. For instance, the therapist felt confident that Henry was reasonably well functioning and well educated (information he gathered in the initial phone call with Henry). The therapist also made quick judgments that FAP-style assessment of the present moment would be well tolerated by Henry, and that what was happening in the moment was likely relevant to his clinical issues. For instance, Henry disclosed on the phone that he was looking for work, and showing up late to appointments is definitely a problem in that realm.

Despite its unique qualities, the story illustrates how much can happen at the beginning of therapy. It represents one (certainly not the only) way of doing FAP. As you can see, both of the core principles of FAP are present:

- Addressing the present-moment interaction, including building connection through vulnerable disclosure and responsiveness to the other's disclosure (such as when Henry admits to considering suicide). Showing the client how the work will go, as well as orienting him to it (as in the last sentences the therapist spoke).

- Beginning to build a functional understanding of the client's issues by integrating what you see in the moment with what the client is telling you about his clinical issues.

In this chapter, we'll discuss how to put FAP principles into action at the beginning of therapy. It's much easier to integrate them at the beginning of a relationship rather than later on, when norms of avoidance are already in place. In turn, if pursued skillfully, we believe the FAP principles of addressing the present-moment interaction and building functional understanding contribute to a strong rapport early on and increase the likelihood that clients will want to return to see you again. Why? Because they experience your understanding of them and their issues and your willingness to work collaboratively with them to make progress.

When therapists feel disconnected or frustrated with a client (or vice versa), the cause is likely found in a failure to attend to this process of connecting. For instance, if the therapist working with Henry had not addressed Henry's tardiness or delved deeper into his presentation to discover the vulnerability underneath, he or she might have been left feeling annoyed or confused. Our assumption in FAP is that it's not any particular differences between client and therapist that cause problems for the alliance; instead it's how these differences are handled that matters. Henry's therapist used direct and compassionate communication to handle his tardiness and invulnerable confidence.

Consider another example: A client might prefer very concrete, linear explanations, whereas a therapist leans toward the abstract. If therapist and client openly discuss this difference and agree to check in on whether the therapist is meeting the client's needs, then they stand a better chance of doing well (in fact, the client might learn something valuable from the experience of navigating this difference). If therapist and client instead skirt the issue, the client may become frustrated by the vagueness of the therapist, and the therapist may be irritated by the repeated requests for clarity.

This chapter is organized around the four main interrelated tasks involved in putting FAP into action at the beginning of treatment:

- Awareness: Noticing potential CRB in the moment.

- Inquiry: Inquiring, from a curious, nonjudgmental, courageous stance, about in-the-moment behavior and how it relates to the presenting problems or the optimal process of therapy.

- FAP rationale: Orienting the client to and seeking informed consent for FAP interventions.

- Feedback: Setting up formal and informal feedback mechanisms to guide the therapy process.

AWARENESS

When you meet a new client, what do you see? Tom, for instance, from part 1 of this book, seemed eager to please and overly polite. Nick was tense and formal. Henry was guarded and overconfident. From the first moments a client appears in the doorway or the waiting room, we are gathering information and making assessments about her. Assessing behavior—and remember, all of what a client does in session is behavior—is the focus of functional analysis. When a client is in front of you, you have access to a high-resolution, responsive, interactive *instance* of behavior. As a rule, what we see and experience in the first session tends to become relevant to a client's clinical problem.

Functional thinking, in turn, leads us to discover *how* this behavior is relevant. In other words, the contextual behavioral science (CBS) standpoint asks you to take a critical next step beyond your immediate judgments and perceptions and observations. Going beyond surface appearance, you must ask this: How does this behavior function for the client? In other words, how does it "work" for her in life? Is it related to a presenting problem? Similarly, we must ask if our reaction to our clients is us simply being idiosyncratic. For example, is my annoyance at Henry's lateness merely reflective of my tight standards about punctuality? Or does my reaction indicate how others likely respond to Henry as well? This discrimination requires self-knowledge. Remember, we are not looking for moral judgments about "the type of person the client is"; we're looking for hypotheses about how the client's behaviors function interpersonally and may create problems that lead to suffering.

An interesting challenge occurs when a client's appearance and behavior in the room differ markedly from the presenting problem she describes. Consider an unusually mild-mannered, thoughtful client who seeks help for anger that escalates when she's getting her children out the door in the mornings. Is it possible that she is overly polite and reserved, such that her kids (and others?) tend to walk over her needs and, in turn, she only effectively gains their obedience through a dramatic change of tone? The general functional question at the center of the analysis is this: How does this striking behavior that I see and experience here and now possibly relate to the clinical problem the client describes? Functional analysis is like a connect-the-dots puzzle, something to be pursued through assessment and investigation. In that process, be prepared to let go of clever hypotheses if they do not appear valid.

Noticing Potential 1s and 2s at the Outset of Therapy

Below are lists of behaviors (1s and 2s) that commonly arise at the beginning of therapy. The behaviors are divided somewhat arbitrarily in the categories of awareness, courage, and love even though many behaviors have multiple functions. These lists are intended to help you generate ideas about the kinds of behavior to look for in your clients and yourself. They are not exhaustive. Of course therapists may have many of the same issues as their clients, but we included behaviors that are only relevant for therapists in a separate list.

Awareness

Client (and Therapist) Behaviors

Not noticing important details about the therapy process (assignments, consent, address, appointment time, and so on)

Not being aware of the impacts of behaviors (not respecting personal space, ignoring questions, talking over the therapist, and so on)

Not using emotion words (for example, anxious, ashamed, irritated, uneasy, content)

Talking excessively about irrelevant details

Offering thin, vague responses

Therapist Behaviors

Being overly focused on a protocol or method of therapy at the expense of empathetic contact with the client or self

Failing to deeply understand or empathize with the client

Overlooking important details in the client's presentation

Not noticing client CRBs until later, in supervision or consultation

Courage

Client (and Therapist) Behaviors

Withholding vulnerable details

Suppressing or avoiding emotion

Presenting a very positive, incongruent picture

Holding back on wishes and needs for therapy

Disclosing a lot very quickly in a way that leads to avoidance or feeling overwhelmed

Being overly assertive, demanding, or critical

Being guarded

Therapist Behaviors

Not asking about more vulnerable topics, such as intimacy, sex, self-harm, or suicide

Asking questions in overly blunt or clinical ways

Not discussing the therapy process or not requesting feedback

Not disclosing more personal reactions

Love (Including Self-Love)

Client (and Therapist) Behaviors

Seldom providing positive feedback or saying encouraging things

Being uncomfortable with or avoidant of warmth or validation

Being overly concerned with offering appreciation or reassurance and doing so in a way that appears inauthentic or excessive

Being overly apologetic about requests or self-care

Therapist Behaviors

Not expressing care for or appreciation of the client

Not accepting praise or appreciation from the client

Overcommitting to the client; for example, by offering extra therapy time or out-of-session support

EXERCISE

Using one of the behaviors listed above, generate hypotheses about how the behavior could function in a way that perpetuates a clinical issue. For example, being uncomfortable with or avoidant of warmth or validation might lead a client to subtly punish others when they offer support; and this behavior, in turn, may make offers of support less likely, leading to a decrease in the client's social support and an increase in feelings of isolation.

INQUIRY

In the dialogue with Henry that opened the chapter, the therapist made a number of potentially evocative statements in response to what he was noticing; for example, he pointed out that Henry was not apologizing for his lateness, asking whether that was a pattern, and he also noted that Henry seemed guarded. These kinds of statements play a crucial role in FAP. Together with other elements, they make up the basic FAP stance in the therapeutic relationship. To understand this stance, let's first review the goals, from a FAP perspective, that should be in place at the outset of treatment.

A very basic goal at the beginning of therapy is to learn about the client; for example, what brings her to therapy, what she is looking for in a therapist, and so forth. Therefore, inquiry is a basic principle of the FAP stance. Active inquiry, of course, forms the basis of functional thinking.

In FAP we also want to pay attention to the process of disclosure that our inquiry invites. That is, how the behavior of disclosure unfolds and responds to what is happening in the therapy interaction. There are several reasons to pay attention to this process. First, if the client is not disclosing openly, therapy is likely to be impeded. Second, the invitation to disclose in therapy may be quite different from what happens in other social settings, so the client may experience quite natural reactions of vulnerability or shame or hesitation as we invite them to disclose. Attending to these reactions and ensuring that we proceed in a way that is attuned to the client's needs is a key part of the therapeutic alliance. Third, it is possible that the client's process of disclosure is CRB—that is, it's functionally related to her presenting clinical issues. The CRBs may involve willingness to disclose or not. They might also involve a variety of other behaviors: for example, a tendency to avoid emotional expression, to ruminate unproductively, to beat around the bush, or to look at things in black-and-white terms. When we attune to the process of disclosure, then, we aim to mindfully and compassionately shape the relationship as an experience of trust and safety; we also want it to be an experience that offers a clear view of how the client's psychology works.

In addition to these goals, it's important to keep in mind that at the beginning of therapy you don't yet know the client or where her interpersonal vulnerabilities lie. If you proceed too boldly in your inquiry—asking invasive questions—you risk damaging the alliance or overpowering the client. If you proceed too tentatively, you risk allowing the interaction to remain superficial rather than proceeding toward the more intimate type of disclosure (and the opportunity to provide responsiveness) that forms a strong therapeutic alliance. Therefore, it's important to proceed in a sensitive, flexible way.

With these goals and our lack of knowledge about the client in mind, the FAP relational stance balances nonjudgmental curiosity and validating compassion with tentative, flexible ventures toward greater directness or courage. Pervasive curiosity and compassion ensure that the therapeutic interaction, as a whole, is appetitive; the client should be richly reinforced for attending therapy and talking with you. There should be no aversive social consequences coming from you related to disclosure of what the client is experiencing.

With directness and courage you can invite slightly more vulnerable disclosures from the client. This may gradually deepen the intimacy and vulnerability (and therefore trust) the client experiences in the relationship. The FAP relational stance sets the scene for addressing CRB directly later on and allows you to observe how the client responds to encouragement for greater vulnerability.

In the following dialogue, the therapist demonstrates some key features of this balanced stance.

Therapist: It sounds like your parents' divorce came at a really difficult time—just when you're figuring out who you wanted to be at college. I can see your pain as you talk about it.

Client: It's the sort of thing everyone has to deal with, I guess, in some form or another. Welcome to being an adult.

Therapist: Yes, I can see you sort of telling yourself to buck up as well. Like, be tough, there's no time to be emotional.

Client: Well what's the point of being emotional? Feeling bad just to…feel bad?

Therapist: Yeah, I see puzzlement there. Why feel bad? It seems so useless…endless. I wonder if what I see in you is a kind of paradox. Because I notice you seem to me to be feeling bad as you struggle against feeling bad. Almost as if you're trying to talk your way out of feeling bad, but the fact remains: you are feeling bad. Am I seeing you right?

Client: Yes, sure. But…then it just seems hopeless.

Therapist: Well, again, I'm just getting to know you, so I might be wrong here. But I notice you are a person with lots of strength. You worked hard through college, despite the chaos happening. You just put your head down and worked. And you're not afraid to ask the hard questions and call it like it is, like "What's the point of feeling bad?" But then I wonder, what if strength—your strength—doesn't work well for all types of struggles in life? What if your tenacity actually doesn't work for this type of emotional struggle?

Client: But how do I change?

Therapist: And there goes your tenacity again. You immediately want to know how to change. What to do. I can hear a kind of hardness in how you're demanding that. Impatience. Do you feel that?

Client: Yes…argh! I'm so exhausted.

Therapist: I know I'm pushing you a bit here. Would you be willing to keep going?

Client: Yes. Of course.

Therapist: Would you be willing to tell me more about that exhaustion? That exhaustion that's behind your impatience, behind your strength?

Client: It feels so weak. Like, I want to just get in bed and cover myself with pillows and cry when I feel exhausted. I feel like a child throwing a pity party.

Therapist: The way you say that makes me feel tender toward you. I wonder if you learned—maybe from someone very important to you, or maybe you sort of figured it out yourself—that it's just not okay to be "weak" or to want to lay in bed and cry. Maybe you learned that people don't respect you if you do that. And then how exhausting to have to just buck up all the time. But how rewarding it must have felt to be strong and to please others, to overcome and be successful. Do I have this somewhat right?

Client: Well, yes. *Buck up,* that's my dad—100 percent. And my gymnastics coach as well. "We do not entertain weakness."

Therapist: I wonder if part of our work together could be about slowing down. Noticing where you are getting caught in the paradox of feeling bad while trying not to feel bad and instead finding a different way of relating to yourself? In fact, it might be a different kind of challenge—a challenge to try easy instead of trying hard all the time.

Client: Yeah, what you say makes sense.

Therapist: What's it like that I'm asking all these questions?

Client: It helps. It's a lot to think about. They make me think about things in a different way, I guess.

Therapist: And I, in turn, respect your strength because it lets us be honest, and direct. I respect your strength in being here, working on what feels so uncertain and hopeless. Working on when your mind says you're weak.

The therapist here is working from an acceptance and commitment therapy standpoint, yet woven throughout the interaction are key elements of the FAP relational stance:

1. **Self-disclosure:** The therapist makes incidental self-disclosures about his internal process: "I'm just getting to know you, so I might be wrong here" and "makes me feel tender toward you." These disclosures help set the norm of vulnerable disclosure.

2. **Collaborative spirit:** The therapist asks for permission to continue the inquiry, acknowledging his potential impact on the client. He also asks if the client would like to buy into what he's suggesting they work on together, once she's experienced a bit of the therapy process. He doesn't impose his view, rather he asks her to try it on. His self-disclosures also communicate collaboration, that he might be off the mark and is open to feedback in order to adjust course. This is not a "my way or the highway" situation.

3. **Accepting and validating:** The therapist reflects the value of the client's strengths. After all, this strength has been strongly reinforced and is in many contexts regarded as a virtue. The therapist balances this reflection with a validation of the cost of being strong all the time: exhaustion. Strength and exhaustion have a very natural relationship. Finally, the therapist recognizes—and hopefully reinforces—the client's participation in the therapy process, suggesting that exploring vulnerability is a different type of strength.

4. **Directness and courage:** In response to the client's question "But how do I change?" the therapist makes a pointed observation: "And there goes your tenacity again." This is an example of courage: saying something slightly challenging in service of building greater awareness. He also recognizes that this challenge may evoke the client's self-criticism. She might say to herself, *Can't I do anything right?* He decides not to explore that possibility in this session, instead opting to slow down and explore the client's response to his challenging. For the client a sense of exhaustion comes up. He suspects that the client will feel more vulnerable sharing that part of herself, so he asks for her permission to go there. In turn, her disclosure of exhaustion naturally makes the therapist feel tender toward her, and he expresses that tenderness, because it is a natural, warm response to her vulnerability. He will, of course, continue to observe and inquire over time about how she actually responds to such statements. Overall, this gradual, attuned movement toward greater vulnerability in self-disclosure also reflects another aspect of courage.

Sometimes it is obvious that a client is guarded—unwilling to open up. At other times, whether or not she discloses vulnerable things about herself is not a matter of willingness; she is actually unable to articulate her internal experience in the moment. At these times, you will not push as hard, because pushing is counterproductive.

Inquiring About the Therapy Process

Clients bring their presenting problems to sessions, but they also react to the process of therapy—filling out consent forms, coming to the first appointment, responding to initial questions. Their reactions can be a valuable window into how they function in life; exploring these reactions can serve as a road to rapport. Accordingly, a FAP therapist might ask in open-ended ways what it is like to come to therapy.

Therapist: I'm curious how it's been for you, leading up to our first appointment.

Client: I was looking forward to it.

Therapist: Any thoughts or feelings about coming here? What were you thinking today?

Client: Not very much at all. It was a crazy day. Our appointment was kind of stuck in the back of my mind. I feel like I'm opening a door and I'm kind of insecure, but I'm a really good actress. I've had to be since I got depressed—to get through life.

Therapist: I want to hear more about that.

You might also inquire about clients' wishes for the session, their reactions to any materials they've already read (for example, your website, your consent form, any flyers or brochures you circulate), their experiences in previous treatments, and their desires to know more about you. All of these areas of inquiry provide opportunities to engage the client in a collaborative relationship and to begin to understand her patterns of behavior. In the following sample, the therapist weaves several of these threads together, shaping an initial understanding of a potential CRB and moving the therapy interaction toward greater vulnerability.

Therapist: What feels important to you for us to get to today? What do you want to talk about? When you came in, did you have certain ideas about what would make this a really good session?

Client: No.

Therapist: So you're going to leave it up to me.

Client: I can help you figure it out. I bet the first session is always hard because there's so much of me that you don't know about. It's always hard to try to get to know people.

Therapist: The first session *is* hard. I never quite know what to expect. I have a list of things to get to today, but one of the things is what's important to you, because it's very important to me to tailor this treatment to you. So, you read my description of this treatment, right?

Client: Yeah. I really like what you wrote.

Therapist: I want to go over that and answer any questions you have. You can let me know what you like and don't like. I want to answer any questions you have about me. You don't know that much about me.

Client: If you're in private practice, I want to know how you got involved with the university.

Therapist: I'm also affiliated with the university. I'm a clinical instructor, and I also teach a class here. Are you curious about my training or background?

Client: Yeah.

Therapist: I got my doctorate here in 1982. I did my undergraduate training at UCLA, and in 1976 I came here for graduate school. I thought I'd go back to southern California, but I never did.

Client: That's interesting.

Therapist: How do you like your therapists to be? It seems that you like your psychiatrist, Dr. L., a lot. Do you want me to be directive or nondirective?

Client: I really like people to be directive with me, but at the same time I'm ultrasensitive. I always have been. And so I always ask the people I work with to be careful—not that anything isn't well-intentioned, but I get a bit sensitive.

Therapist: Can you give me an example of something that's happened?

Client: Sure. Once with Dr. L., I left feeling worse—angry and upset. I have all this debt, and I felt like she was kind of hard on me about it, which surprised me. I just wanted to talk about it and get it out. I felt really uncomfortable because I owed her money. I owe all of my health professionals money. When I left I felt awful.

Therapist: Wow. Okay, well I want to be really sensitive to how hard it is for you to talk about things and make sure I get that right for you.

Client: I'd appreciate that.

Therapist: You know, this is a good moment, because as you read in that description of our therapy together, one focus of our treatment is going to be our relationship and how it connects to all your other relationships. I notice that you've got some other good relationships going.

Client: I'm lucky.

Therapist: It's not just that you're lucky. I think you're pretty socially skilled. You're saying you know how to put on a good act and doing so is exhausting, but it's also a skill that you have. But in here I want us to look at what's effective in terms of how you relate to me and how I relate to you, and maybe we can look at getting more skilled at being authentic. For example, if I don't get something right, you can tell me. Did you tell Dr. L. how you felt?

Client: No.

Therapist: Yeah, I understand how hard that is. It seems that on the one hand you have really good relationships, but on the other hand you feel lonely. Maybe not speaking up is part of it. Is that an area you want to work on?

Client: I haven't figured out how to feel less lonely. One thing is that I live alone. And I've noticed a trend that over the past year and a half I've pulled back more and more from socializing.

Therapist: What does it feel like to feel lonely? Do you feel lonely right now?

Client: A little bit…maybe empty.

Therapist: Where do you feel empty?

Client: My heart…my chest. I notice not so much something missing but more of an emptiness.

Therapist: When did you last feel more full?

Client: I'm not sure I can remember. I think probably during my last long-term relationship.

Therapist: How long ago was that?

Client: Three and a half years ago.

Therapist: So when you talk about your relationship, it seems you still have a sense of longing. Do you long for that relationship, or just a relationship in general?

Client: A relationship. (Pauses.) I feel emotional.

Therapist: You feel emotional talking about your loneliness?

Client: I think so. (Cries.) The whole thing is difficult. May I bother you for some tissues? I can kind of deny my miserableness on paper, but if I to have to talk to somebody about it, it's painful.

Therapist: Well, you're talking right now, to me, and it's really helpful to me. How much hope do you have that this treatment will help you? What are your hopes and fears?

Client: I have a lot of hope actually.

Therapist: Tell me what you feel positively about.

Client: My life. I didn't focus on anything with Dr. L. I haven't been working on anything, or don't feel like I have. I feel like I've been treading water for a long time, and this therapy feels like something I need. I need a direction.

Therapist: I'm good at giving direction—and at hand-holding.

Client: You seem like you are. You have very kind eyes. I am hopeful.

Therapist: I'm really glad that you're hopeful. And I'm glad you notice the kindness in my eyes—the kindness I'm feeling for you already. One of the things that's important to me is that this is a sacred space for you. When I'm here, I'm not thinking about anything else; this space is protected. I take it really seriously. I want to respect the effort and risk you put into being here.

Client: It reminds me of something that happened. You know how at a drugstore you often see those pamphlets on quitting smoking? They usually have a little saying. One time I saw one that said something like, "In order to get anywhere in life, you have to decide you're not going to stay where you are." This reminded me that the first step is simply deciding you're going to move.

Therapist: And that's what you're doing. You're taking a risk by being here. So, given what you said before, I wonder, what's the difference between acting like you're taking a risk and actually taking a risk? One of the things we can do in here is help you really take risks, and take the right kind of risks.

Client: That's going to be hard—good, but hard.

Therapist: I know. I'll appreciate how hard it is for you.

Inquiring About CRB with In-the-Moment Functional Analysis

As we mentioned earlier, part of the functional analysis process is linking the behaviors you see here and now with the presenting problems the client describes as happening in daily life. Making these connections eventually gives you the opportunity to identify and work on changing CRB in the moment. In the interim—even in a first session—this linking of in-session and out-of-session behavior can help you better understand the client's presenting problems and related behaviors.

For example, let's say a client describes how his wife often interrupts him or grows impatient with him. You notice that he tends to talk at length, to the point that it's not clear when he will stop to let you talk. You might delicately share this observation with him and ask whether he tends to talk in this lengthy way with his wife.

Therapist: If I might share something delicate: I notice that you do tend to talk at length. So, I wonder if that might be one factor that contributes to your wife interrupting? That she gets impatient with how you are talking?

Client: Well, I suppose. I always talk like this and I've been given crap for it my whole life. I get tired of people wanting me to be different. When I was in the fourth grade they used to call me motormouth. There was this one teacher who used to interrupt me on purpose whenever I was giving answers in front of the class...

Here, the therapist uses what she observes in session to make a hypothesis about what might be going on outside of session. In turn, it can be useful to explore differences between what you observe in session and what is reported about out of session.

Therapist: Well, I recognize my pointing out that you do talk a lot might put you on edge. But I appreciate that openness, and I hope we can have a spirit of "let's put all the facts on the table." I notice you do seem willing to take that feedback from me, and to consider the effect of your talking. But I heard you say that with your wife, if she tries to give you feedback, you respond quite differently.

Client: Yes, I'm very defensive. We argue about it every once in a while, then we go back to a resentful avoidance.

Therapist: So what is different here—that you are willing to hear my feedback?

Client: Here I trust that you want to understand me and you want what's good for me.

By contrasting the in-session and out-of-session contexts, the therapist discovers an important misalignment in the client's relationship with his wife: he doesn't trust that she wants to understand him compassionately.

You can also compare in-session and out-of-session context using the following questions:

Would [some clinically relevant behavior that happens in daily life] ever happen in here with me?

If [that behavior] happens, would you tell me?

These questions are especially useful when the client's daily behavior involves not disclosing what is happening to the other people involved. For example, if a client gradually feels more resentful toward naturally assertive people because of the way they unknowingly step on his unvoiced needs, until he eventually blows up at them, you might explicitly ask whether such resentment might conceivably show up in the therapy relationship. This could be an especially important inquiry if you know yourself to be a naturally assertive person. Again, such questions set the tone for an open, disclosing therapeutic relationship.

Responding to Possible CRB2

Sometimes clients engage in significant and risky vulnerable disclosure in the early stage of therapy because they think that is what they're "supposed to do," or because they're so understandably exhausted from suffering in isolation that they take a chance and share their burden with a sympathetic listener. For example, in the dialogue that opens this chapter, Henry discloses suicidal ideation, something he admits that he has not told anyone else. The therapist then takes a risk by responding in a very direct and personal way. While this shift is not explicitly indicated in the dialogue, the therapist's response is marked not just by his words, but also by a change in voice tone and posture that reflect a genuine emotional response to Henry's distress. The therapist hopes that his response reinforces Henry's disclosure and that more vulnerable disclosure will follow.

At an early stage in therapy, however, the therapist cannot be certain that the disclosure from Henry really is CRB2 (honest disclosure about his suffering) nor whether his heartfelt response will reinforce the disclosure. Henry might actually find the response off-putting. Nevertheless, as therapists we sometimes have to guess, especially with issues of vulnerable disclosure. It's worth making these guesses, because the harm of failing to respond receptively to a significant disclosure early on can be meaningful; responding genuinely sets the precedent of genuineness and also the precedent of addressing directly what is happening in the here and now. Be sure to respond to vulnerable disclosures in ways that are natural. (More on that in chapter 9, which focuses on responding to CRB2.)

OFFER A FAP RATIONALE

At the beginning of treatment, it's also useful to orient clients explicitly to how you will use the therapy relationship in your work together. In other words, provide a FAP treatment rationale ("FAP rap" for short). The FAP rap is typically delivered as soon as you know that FAP interventions will likely be part of your treatment plan. The core of the FAP rap is simple and can be presented along these lines:

Therapist: When the issues you're working on show up here and now in therapy, it's useful to notice them, giving you an opportunity to change the behavior you're working on right here and now in the moment, and giving me—your therapist—an opportunity to respond to you in a way that gives you support and useful feedback about what you're doing.

A less formal variant looks something like this:

Therapist: I find it's useful in this work to be able to slow down at certain points so we can look closely at what's happening in the moment. For example, certain interactions between us can be useful moments for you to learn about yourself. You can get feedback from me in the moment about how you're coming across, or how others might see you in

131

those moments. You can also then practice responding differently, if that seems useful. How does all this sound to you?

You can also be more explicit about FAP if doing so fits your style or if a client has requested to know what type of therapy you practice:

Therapist: I do a type of therapy called functional analytic psychotherapy, or FAP. Yes, it's a silly acronym. A key part of FAP is using our interactions, here in therapy, as a way to understand who you are and how you want to change. For instance, you've told me you want to learn to be more aware of yourself, how you impact others, and how you get stuck or hold yourself back in interactions with others. Together we can watch for moments when you do these exact things with me, and we'll see how we can shift what happens in those moments. How does that sound to you?

Finally, some FAP therapists phrase their rationale with more evocative language and seek a more explicit commitment to interpersonal depth and FAP work in general:

Therapist: I feel privileged to be embarking on a journey of exploration and growth with you. One of the first and most important things I want you to know about our work together is that FAP emphasizes that we form a bond. It will be a major vehicle in this journey. I'd like to have a real relationship with you. I commit to you that I will be a genuine person in this room with you; I will not be fake or hide behind anything.

I know how hard it is to be vulnerable and to talk about difficult things. I also know how important it is. So I commit to make therapy feel like a sacred space for you, a place with unusual levels of safety, understanding, caring, and support. I will do this so you can join me in really working, exploring, and growing. I want to create a feeling between us that lets you know you have 100 percent of my attention; I'm able to deeply see, accept, and respect who you are at your core, both flaws and strengths; and I'll hold with reverence and care all that you share.

I'll be investing a great deal of care and effort into our work together, and I expect you to do the same. Based on your goals for therapy, and with your permission, I'll challenge you to be more aware, present, open, vulnerable, and loving. I'll check with you about what's working well for you in our relationship and what needs to be changed. And if difficulties come up with me that also come up with other people in your life, we'll zero in on our interaction, either positive or negative, and look at what's going on and what we can learn from it. These will be key moments for us, and I'll always be looking for them. There are also exercises we can do to get these issues directly in the room with us. Our therapeutic relationship will be an ideal place for you to practice how to navigate these moments in a way that feels like you're really being who you want to be, with me, with others, and in life. From here, we begin to foster change and growth so you can live the life you really want. How does all of this sound to you?

You should develop a FAP rap that fits your values, way of speaking, cultural context, and clinical context.

Linking to Client Problems

The preceding examples of the FAP rap were fairly generic—even the final, very heartfelt one. You can often make the FAP rap more meaningful and persuasive by linking it to what you understand about the client and her presenting problems. Here's an example:

Therapist: You mentioned that you struggle with feeling at ease around people, especially when it's not clear what your role is. For example, at cocktail parties you tend to feel very awkward, whereas at your job you know exactly what to do. In our work, there might be moments when there is similar confusion about what your role is. It's like what you said at the beginning of our meeting today, that you were a little anxious about what you were supposed to tell me about yourself. So here is a version of that very situation you struggle with, here in the moment. It can be quite useful to work with that experience here in the moment, as it happens between us, rather than just talking about it from a distance. How does that sound to you?

For clients with presenting problems related to social disconnection, it might be useful to highlight the aspects of connection—vulnerable disclosure, and so on—that naturally occur in the therapy relationship:

Therapist: You've said that trusting and being vulnerable with others is really scary for you, and I know that therapy can be a really vulnerable process. You come in here and tell me things that are very personal that you don't tell anyone else, and that can be scary. I want you to know how important that honesty is. I can help you most effectively when I know what's happening for you. What I hope is that, as you open up to me, I'll respond in ways that help you come to trust me. And believe me, nothing is more important to me than being trustworthy as a therapist. And in turn, you might learn to become more confident in opening up to other people in your life who are also trustworthy.

Therapist Self-Disclosure

Another key element of the FAP rap is therapist self-disclosure. At this point in the book, you've seen again and again how a therapist disclosing her reactions to the client and the process in the moment plays an important role in FAP. Some clients expect the therapist to be a "blank screen"; they may be reticent to ask the therapist direct questions, or they may be surprised to hear the therapist sharing personal reactions. It can be useful, therefore, to orient explicitly to the value your own self-disclosure can bring to the relationship, as well as your full presence and availability.

Here's an example:

Therapist: As I said, therapy is a vulnerable process, so I want to do things that make it easier for you to feel trust and respect in our relationship. In the service of building that trust and understanding of each other, if there's anything you're wondering about me, or if you're ever wondering what I'm thinking, such as my reaction to something that happened to you or what you said, I invite you to ask me. Is there anything you want to know about me right now, as we get started?

You might also establish that you'll offer honest responses and describe how you'll do so:

Therapist: A way that therapy can be helpful is if I show up to our sessions not as merely a therapist but as a full human being. As such, I might sometimes have responses to you that could be useful for you to hear. For instance, I might be moved by something you say. Or—and this could be more difficult to talk about—I may be challenged by something you say or might disagree with you. I'd like to have your permission to share my honest reactions with you, in a way that's sensitive and that I think will serve you. Is that okay?

Again, none of these rationales should be offered as boilerplate. They should be adapted to the context, the individual client, and what the functional analysis reveals about the client. For example, if asking lots of questions of the therapist appears to be a CRB1—a way of avoiding more vulnerable but useful therapeutic topics—then the rationale should be adjusted.

EXERCISE: FAP RAP INTENSIVE PRACTICE

Your skill at delivering FAP raps can rapidly improve with intensive practice, especially in a group format in which you can benefit from the modeling and feedback of others. Therefore, we recommend some deliberate practice:

1. Think of a client with whom FAP might be productive.

2. Write (or think or talk through) a FAP rap that feels genuine to you and relevant to this client.

3. Read or speak your rap out loud, either to yourself, an audio recorder, or, better yet, a colleague who can give you feedback about what works well and what can be improved.

4. Improve the rap as needed.

5. Offer the rap to your client and notice what went well and what you could improve. Capture what you learn by writing it down.

6. Repeat!

FEEDBACK

A final, important FAP element to establish early in therapy is open and mutual feedback. And, beyond merely talking about it, it's vital to put this exchange of feedback in motion. Broadly speaking, feedback is information that changes the process of therapy. You'll notice that feedback is woven into the earlier examples presented in this chapter. For instance, the therapist offers various forms of feedback about how the client is coming across. The therapist also asks for feedback from the client about how his questions affect her. The FAP raps in the previous section also mention the importance of feedback for keeping therapy on track and for responding to key moments in therapy, such as when a client's issues show up in the room. And as the work of therapy unfolds, FAP asks you to keep in touch with how the work is going for the client (as prescribed by rule 4; more on that in chapter 9). In all these ways, FAP asks you to engage in various forms of feedback exchange.

Building on the process of inquiry described earlier in this chapter, at the end of each session it can be useful to recap and summarize in ways that invite vulnerability and honesty. For instance, you might express appreciation for the important steps forward the client is making by choosing to participate in therapy. Here's an example:

Therapist: What are your thoughts about our first session as we are coming to the end of it?

Client: Good. I feel encouraged.

Therapist: What stands out to me is your perseverance. You've been depressed since you were thirteen, and there's something about you that perseveres, some incredible strength inside you that keeps you growing and keeps you hopeful. Something else that stands out is that you like the risk-taking poem. I'm excited about that, because if you like to take risks you and I are going to get along really well. What stands out to you?

Client: I was able to cry. I don't spend a lot of time crying alone. I feel a little better.

Therapist: After you cried?

Client: Yeah. I'm surprised and encouraged.

Therapist: You're surprised that you were able to cry?

Client: I push it away and push it down.

Therapist: It's good for me to know that you feel encouraged that you could cry.

One additional feedback mechanism is the session bridging form (Tsai et al., 2009). The first part (A) of the form, filled out shortly after session, asks the client to reflect on various aspects of the session. The second part (B), filled out just before the next session, asks for a brief synopsis of events between sessions and the client's wishes for the next session's agenda. Some therapists prefer to receive the form in advance of the session; others read it at the beginning of the next session. The form can be introduced in a simple way:

Therapist: In terms of homework, here's a worksheet that will help us focus and make the most of our time during each session. It's called the FAP session bridging form. There are two parts to it. Fill out the first part right after our session. Fill out the second part right before you come to our next session. If you have any questions between now and then, feel free to e-mail me.

As your assessment of CRB develops, you can individualize how the form is used; for example, you can tailor it to focus on vulnerable disclosure, make direct requests, or share appreciation. Or you may introduce the form at the beginning of therapy in a way that links more directly to your understanding of the client's potential CRB.

The form offers several unique values. It provides an alternative medium for processing events in the session. Sometimes clients will write things on the form that they would not say in person, and this openness is very productive. The form also provides a written record of what happened in each session, so there is less forgetting and more sense of continuity between sessions (that's why it's called the "bridging" form). On the therapist side, if the client invests effort in the form, assuming that effort is a 2, be sure to reinforce the effort by putting aside time to read and respond to the form! In other words, completion of the form offers the opportunity to reinforce a 2.

Again, various CRBs (and T1s and T2s) might occur around the session bridging form. Some clients are fastidious about doing the form "right." Others are lackadaisical. All of this is grist for your functional analysis.

SESSION BRIDGING FORM

Name: _____ Date: _____

Part A (to be completed shortly after therapy session)

1. What stands out to you about our last session? Thoughts, feelings, insights?

    _____

    _____

2. On a 10-point scale, how would you rate the following items, *a* through *d*?

Not at all		A little bit		Moderate		Substantial		Very Substantial	
1	2	3	4	5	6	7	8	9	10

    a) Helpfulness/effectiveness of session: _____

    What was helpful? _____

    What was not helpful? _____

    b) How connected you felt to your therapist: _____

    c) How engaged/involved you felt with the topics being discussed: _____

    d) How present you were in the session: _____

3. What would have made the session more helpful or a better experience? Anything you are reluctant to say or ask for?

    _____

    _____

4. What issues came up for you in the session or with your therapist that are similar to your daily life problems?

    _____

    _____

5. What risks did you take in the session or with your therapist or what progress did you make that can translate into your outside life?

_____

_____

Part B (to be completed just prior to the next therapy session)

6. What were the high and low points of your week?

_____

_____

7. What items, issues, challenges, or positive changes do you want to put on the agenda for our next session?

_____

_____

_____

8. How open were you in answering the above questions, 1 through 7 (0–100%)? _____

9. Anything else you'd like to add?

_____

_____

_____

_____

_____

SUMMARY

- FAP processes may be woven into therapy from the first moments of your first session.

- Notice potential CRBs as the client engages in the process of therapy.

- Inquire about the relationship between what you notice in the moment, your client's description of his or her presenting problems, and your client's description of the behaviors related to those problems.

- Offer a rationale for the focus on the therapy relationship and the FAP interventions.

- Set up informal and formal exchanges of feedback about the process of therapy. Use the session bridging form between sessions to collect written feedback.

CHAPTER 8

Call Forward into the Moment

We are moving away from the world of fixed nouns and toward a world of fluid verbs.

—Kevin Kelly

You've been working with Jennifer for a month. She came to you struggling with long-standing depression and social isolation. She has a stable job but is working well below her capabilities. However, as she puts it, she continuously self-sabotages. She often spends whole weekends at home alone, watching television, feeling almost continuously guilty and ashamed but in too much pain to mobilize. She avoids paying bills until late fees and credit issues pile up.

Early in treatment you learned that Jennifer suffered major betrayals when she was young. She learned from those betrayals, at a visceral level, that sharing her emotions is dangerous. She also internalized a very harsh self-critical voice. You agreed with Jennifer that learning to break down that voice—and the wall she maintains—will likely be an important part of treatment, moving her toward goals of feeling more connected with others.

Given the amount of fear that Jennifer reports about being vulnerable, you are gentle in your approach. You allow time and space to build trust. At the same time, Jennifer is extremely appreciative of your efforts and works hard on early homework assignments. In fact, you feel somewhat seduced by her praise. At the same time, it is clear that Jennifer has a range of ways of avoiding vulnerability in the moment. You focus on building a sense of safety in the room and gradually build awareness of these avoidance moves.

This week, as often happens a few months into therapy dealing with long-standing issues, there is a drop in her mood. Jennifer is markedly more withdrawn and anxious when she enters the room.

"How are you feeling today?"

"I'm okay. Well, no, I'm having a hard time."

"I see that, I think. You look tense, guarded. What's going on?"

"It's been a hard week. This is where I end up. I know it's not rational… Okay, so what are we going to talk about today?" She flashes a tense, fake smile and raises her shoulders as if to say, *Let's move on.*

You take a slow breath. "You want to move on, and it feels unnatural to leave your feelings. I want to know more about what you're feeling right now. Would you be willing to slow down and tell me more?"

"I don't know." She glances around nervously. "I feel…empty. But it doesn't do any good to talk about it."

You remember that Jennifer struggles with a ton of self-criticism—crippling self-criticism. You notice she is pushing you away.

"I don't think you mean to do this, but I have the sense you're pushing me away right now. I'm also wondering if you're feeling a lot of self-criticism, and if you want to hide your terrible self from me. Is that happening?" You speak kindly, tenderly.

"You're right. I'm sorry. I don't mean to push you away." She flashes a look of shame.

"It's okay, you know, if you do want to push me away. It makes sense to me."

She takes a deep breath. Then she speaks with a lower voice. "Actually I do, in a way. I don't want to dwell on the negative; I spend enough time there. I don't need reassurance or anything. I want to move forward. That's what would be helpful for me right now. So it's not that I want to push you away, but I don't want you to just focus on how bad I'm feeling."

Something is suddenly clear. This is about a request, not experiential avoidance.

"Ah…well that makes a lot of sense. Now I'm glad I pushed you to explain that. I think something else just clicked for me. It's like sometimes what you're trying to do here is be brave, keep moving toward what you care about? Is that it?

"Yes."

"It's like you're a marathoner, and sometimes what I've done is become the voice in your ear saying, *Oh, this is so painful.* When what you really want is to just keep running."

"But it wasn't your fault!"

"I appreciate that. I don't think it was my fault. I thought you needed soothing and the time to process your emotion. And I take responsibility. I didn't understand that you also want to just move forward. I always want you to make that sort of thing clear to me. I'm glad you are making it clear to me now. You weren't stuck because of how you're feeling, but because you're dreading that I'm going to make you dwell in a way that doesn't feel right."

She's looking at you squarely now.

From the FAP perspective, "How are my client's issues showing up in the therapy process?" is one of the most important questions you can ask. "Am I addressing these issues therapeutically?" is another. With Jennifer, what shows up is a reticence to make her needs known, to risk hurting or disappointing the therapist.

Despite the fantasy that we are all perfect technicians, the reality of clinical work is that things are often murky. As therapy unfolds, sometimes we have to slow down the moment, to press into a feeling that seems too scary, to clarify a confusion that lingers, or to address some unspoken but felt tension. These steps are necessary not just to keep the process of therapy moving, but also because what blocks the process is sometimes what blocks the client in his or her life and is the reason the client is seeking treatment. In terms of the FAP rules, this mix of exploration, functional thinking, noticing, and evoking represents rules 1 (notice CRB) and 2 (evoke CRB).

In the example with Jennifer above, this exploration is crucial. The therapist starts with the assumption that holding back emotion is the key CRB1. In retrospect, however, Jennifer was very open about her emotion. What she was holding back was a request to move therapy forward in a different way rather than spending an hour in what would feel like an emotion-focused pity party. Her initial statement, that she does want to push the therapist away, is a crucial 2—wobbly and uncertain, but a 2 nonetheless. The therapist in turn realizes her error. The exploration leads to this clarity. The vulnerability of both Jennifer and the therapist and the commitment to thinking functionally allow this to happen. In this way, Jennifer and the therapist also learn a deeper lesson about connection: that there is more resilient connection in the tenacity to find understanding, despite misunderstanding, than in perfect understanding. This entire process started, however, because the therapist was willing to push deeper into what was happening—and she kept pushing.

WHAT IS EVOKING?

Read through the questions and statements below, imagining that a supervisor or close friend is saying each one to you:

What do you feel about me right now?

What are you avoiding saying to me right now?

There seems to be a pattern that plays out between us, and I want to share it with you because I think it's happening again.

I'm not sure if this is the right thing to say, but it feels right. I want you to know that…

What do you need from me right now?

How can you open up to how much I value and appreciate you in this moment?

I'm feeling afraid of making you angry right now, and I wonder if you can notice your tone?

I notice you're not looking at me much today, and I don't feel as connected to you. I'd like to connect with you. Can you look at me?

The word "evoke" comes from the Latin word *evocare*, which means to "call out" or "summon," and is based on the root verb *vocare*, "to voice." To evoke is to call forward with your voice. These questions and statements are evocative, then, in the sense that they call forward a different behavior, even if that behavior is simply awareness of what is happening: "Notice what is happening between us right now."

This kind of calling forward into the present often takes courage because it is uncomfortable. There tends to be a natural intensity to orienting attention in this way. The stimulus of judgment or rejection is immediate. The uncertainty is palpable. The emotion is raw. Bringing attention to the present is a much more vulnerable endeavor than talking about things from a distance, that is, experiences of the past or the possible future.

When practicing FAP, the aim is to use evocative questions and statements not in a reckless way, but rather in a way that's strategic, sensitive to case conceptualization, and monitored over time to ensure they lead to therapeutic ends. Specifically, we aim to evoke, in the moment, the exact behavior that matters for a given client's growth or recovery at this point in his life. Evoking effectively requires clear functional thinking, and to evoke boldly you must have confidence that you are doing so therapeutically. Only functional thinking can give you that confidence. But evoking also informs the functional analysis because it calls forward behavior and disclosure and allows you to explore what is happening in the moment. Remember, while we aim to be strategic as therapists, we will not always be right. So evoking is often just the beginning of an exploration, a moving toward something that seems to matter. In evocative moments, all the elements of FAP come together: trust, vulnerability, courage, compassion, and functional thinking.

In this chapter, we describe some of the common principles of evoking.

WHEN YOU SEE A POTENTIAL CRB

Evoking skillfully requires noticing behavior that is potentially CRB, as rule 1 states. In the example of Jennifer, the therapist notices that Jennifer is emotional, and that in the context of feeling emotional she seems to want to move away from the emotion and keep the therapist away from it as well.

The evoking, then, is to call something different forward. Inherently, evoking tends to interrupt what is already happening. It is disruptive. This disruption can take a lot of different forms and vary widely in intensity. When you think of evoking, imagine a continuum between gentle interruption and bold confrontation.

The gentle interruption is like a soft, extended hand slowing reaching forward: "May I slow you down?" It balances the gentleness of asking for permission with the assertiveness of interruption. Even though it is gentle, its disruption may be startling: "May I slow you down? I think you are perhaps terrified to say what you are really thinking right now."

In contrast, bold confrontation is like a fist that grabs attention: "Let me stop you there." It takes the moment, but it need not take away choice, because in the next moment you can powerfully give choice back: "Let me stop you there. What is it that you really want?"

Different moments in therapy will require different positions on this continuum. As always, it's important to ask yourself this: How does my evoking function in this moment?

EVOKING IN WAYS THAT ARE HEARD, SEEN, AND FELT

Evoking functions at many levels beyond the words that are spoken. Often the most effective evoking disrupts not just through content but through how that content is voiced, meaning the facial expressions, hand gestures, and body posture that accompany the words.

Imagine that you're working with a client who tends to get lost in his head, telling the same circular stories about a situation in which he was wronged as though you haven't already heard these stories and communicated your understanding of his pain multiple times. Imagine his 2s involve slowing down, breathing, describing how he's feeling, and voicing his needs. In this situation, your evoking might embody these various 2s at numerous levels:

You sit forward in your chair and make eye contact.

Your hand comes forward in a gentle gesture of interruption.

You breathe deeply into your belly.

You focus on your intentions: to communicate with your tone the empathy you feel for the client's pain as well as to talk in a more productive way.

Finally, your words arrive: "I really want to help you move beyond your pain, and I'm wondering if you're telling me the same story over and over again because you aren't deeply feeling the anguish of what you're telling me, or because you're not receiving my validation of what you're saying. Would you be willing to slow down and notice the visceral sensations you're feeling in your body, one sentence at a time, as you talk to me and as I respond?"

FORMS OF EVOKING

Evoking is defined by its function, not its form. However, evoking does tend to take a few common forms, and it's useful to consider these in order to understand the range of possibilities. In the following section we will consider these forms:

Describing what you notice

Prompting clients to notice

Requesting and inviting

Bold requests

Expressing empathy and love

Describing What You Notice

Describing what you notice happening in the moment is a very basic way of evoking CRB: "I noticed that you looked away from me when you said that." The awareness the statement prompts is sometimes sufficient enough to prompt, in turn, a shift in CRB. Or it opens up a useful exploration.

Prompting Clients to Notice

Another basic way to evoke CRB is to prompt clients to share what they notice. This directs their attention, which may disrupt avoidance, and also evokes self-disclosure. Consider a prototypical therapeutic question: What are you feeling right now? This tends to evoke sharing of what the client notices. You could also evoke noticing alone: "Can you notice what you're feeling right now? You don't have to share anything with me; just notice and experience it on your own." This isn't an academic distinction. For some clients, a pure focus on awareness and private experience may be exactly what they need, and attempting to evoke self-disclosure might take them too far out of their comfort zone and feel too perilous. You might take these further steps with such clients over time, but starting with pure awareness and experiencing might be more effective than asking them to also share what they notice.

Sharing intimate, vulnerable experience, especially about emotions, is difficult for many people, yet it leads to a sense of connection that many people crave in their relationships. Sometimes a robust FAP process can unfold entirely around the process of sharing, back and forth, moment by moment, what both client and therapist are experiencing. FAP therapist Tore Gustafsson calls this "affective mirroring." Here's a brief example:

Client: I feel a flash of shame. I feel my cheeks flushing as I say this to you.

Therapist: I feel your discomfort, and that you're not looking away. This makes me feel tender toward you. There's a warm feeling in my stomach.

Client: I feel myself shudder as you say that. Part of me wants to push you away. But it feels so nice to be seen, to be cared for.

Therapist: I'm happy you're not pushing me away. Part of me is uncomfortable too. I notice my hands are restless. And yet as I look at you, I feel everything else fading away. I feel peaceful.

Requesting and Inviting

Sometimes stating what you notice suffices to evoke CRB. At other times you might add a specific request or invitation; for example, "I've noticed that you're not looking at me. I want to feel connected to you because what you're talking about feels very important. So—and I know this is hard—can you look at me right now as you talk?" Such invitations name and request the 2 directly.

Bold Requests

We distinguish bold requests as a separate category based on the intensity of the disruption or the degree of change they invite. Of course, this degree is entirely contextual. Therefore, for some clients or therapists, the example request in the previous section may be quite bold. Because of their intensity, bold requests should be used sparingly; otherwise their impact is diminished or there is a high risk that therapy will become aversive. The response to a bold request should have the quality of "I'm only willing to do this because you've built up a lot of good will and trust and because I know you're right that this is good for me." There is willingness to respond, but it is strained to the limits.

Here's an example of a bold request in a challenging context in which a great deal of sensitivity to the client is required. The client has been ruminating about suicide for weeks and is unwilling to commit to life but nevertheless continues to come to therapy. His therapist notices that recent therapy sessions have revolved around the client's suicidal rumination in a way that seems unproductive; in fact, the therapist has noticed that the client's in-session behavior parallels his pattern of avoiding commitment and avoiding active coping with challenging issues, such as his failing marriage and stalled career. So, with the utmost empathy and attunement, the therapist says, "I want to make a bold request of you. And I recognize that when I say this, I'm asking for a lot. I notice that we keep going round and round about suicide. You don't want to give up the idea of checking out. But what I see at the core of that is something else that I think is scarier for you: you're really scared to face the problems in your marriage and feeling like you're in a dead-end job. There's a way in which talking about suicide is easier. So this is my request: Can we stop acting as though whether to commit suicide is the real problem here, and instead focus on what's making you want to kill yourself? Would you be willing to stay in that conversation with me?"

Expressing Empathy and Love

Receiving empathy and love can be just as evocative as any request. A simple, empathic reflection—such as "That must be so painful"—can evoke a range of potential 1s: dismissal, skepticism, cynicism, various forms of avoidance, and so on. There might also be parallel 2s that come forward from acknowledging or openly receiving the therapist's empathy or caring.

BALANCING COURAGE AND LOVE

Again, the above categories (describing what you notice, prompting clients to notice, requesting and inviting, bold requests, expressing empathy and love) only suggest some of the ways you can evoke behavior in session. Various forms of behavior may also accomplish the desired function. We have also found that balancing courage and love is another quality that is important for evoking therapeutically.

Notice that in the earlier example about suicide, the therapist prefaces her bold request with an acknowledgment of the client's perspective—that she's asking the client to face what he fears more than suicide. This prefacing is an example of an important general principle of evoking in FAP: to the extent that evoking demands courage of the client, it should clearly come from a perspective grounded in empathy and love. Acknowledging the client's perspective or the likely emotional impact the evoking may have or asking for permission are all ways of expressing empathy and love. In turn, communicating empathy and love can change how the request functions, transforming it from a more aversive demand ("Do this or else") into a more inviting invitation to move toward something meaningful. Consider the differences in these examples:

- I know this is a bold request and it might make you uncomfortable, and I'd really like you to dig for some critical feedback you could share with me. (Compare with "I want you to dig for some critical feedback to give me.")

- I hear you saying how alone you feel right now. You're right that I can't know exactly how you feel. And I want you to know that I do want to understand. Would you be willing to tell me more? (Compare with "Tell me more right now.")

- I can feel how difficult this is for you to talk about. Is it okay if we stay with this topic for a while longer? (Compare with "Let's talk about this some more.")

As a corollary, if a client reacts with defensiveness, resistance, or avoidance, a good rule of thumb is to amplify your empathy and expression of love in order to increase the appetitive function of the evoking. You can achieve a similar effect by linking the evoking directly to the client's goals.

SLOWING DOWN AND ALLOWING

Going further, whatever form evoking takes, even if it is firm or striking, in general it shouldn't feel like forcing. Invoking should feel like inviting, suggesting, encouraging, or collaborating. The statements in the previous section are good examples of such noncoercive evoking. Our assumption in practicing FAP is that voluntary participation and choice are, as a rule, the foundation of effective therapy. We are not coercing or placing clients under aversive control ("Do this or else something bad will happen."). We are not asking clients to do what we say because we say they should. We want clients to choose what is right for them based on their values and their experience. If we ever force or confront, it's typically strategic, in service of getting the client more in touch with choice.

It's useful to remember, then, that often the medium in which choice arises is spaciousness of time, especially if emotion, confusion, or conflict is involved. We must provide time—through silence, through listening, and so on. This isn't untethered spaciousness; your presence holds clients in the moment and invites them to feel what they haven't fully felt, think what they haven't fully thought, and choose what they haven't fully chosen. To that end, your presence may need to be more or less prominent and more or less active.

Sometimes, for example, the single best strategy is to hold your tongue after making a bold request. Let silence create space in which influence sets in. Silence can also be stultifying—perpetuating the space in which a familiar pattern or confusion consumes clients, or in which unspoken thoughts are buried even more deeply. In these cases, you need to evoke again; for example, "What are you thinking right now that might be hard to tell me about? What are you avoiding saying to me right now?"

Silence itself is evocative. Pay attention to the function of silence: What does it evoke? Pay attention as well to your T1s and T2s when it comes to silence and filling silence. If you tend to talk too much—or not enough—you are leaving valuable opportunities to shape client behavior on the table.

EXERCISES

Besides the more unstructured, process-based forms of evoking described above, you can also make use of various exercises, structured or unstructured, to evoke CRB. The life history exercise, FAP session bridging form, and various assessments—in fact, any aspect of the therapy process or structure—can all evoke CRB. In chapter 12, we offer a sampling of exercises precisely for their evocative value. The only thing that sets these exercises apart from other ways of evoking is that they tend to be somewhat structured.

A LONG LIST OF EVOKING

Below we offer a long list of sample questions and statements you can use to evoke CRB. They are organized into the functional classes of awareness, courage, and love (ACL) and the subcategories of each outlined in chapter 4. However, most of them are useful across a broad range of functional analyses. (In fact, many of them could be fit into one or both of the other ACL classes.) Please don't view these examples as rule 2 "scripts" to employ verbatim with clients—although there may be times when the language we provide is a perfect fit. Rather, we hope these lists will stimulate you to think of ways to evoke CRB for specific clients in context. We also hope they will inspire you to evoke CRB in bold and courageous ways while also being attuned to the needs of clients.

Awareness of Present-Moment Bodily Sensations, Thoughts, and Feelings

Can you slow down right now, take a deep breath, and connect with your body?

Can you really notice and become aware of what it feels like in your body to hear this from me?

Can you find what's good and pure and strong in your own behavior right now?

Can you notice what you're feeling right now?

I notice that I'm not sure if you're tracking me as you're talking. I notice that I'm not as tuned in as I'd like to be because you don't seem very connected to me or to what you're saying. Can you see that?

You've told me that it's hard for you to figure out what you're feeling. How about if I name some feelings that you might be having? Your job is to just pay attention and notice when an emotion word feels like it fits.

There was this momentary flash of emotion as you were talking. Were you aware of what you were feeling?

Did you notice that you quickly moved on when I gave you that feedback? I had the sense you were brushing me off.

Awareness of Values, Needs, Goals, and Identity

Do you know what you need or want right now, from today's session?

What feels really vital and meaningful for you in this moment?

As you're talking to me, are you aware of why you're here and what you're trying to work on?

What do you long for?

What goal feels the most difficult to approach right now?

What are the most important skills you've learned that you want to keep implementing in your life?

In what areas do you feel disappointed about the progress you've made?

I'm having a hard time following what's important to you in this. Can you help me understand?

Awareness of Others

What do you think I'm feeling?

I am wondering if you could pay more attention to my face, my expression, and my eyes right now. Really notice me.

What could you do to improve our relationship?

What are some seemingly inappropriate reactions you've had to me?

What do you think I'm feeling about your progress?

Are you aware of how I'm reacting to what you're saying?

You seem very tuned in to how I'm reacting right now. What are you noticing?

It seems that you're comfortable with a lot of conflict with your relationships, and you're interacting with me in that way. What do you think it's like for me and other people who care about you?

As you know, part of making relationships work well is being tuned in to the other person. How aware are you of how you're impacting me in terms of...?

Courage: Choosing to Experience Vulnerability and Emotion

What were you thinking or feeling on your way to therapy today?

What were you thinking or feeling while you were waiting for me out in the waiting room?

People have different ways of suppressing their feelings. One client told me that she counts backward from one thousand by sevens. Another one holds his breath. What do you do to suppress your feelings?

It's hard for me to know what you're feeling based on your facial expression, or lack of it. Can you describe the visceral sensations you're having?

What's your reaction to what I just said? [...to the rationale I just gave?...to me as your therapist?... to agenda setting?...to structured therapy?...to the homework assignment?]

Let's spend five minutes really talking about how we're feeling right now, in this moment, from the heart.

What are you feeling right now?

What thoughts and feelings are you having about the end of this therapy relationship as it approaches?

What's it like for you to hear my feedback?

It's painful for you to hear me say that. I want to acknowledge that. Can you tell me more about how it feels?

I have the sense that you're being very careful about your words right now. What are you avoiding saying? If you were less careful, what would you say?

I know our disagreement is hard for you to stay with. Are you willing to keep talking with me about this?

You seem angry but your words don't reflect that. What if you put your anger into words?

Can you express the hurt beneath your anger? That would make it easier for me to hear what you're upset with me about.

What does it bring up for you that we're getting closer?

It means a lot to me that you just shared something with me that you don't usually tell people, but you're acting like it's not a big deal. What are your feelings about having told me what you just said?

I'd like you to slow down and say that to me again. Can you feel what you're saying?

Courage: Offering Self-Disclosure

What would be hard for us to talk about?

What do you not want to talk about?

What do you have a hard time expressing about yourself?

What's difficult for you between sessions?

What's happened that's been painful for you to discover?

What are the hardest parts of our time together?

Which of your behaviors tend to bring closeness in your relationships? What do you tend to do that decreases closeness in your relationships? How would you feel about us watching for those behaviors in here?

What's hard for you to tell me about yourself?

In what area do you feel disappointed about the progress you've made?

What happens during sessions that makes it hard for you to manage your feelings?

What stands out to you most about your interactions with me?

What situations, thoughts, or behaviors make you vulnerable to feeling [insert presenting problems here], and how can you deal with them to decrease the likelihood or severity of what you were experiencing when you first came in?

When do you feel closest to me?

What powerful experiences have you had because of our work together?

From your heart, what's most vulnerable for you to say to me as you say good-bye?

What regrets do you have about the therapy or what would you like to have gone differently?

Is there any negative feedback you'd like to share with me?

It seems that you're really making therapy a priority. Can you tell me what your therapy relationship with me means to you?

Courage: Asking for a Need to Be Met

What do you not want to talk about?

What can we do to connect right now?

What do you need from me right now?

What do you want to change about your therapy?

What's an area that's important for us to continue talking about?

How do you wish I would change?

What's hard for you to say to me?

What do you wish I'd do differently?

I hear a need in what you're saying, but it's not quite clear to me. Can you help me understand?

I notice that you're working really hard to take care of me right now. Who takes care of you? How can I take better care of you?

I think it's very hard for you—scary even—to ask for what you need here. Would you be willing to ask me despite your fear?

I have the sense that your anger is overwhelming everything else right now. What do you think is needed?

Love: Providing Safety and Acceptance

Can you express acceptance to me? What do you really love and accept about me and how I interact with you?

You seem kind of scary to me right now. Is there a way you can be less scary while still remaining true to what you feel?

Love: Expressing Understanding, Validation, and Empathy

What do you feel is important for me to know right now?

When do you feel closest to me?

What do you like and appreciate about me? What will you always remember about me?

It means a lot to me that you're listening to what I have to say right now. Often you're very focused on telling me your story, so it means a lot to me when you tune in to my input.

Love: Giving What Is Needed

What could you do to improve our relationship?

I feel like it would help me connect with you if…

I'm wondering what you appreciate about our work. Would you tell me?

It seems that anger is your go-to emotion, and it can really push people away. Can you express your anger to me in a way that brings us closer?

It's hard for me to tell you this because I don't want you to feel distanced from me. But you express your feelings in a really intense way sometimes, and it scares me. I want to stay present with you, and it would be helpful for me if you lowered your voice and slowed down a bit. What do you think?

I noticed that you just changed the topic. Can we go back?

I notice that you're not looking at me as you say that. Can you look at me?

Love: Reciprocal Disclosure

Are you upset with me?

What do I do that bothers you?

What are some things I've done that you felt were insensitive?

What are some things that I've done to hurt you or make you feel angry?

When do you feel closest to me?

I want you to know that I respect your anger about this. I'm sorry about what I did. Are you willing to let me try to repair the situation?

Would you be willing to compromise with me?

It seems that when you're unhappy with something, you tend to blame other people, including me. Can we each look at what we're contributing to this conflict we're having?

The ability to forgive another person's mistakes is essential in maintaining close relationships. I get that you're really mad at me and want to walk away from our relationship right now. But that would just be a repeat of what you've done with everyone else who's cared about you. Are you willing to do something different this time? Will you work on forgiving me for my mistakes?

Self-Love: Self-Acceptance

What do you have a hard time expressing about yourself?

What can you accept in yourself right now?

What do you like and appreciate about yourself?

It seems like you're being really hard on yourself right now. What can you appreciate about what you're doing in this situation?

Self-Love: Accepting Love from Others

What does it feel like in your body to hear this appreciation from me?

Can you accept my appreciation of you?

How accepting of my appreciation are you right now?

Self-Love: Self-Care

What do you need from me right now that would help you take care of yourself?

How can you take care of yourself in this moment?

If you were to make our session today the most nourishing and supportive for yourself, how would you approach it?

RESPONDING TO CLIENT 1S

When you evoke, you call something forward in the moment. You step into the stream of behavior and divert it in some way. Of course, the stream has its own momentum. It doesn't comply immediately to your suggestion. It might bowl you over. It might twist around you and create havoc downstream. It might silently conform and then immediately resume its course.

To evoke then is merely the first step, and often when we evoke we find ourselves contending with the momentum of the behavior we are seeking to change. Consider these examples of client CRB1:

- The client has a dozen ways of distancing from her experience of anxiety.

- The client plunges into anxious objections to any path of action.

- The client believes rigidly that one "simply can't" do certain types of things and argues with suggestions to try doing them.

- The client feels anxious and offers various charming, self-deprecating jokes when she is vulnerable.

The CRB1 in all these examples functions to push away, escape, or avoid something that is aversive for the client. The CRB1 is reinforced when the behavior accomplishes that function. When a CRB1 occurs in response to evoking, then, the key question is: what happens next?

One possibility is that the CRB1 is aversive to you or otherwise pulls you away in a less therapeutic direction. (Remember, in this context "therapeutic" is defined as evoking CRB2.) In fact, you might have a countertherapeutic effect by somehow reinforcing the client's CRB1. This is not unusual.

Here's an example. Imagine a teenage client whose daily life problems revolve around not completing important tasks because of her tendency to get wrapped up in her emotions. In therapy, the mutually agreed-upon core CRB2 is to do what's important despite feelings that come and go:

Therapist: So, your homework was to have a really important conversation. I'd like to hear how it went.

Client: I really don't want to.

Therapist: Why not? (Sensitively.)

Client: I just feel so overwhelmed. (Tearing up.)

Therapist: (Leaning forward.) Tell me more.

Here the therapist may be getting pulled away from the core CRB and the corresponding evocation, instead engaging in her own T1 of avoiding the possibly more challenging topic of the avoided homework. Attending to the emotion might be functional, before looping back to address the homework, but as therapists we don't always close the loop. The therapist in this situation may be absentmindedly reinforcing the client's avoidance, and she may kick herself at the end of the session when she realizes that very little outside of the status quo has been accomplished.

Responding to CRB1 in a contentious way that seems to challenge the client to step up but in fact fails to evoke CRB2 can be just as dysfunctional:

Therapist: So, your homework was to have a really important conversation. I'd like to hear how it went.

Client: I really don't want to.

Therapist: Too bad. We gotta.

Client: Fine. Whatever.

Therapist: So how did it go?

Client: Fine.

Therapist: *(Waiting.)*

In contrast, despite a client's attempts to steer you away and avoid, despite the aversiveness of the moment for you or the client, there is a way of gently staying with the evoking without forcing it or reinforcing the client's 1. Much of the skill is essentially lingering and making the moment as appetitive as possible, such that the client becomes willing to stay there with you to find the behavior that is a 2 for him. For example:

Therapist: So, your homework was to have a really important conversation. I'd like to hear how it went.

Client: I really don't want to.

Therapist: Yeah. I can see your emotion. Are you willing to tell me what happened—whatever it was? This was such an important conversation. And so much is at stake.

Here the therapist balances validation, asking for permission, and highlighting the importance of the homework while repeating the evocation. Such a gentle and insistent repetition of the evocation is probably the simplest response to a CRB1. In this context, the therapist may now be looking for any slight movement toward talking about the homework or the emotion about what happened. In this way, the therapist shapes the gradual movement toward a more fully developed CRB2:

Therapist: Yeah. I can see your emotion. Are you willing to tell me what happened—whatever it was? This was such an important conversation. And so much is at stake.

Client: *(Tears up.)*

Therapist: It looks like whatever happened was really painful.

Client: Yes.

Therapist: It's okay. Take your time.

Client: I feel so embarrassed.

Therapist: Tell me what happened.

Moments like this often have to unfold gradually, with a broad, flexible sense of the CRB2 that you and the client are shaping. There should be a sense of exploring the experience, with empathy. Here is an extended example of an exploration that gradually leads to a CRB2 related to emotional expression.

Therapist: You're looking at me like this (eyes looking up, tilted down). I'm wondering if you can look at me more directly. That would help me feel more connected.

Client: All right. (Looking at the therapist.)

Therapist: What are you feeling right now?

Client: Anxious. I don't know why I'm anxious.

Therapist: How do you know you're anxious?

Client: I'm more tense.

Therapist: Where do you feel tense?

Client: Physically. My whole body is rigid. Looking at you is harder than it's been before. (Looking away slightly.)

Therapist: I'm asking you to look at me more directly.

Client: How's this? Is it better?

Therapist: You do look more emotional.

Client: Yeah, I'm sad. When I start to think about the play I saw last night, there's sadness, crying—there's tears here, in me, now…somewhere.

Therapist: You're smiling. What happens when you smile? Does it block your tears?

Client: Yeah, I guess.

Therapist: See, you're doing it, you're making your sadness go away. It's hard to be sad when you're smiling and kind of laughing.

Client: It's true.

Therapist: It's a very effective technique. I'd like to hear more about your sadness. How do you experience it in your body right now? What are you feeling? Get basic: A lump in your throat, a heaviness in your chest? What do you feel?

Client: Hmm. I'm not sure what it is I'm feeling.

Therapist: Do you notice the sensations in your body?

Client: I notice shallower breathing.

Therapist: You're doing a good job of staying with yourself and not smiling—not going into your head. Are you holding your breath?

Client: Yeah, holding my breath.

Therapist: What would happen if you would just let yourself cry?

Client: Nothing. I don't understand why I can't do it. I'd just get sad. I don't get it. I don't know why I can't do that.

Therapist: You actually do that better than a lot of men. You let yourself get teary, sob at times. I think you'd feel much more liberated if you were in touch even more with your feelings and were more expressive. The big thing for me about your emotional expression is the incongruence, the smiling. The first thing I want you to do is to cut that out. You know that when I am working with my clients and they're saying sad things and start grinning, it's difficult to be on the receiving end of that. And I don't know what it feels like for you; it seems invalidating for you, a very effective way of cutting yourself off from your feelings. And I'm wondering how that came about. Did you have to smile for your parents, and let them know everything's okay? I'm checking to see how you're breathing.

Client: Shallow. I'm sweating in my chest and legs. I'm anxious.

Therapist: What's percolating that you're anxious about? What do you need to say that you're not saying? Just blurt it out.

Client: You said my smile cuts me off from my feeling. I was thinking I don't want to be cut off from my feelings. I don't want to put myself in a box. My parents contained me in a box.

Therapist: I feel sad when I hear you say your parents put you in this box.

Client: It is sad.

Therapist: Can you say "I feel sad?"

Client: I feel sad.

Therapist: Say "I feel sad when I think about my parents putting me in a box."

Client: You want me to say that?

Therapist: And try not to smile.

Client: I feel sad about my parents putting me in a box.

Therapist: Say that again.

Client: I feel sad about my parents putting me in a box.

Therapist: I feel sad too about your parents putting you in a box. Your voice is really low. Say it in your own voice like you mean it.

Client: I feel sad that my parents put me in a box.

Therapist: What do you notice in your body?

Client: I'm tight, I'm not breathing, I'm not really moving. Was that my own voice? No? What do you notice?

Therapist: I'm wondering what you're doing to cut yourself off from your feelings. You're not smiling, which is really good, but you're constricted. I'm really struck by how subdued you sound. I guess that's exactly what you're telling me about…being put in a box, being medicated. You seem to have so much grief under the surface. It seems like you're doing everything you can to keep it there.

Client: I'm clenching my teeth. This is fucking crazy.

Therapist: I think you're a little hard on yourself, because you're not fucking crazy. What do you expect? You grew up in this environment with your parents. They medicated you because you were a little too much for them. And what do you think you're going to do, emote like crazy? Not yet.

Client: I am so hard on myself. I'd like to try and get to the emotion…I want to emote.

Therapist: I want you to.

Client: (Cries briefly.)

Inviting Growth or Change

Notice in the previous example that evoking CRB2 is not as simple as offering a deliberate choice. It is not a matter of willpower or choice. Instead, evoking CRB2 is a matter of creating a context that is challenging enough, compassionate enough, and aware enough for something new to emerge. The therapist is compassionate throughout, while remaining focused on evoking CRB2.

It is often important to be just as compassionate toward CRB1 (or the person engaging in CRB1) as we are toward CRB2. This is a critical point! This stance counteracts our tendency to be frustrated or disappointed with "problem" behavior. Why does this matter? Clients are often amply frustrated and conflicted with their CRB1. In that case, our own frustration doesn't offer anything new or disruptive. In addition, the threshold at which CRB1 turns into CRB2 is often riddled with fear or vulnerability—aversion that tends to evoke avoidance. Our aim is to make that pathway as appetitive as possible.

At the same time, this stance of compassion toward CRB1 does *not* mean being soft or tolerant in any broad sense of CRB1. We can empathize with the history and the function behind CRB1 and, at the same time, remain aware of the terrible cost it has wrought over time. Our goal is to help the person recognize that he or she is able and capable of stepping through the experience of vulnerability toward a CRB2.

Of course, the particular style or tone of this balance between compassion, acceptance, and firm evoking varies between clients. Many therapists tend to err on one side or the other—either too soft and compassionate or too harsh and demanding—with similar results: they don't evoke much change.

With all clients you should be guided by functional thinking and observation of what is happening. Ask yourself how your evoking is functioning. Are you being too lenient or too harsh? Adjust accordingly.

See the 2 in the 1

When navigating the conflicted flow of CRB1 or emerging CRB2, to "see the 2 in the 1" is an invaluable concept. Consider this example:

Therapist: What are you feeling right now?

Client: Nothing. I want you to take a leap out the window.

Therapist: I know you're angry at me. Can I see if I understand why?

Client: Good fucking luck.

Therapist: Well, I think that basically what we've been trying to do these last few weeks is not working. And then in that context, I kept challenging you in a way that must have felt really frustrating. And now things have really fallen apart at your job. So you're sitting there going, *How the fuck is therapy worthwhile again?*

Client: Pretty much.

Therapist: It's crap, there's no way around it. I'm sorry.

In this example, there might be a tendency to see—even without context—the client's first statement as an aggressive, avoidant CRB1. It was indeed aversive for the therapist, and in many contexts it would have been ineffective. The therapist, however, recognizes that the client's mere presence in therapy (rather than being at the liquor store) and her verbal engagement with him, in this context, is CRB2. In other words, the client's life would be worse if this behavior were not happening.

In turn, the therapist responds to the client's statement as though it is a CRB2 of accurately expressing anger. The therapist aims to reinforce this statement by reflecting the anger and, in turn, evoke further vulnerable engagement with the client by asking if he can explore why she is angry.

Again, the client responds in a vague, aggressive way—congruent with her emotion—but also in a way that invites the therapist to proceed. And again, there is a CRB2 in that prickly statement. The therapist offers a validating, event-based explanation of the client's anger, admitting his own contribution to the situation. The client then finally offers a more neutral, perhaps even agreeable, response. From here, the discussion continues to move in a constructive direction.

If the therapist had responded more directly to the aversive CRB1 aspects of the client's response, or had he been unable to see the 2 in the 1, the outcome would likely have been much less constructive.

Ignoring—When and How

Besides gently blocking or evoking 2s in response to 1s, you may experience the impulse to ignore 1s. For instance, if the client vaguely asks for reassurance, and seeking reassurance is a 1, the therapist might ignore that request and respond to another part of the message. Or if the client sends a message venting about frustrating events after-hours, the therapist might ignore the message.

Ignoring does not work well when the client is making a specific request of you and/or is expecting a response. For socially attuned human beings, conspicuous ignoring creates uncertainty, and anxiety or irritation may follow. The uncertainty arises because ignoring rarely comes with an explanation; for example, "I'm going to ignore what you just said." Ignoring is intrinsically vague: *Is he ignoring my message? Why is he doing that? Is he considering it a 1? It seemed reasonable to me. Or is he just busy? Did I do something wrong? Is he angry at me?* This kind of unspoken uncertainty often corrodes trust. It creates a special kind of paranoia; for example, "Are you doing behavior modification on me by ignoring my response?"

However, if there is a clear, shared rationale for ignoring, the function may be quite different. Consider this: "When you send me venting messages on the weekend, because I'm quite busy, and because those messages are generally about you avoiding doing what you need to do, we agree that I won't respond." Or "Sometimes I can't provide everything you need, nor can anyone else. So from time to time I may not reply to your messages, because life gets in the way. When that happens, are you willing to work on accepting that?"

In addition, ignoring can sometimes work pragmatically: for example, if there is plenty of other stuff to respond to, you simply can't respond to everything or it may work to focus on specific things or perhaps the client hasn't specifically requested that you respond to a given item. And there is a behavioral rationale for ignoring: ignoring may be the "least-reinforcing response," and as such it ensures that a 1 is not reinforced. Principles aside, as always, before ignoring we should ask how doing so will actually function for the client.

Without a clear rationale for the value of enduring the disappointment, the cost of breach of trust outweighs the potential that the client will stumble upon the therapeutic benefit of being ignored. Responsiveness is too important; nonresponsiveness is too confusing. In the majority of cases, when a response is expected, the superior therapeutic stance is to address the expectation of response with honesty and adult social skills.

NAME THE PATTERN AND STEP OUT OF IT

In our consultations with therapists, we have found, again and again, that there is a special kind of evoking that is useful when therapy is stuck. In FAP terms, "getting stuck" in therapy means the therapeutic relationship is no longer exerting a therapeutic influence on the client's patterns of problematic behavior. Instead, the therapist's behavior has been shaped by client responses (or other factors) to the point that the therapy is no longer therapeutic.

Consider these examples:

- The client becomes angry at you every time you suggest behavior change, and now you've given up on suggesting change.

- You struggle through the same protocol over and over again, but the client doesn't "get it" and you don't know why.

- You both like each other a lot, but there is a nagging sense that nothing is really changing.

These examples all boil down to this: behavior isn't changing. It's not a matter of progress being a slow, gradual grind, rather the therapy is stuck.

When this happens, you need to do something different. Functionally speaking, you need to vary your own behavior in order to evoke something different. Sounds simple, right? The approach we typically recommend in this situation is called "name the pattern and step outside it." In the sections that follow, we describe the steps involved.

Step 1: Describe the Pattern

The first step is to describe—using basic and nonjudgmental behavior terms—exactly what the pattern of behavior is that that you and the client engage in. You are not going to share this with the client yet. You are writing this description just for yourself.

Sometimes there can be a relatively stable holding pattern of behavior, but more often than not the pattern is more of a cycle: this phase leads to that phase that in turn loops back to the beginning. The tricky thing about cycles is that some part of the cycle might present itself as an escape from the cycle, but in reality it's just another part of the stuck cycle. Consider this example of a pattern of behavior written from the therapist's perspective:

> First we try to shape commitments that you will follow through on to move you toward your goals and activate out of unproductive avoidance. We drum up motivation. Then you tend to fall short in some way. Then you feel frustrated with therapy and miss a session and question the whole enterprise. Then I feel bad, and then we talk about hopelessness, and we usually arrive at a point where we feel more connected. Then we get hopeful again. Then we shape commitments again…and the cycle repeats. We've repeated this cycle three times in the last three months.

Describe the pattern at whatever level of detail is sufficient to capture it. Your description should be detailed and accurate enough that, having read it, both you and the client would give a head nod of recognition: yes, that's what happens between us.

Step 2: Take the Client's Perspective

Next, from the client's perspective, review the description that you wrote. It must avoid laying blame on the client. It should convey that there is a 100 percent reasonable explanation for the current situation—a sense of, "Of course this is what happens, because this reflects exactly how your behavior was shaped by your history, and it is exactly why you are seeking help from me." Does your description convey that sense?

For example, we might expand the example from above in the following way:

> First we try to shape commitments that you will follow through on to move you toward your goals and activate out of unproductive avoidance. We drum up motivation. Then you tend to fall short in some way. **This is understandable, because I think we're not great yet at estimating what is doable; we tend to get too ambitious. You're also still struggling with a lot of difficult emotion.** Then you feel frustrated with therapy and miss a session and question the whole enterprise. **Again, that makes sense—even though I think it's self-defeating—because empirically therapy hasn't moved you forward much yet.** Then I feel bad, and then we talk about hopelessness, and we usually arrive at a point where we feel more connected. Then we get hopeful again. Then we shape commitments again…**We have the best of intentions. We think we won't make the same mistake again.** And the cycle repeats. We've repeated this cycle three times in the last three months.

What validation do you need to add to your description?

Next, consider more broadly how the client will hear your description of the pattern. What objections or explanations will his self-critical mind give? Will there be shame? Hopelessness? Fear that you are giving up on therapy? Add some validation or assurance that responds directly to that voice:

I'm afraid that saying this will make you think I'm giving up on our therapy, but I'm actually reaffirming my commitment.

I want to own my part in what has happened. You're right to be disappointed and frustrated with this process.

I expect you may find this pattern to feel hopeless. But I think that by naming the pattern we can begin to step out of it.

Step 3: Find Other Avoidance

Often, the main thing that is being avoided is calling out the stuck pattern, and naming the pattern directly is the most important, disruptive step forward. However, sometimes there are other points of avoidance that don't come clearly into focus with the initial description of the stuck pattern. Addressing this avoidance can be critical.

To address this possibility, consider these questions:

What are you not talking about or accepting in relation to this client?

Are you or the client failing to meet your commitments to each other?

Is there significant unspoken frustration or disappointment in the relationship?

Has one of you shut down or refused to address something the other considers important?

Is the client resisting your input?

Are you resisting or failing to understand the client's input?

What else do you feel about this client that you are not accepting?

If there is something important that you are avoiding facing, consider yourself lucky that you've discovered it. Reflect on how that avoided thing fits into the stuck pattern. About nine times out of ten it will fit in a very clear way. For example, the therapist might build on her perspective of where therapy is stuck in this way:

First we try to shape commitments that you will follow through on to move you toward your goals and activate out of unproductive avoidance. We drum up motivation. Then you tend to fall short in some way. This is understandable, because I think we're not great yet at estimating what is doable; we tend to get too ambitious. You're also still struggling with a lot of difficult emotion. Then you feel frustrated with therapy and miss a session and question the whole enterprise. Again, that makes sense—even though I think it's self-defeating—because empirically therapy hasn't moved you forward much yet. Then I feel bad, and then we talk about hopelessness, and we usually arrive at a point where we feel more connected. Then we get hopeful again. Then we shape commitments again...We have the best of intentions. We think we won't make the same mistake again. And the cycle repeats. We've repeated this cycle three times in the last three months.

I think one thing we've been avoiding dealing with is recognizing that we don't have a clear bead on what's going to make your life more meaningful and rewarding right now. Part of this is related to the bankruptcy hanging over your head and the uncertainty about whether your job will continue past the fall. I think these issues insidiously undermine all the motivation we try to build.

Perhaps you're thinking, *Therapists just can't say things like that,* or *I can't say that!* If you feel constricted by such thoughts about addressing the things you've been avoiding, try reflecting on the following:

If you weren't concerned with being a "good therapist," and you were at your best as a compassionate human being, what would you say to this client? For example, if the client was a close friend or family member, what would you say? How would you say it?

If you weren't constrained by a treatment plan, therapy principles, case conceptualization, and so forth, what would you think is the most important thing the client needs right now?

What single issue, if you could resolve it, would make the biggest difference for this client?

Now ask yourself these questions:

How does my avoidance of this topic, or of saying what I would say to a close friend, function for me and for the client in our relationship?

In other words, what do I do when I am avoiding that topic? How do I feel? What do I think? What happens next? What is the cost of that pattern of avoidance?

Step 4: Take Responsibility

If you haven't done so already, answer this simple question: What have you done to contribute to the relationship being stuck? The avoidance identified in the prior step might be a key part of your contribution. Then incorporate your response into your understanding of the situation. Consider this example:

First we try to shape commitments that you will follow through on to move you toward your goals and activate out of unproductive avoidance. We drum up motivation. Then you tend to fall short in some way. This is understandable, because I think we're not great yet at estimating what is doable; we tend to get too ambitious. You're also still struggling with a lot of difficult emotion. Then you feel frustrated with therapy and miss a session and question the whole enterprise. Again, that makes sense—even though I think it's self-defeating—because empirically therapy hasn't moved you forward much yet. Then I feel bad, and then we talk about hopelessness, and we usually arrive at a point where we feel more connected. Then we get hopeful again. Then we shape commitments again... We have the best of intentions. We think we won't make the same mistake again. And the cycle repeats. We've repeated this cycle three times in the last three months.

I think one thing we've been avoiding dealing with is recognizing that we don't have a clear bead on what's going to make your life more meaningful and rewarding right now. Part of this is related to the bankruptcy hanging over your head and the uncertainty about whether your job will continue past the fall. I think these issues insidiously undermine all the motivation we try to build.

I think my contribution to this pattern has been wanting to believe that the simpler path of just getting activated under these circumstances is enough for you, that somehow you'll be able to gut your way through. But clearly more than that is needed.

Notice any reactions—defensiveness, shame, hopelessness, and so forth—that come up as you take responsibility. In order to face the situation and move the therapy forward, are you willing to have these feelings?

Step 5: What Else Needs to Be on the Table?

When a relationship is stuck, about 95 percent of the time the first thing that's needed is for the therapist and client to collaboratively look at it and seek to understand why. Because that understanding typically develops from a dialogue, don't become overly invested in a specific solution too early. What is needed early on is the willingness to look at the pattern, facing whatever feelings come with that willingness.

Next, get in touch with the cost of the pattern. Complete the following sentence: If this pattern continues, the most likely outcome is that... For example:

If this pattern continues, the most likely outcome is that we'll both feel more and more frustrated. We won't get anywhere, and you'll walk away with another experience in which you weren't enough and nobody could help you.

Finally, consider why it will be worthwhile to break the pattern. Consider what the client aspires to be and what the client values. Consider what you genuinely believe the client must learn to move forward. Building on the therapist perspective from earlier steps, consider the following additions:

First we try to shape commitments that you will follow through on to move you toward your goals and activate out of unproductive avoidance. We drum up motivation. Then you tend to fall short in some way. This is understandable, because I think we're not great yet at estimating what is doable; we tend to get too ambitious. You're also still struggling with a lot of difficult emotion. Then you feel frustrated with therapy and miss a session and question the whole enterprise. Again, that makes sense—even though I think it's self-defeating—because empirically therapy hasn't moved you forward much yet. Then I feel bad, and then we talk about hopelessness, and we usually arrive at a point where we feel more connected. Then we get hopeful again. Then we shape commitments again…We have the best of intentions. We think we won't make the same mistake again. And the cycle repeats. We've repeated this cycle three times in the last three months.

I think one thing we've been avoiding dealing with is recognizing that we don't have a clear bead on what's going to make your life more meaningful and rewarding right now. Part of this is related to the bankruptcy hanging over your head and the uncertainty about whether your job will continue past the fall. I think these issues insidiously undermine all the motivation we try to build.

I think my contribution to this pattern has been wanting to believe that the simpler path of just getting activated under these circumstances is enough for you, that somehow you'll be able to gut your way through. But clearly more than that is needed.

You've said again and again that you care about your freedom. But again and again we keep getting caught in this pattern, which is the opposite of freedom. What I want is that we find a way to step out of this pattern. Part of me says the pattern is genuinely about facing failure, being willing to learn from failure. And I think part of it is about being willing to face the bigger questions looming over your head.

Step 6: Prepare Your Opening Statement

Pulling together everything you've considered in the previous steps, you'll now prepare a brief, one-to-two-minute opening statement that you'll say to the client to begin addressing and talking openly about the stuck pattern.

To get you started, here's a template of sorts that you can use to construct your opening statement. You shouldn't stick to this exact wording (unless it works well for you):

1. I want to talk about something I've been noticing in our therapy. I want to share it with you so that I can get your input.

2. What I've been noticing is that we seem to be in a pattern. The pattern is [describe the pattern].

3. What I've contributed to this is [describe your contribution].

4. I think the cost of this pattern, if we let it continue, is that [describe the cost].

5. I want us to step back and talk about this pattern so we can find another way forward.

6. In talking about the pattern, I think we may have to face [name something you've been avoiding].

7. In turn, I think the reason to step back, to step out of this pattern, is that then we can move toward [name the payoff].

8. What's your view on what I'm describing? I would really value your honest perspective.

Rehearse your statement a few times and make sure that you balance courage and love while delivering it. Be aware that sometimes a mere request to engage in dialogue about the process can be quite intense for clients, so don't make this request lightly. Offer the validation your client will need to hear you clearly, with less sense of threat. At the same time, don't let your efforts to validate the client's perspective and communicate safety and openness undermine the clarity and directness of your request to disrupt the dysfunctional pattern.

Here's an example of an opening statement that's quite brief but covers all of the important points:

> I want to talk about this pattern that I think keeps happening between us. What I've noticed is that during the last few weeks I've been giving you lots of ideas about what to do. I feel this kind of urgency to give you stuff to do. And then you end up doing very few of the things I suggest during the week, and you still feel distressed, and you still feel urgently like there's something you need to do differently. And then I jump back on the train of trying to urgently give you stuff to do. I think it's really important that we step back and figure this out. Otherwise I fear you'll continue to be frustrated and we won't move forward. More importantly, I think this loop that we are stuck in—you and I—is probably something that happens more broadly in your life. Do you recognize it? A sense of urgency, and of grabbing after what you should do but not being able to actually embody the change you are grasping for. Of course I've contributed to this by feeding your urgency, buying into it right alongside you. The upside is that now I know what it feels like to be in your life, at least somewhat. And I have a hunch that what it will take to break this pattern is gradually slowing down and feeling something different or uncomfortable. What do you think about what I'm saying? Do you recognize what I'm talking about?

Step 7: Have the Conversation

The next step is to actually have the conversation with your client. Although you've hopefully rehearsed your opening statement, once you begin talking to the client, focus on the moment and connecting with your client rather than trying to remember the script you set out to deliver. If you start into your opening statement and it doesn't feel right, feel free to abandon it and speak to what seems more to the core: "You know, as I say this, I realize I don't quite know what matters most, or how to solve it. I just know we need to talk about this. What we've been doing doesn't seem to be getting us where we want to go."

Once you've opened the conversation, whatever form that takes, let go and listen. It's possible that the client will engage in CRB1 in response to your invitation, either immediately or as the conversation proceeds. If this happens, accept it, respond with compassion, and stick to your goal of disrupting the status quo. Be persistent. Sometimes you'll have to approach the conversation multiple times, perhaps across multiple sessions, to create a productive shift.

Step 8: Follow Up

Follow-up to the conversation is just as important as the initial conversation. If both you and the client are uncomfortable with the conversation and the pressure or uncertainty of change, there might be a tendency to shift back into a relative comfort zone after an intense dialogue. The pattern you set out to correct could drift back into the therapy process. The rule of thumb is this: After a disruptive conversation, revisit the conversation and the commitments both you and the client have made to shift the process; follow up on these commitments *in every session* and whenever relevant CRBs or T1s or T2s happen until doing so is clearly no longer necessary.

SUMMARY

- "Evoking" means calling forward CRB in therapy in order to give you and the client the opportunity to shape more effective responses (CRB2).

- Evoking is guided by functional thinking.

- The balance between courage and compassion ensures that evoking remains appetitive for clients rather than coercive or aversive.

- It's often important to be just as compassionate toward CRB1 as CRB2.

- See the 2 in the 1: notice the adaptive, therapeutic function in the behavior that might seem ineffective on its surface.

CHAPTER 9

Respond to Growth

What is love...except another name for the use of positive reinforcement?

—B. F. Skinner

"I'm wondering if this, right now, is an example of you not being... How did we phrase it last time? Not being who you are without hiding."

"Yeah."

"In other words, there's another way you and I could be interacting right now, instead of me just getting lucky and sometimes figuring out who you are. I guess my question is this: What would it take for you to be more okay in here with truly expressing who you are and how you feel without reservation?"

"Yeah, yeah."

"I mean, how could we get there?" Ryan laughs. "What do you need from me, right now, to make that happen more?"

He laughs again. "Yeah. Well, my life is pretty boring. Nothing, really."

"So here's the thing, I really want you to be able to be different with me. Your life isn't boring to me; it's important."

"Okay."

"So how can you take a risk with me? Is there anything you're not saying? Is there a way you can be more fully you, with all of your fears and worries and concerns and anger and hostility and I don't know exactly what else? I mean, what do you really want from me—right now?"

"Well, I'm thinking, *Should I say this right now?*"

"Just say it."

"It sounds so cheesy."

"Is it who you are?"

"Yeah."

"Then say it."

Ryan stops laughing, straightens himself up, and, with a lot of emotion and a shaky tone, says, "I really need you to support me. You know, I don't have anybody to support me and my endeavors. I know it's weird, but it's true."

Up to this final point in the interaction, the therapist had been trying to evoke CRB2 in Ryan, but mostly he was getting CRB1 in the form of brief responses and laughter. When Ryan shifted toward CRB2 at the end of the exchange—did something different—the therapist's persistence paid off.

From a FAP point of view, that last, heartfelt statement from Ryan reflects a key moment. For another client, that kind of statement might not be a big deal, but for Ryan it was. It was the first time in his work with the therapist—and perhaps in his entire adult life—that he specified what he needed and asked for it so directly. It wasn't a perfect request; in fact, exactly what he meant was unclear, but it was a huge step for Ryan. Because of the time they had spent together, both the client and the therapist understood the significance of the moment.

In FAP terms, Ryan's statement is pure, obvious, and perfectly imperfect CRB2. It is directly about his relationship with the therapist, and it is also directly related to what Ryan was struggling with in life and how he wanted to change. Sometimes CRB2s are smaller, less obvious, or less dramatic. Sometimes they don't require so much evoking, and sometimes they require more. And sometimes CRB2 is mixed with CRB1. But in all cases, the key question is how to respond. How can you use your response to maximize the therapeutic impact of this crucial step? In behavioral terms, how do we respond so as to maximize the chances that this step forward will be reinforced?

This chapter discusses how to respond to CRB2.

WHAT IS REINFORCEMENT?

Let's start with a quick review. "Reinforcement" is the process by which a behavior becomes more likely to be repeated in similar circumstances due to the consequences the behavior produces.

Is the therapist's response below reinforcing?

Client: I am sad.

Therapist: Ah… I'm so glad you said that!

If you know a little bit about contextual behavioral science (CBS), you might say no. It is incongruent to respond to an expression of sadness with happiness. This therapist is falling into the trap of offering a glib, positive response in an apparent effort to reinforce the expression of emotion. She is conflating positive affect or praise with reinforcement. She might as well give the client an M&M.

Reinforcement, you might remind yourself, is *not* about doing something nice or making the client feel good. Reinforcement is a process by which a behavior becomes more likely to recur. Whatever response from you produces that result is reinforcing. Reinforcement has nothing to do with the form of your response.

But hold on a second. If the form of your response—its emotional tone, its meaning, and so forth—has nothing to do with whether or not it is reinforcing, then how can you say that the response above is *not* reinforcing?

You can't. Congratulations if you realized this already. The best answer to the question "Is the therapist's response reinforcing?" is "We can't tell. It depends." In other words, we can't tell if the response is reinforcing based only on its form. What matters is the function of the response for the client—what effect does that response actually have on the client? This is the essence of functional thinking. (Forgive us for the trick question. And we hope you passed that little test.)

We might be able to make an informed guess about whether the response will be reinforcing by seeing more of the context around the response. For example, consider the following situation with a client who is struggling with burnout at work and whose CRB1 revolves around hiding and being out of touch with her own needs and emotions:

Client: I just feel lost. I don't want to move forward; I drag every day. I love the project but...

Therapist: It's like there's something missing. It still doesn't make sense. What else do you think is there?

Client: I am sad.

Therapist: Ah...I'm so glad you said that! Yes, now it clicks. Sad about losing Rod, losing your team. Of course. Sorry I didn't get that before.

Client: Yeah, I think the sadness is a big part of it. I've not wanted to admit that.

Or consider this example, with the same client:

Client: I just feel lost. I don't want to move forward; I drag every day. I love the project but...

Therapist: What else are you feeling?

Client: Um...I am sad.

Therapist: Ah... I'm so glad you said that! Thank you for expressing your emotions.

Client: Um. okay.

In which of these two examples do you think the client is more likely reinforced for expressing her emotions to the therapist? In other words, in which example is the client more likely to continue to share how she feels?

In the first example the therapist more closely tracks the meaning of what the client is saying. Her evoking ("What else do you think is there?") comes with some explanation of why she is asking. She also explains her own reaction to the client's disclosure in relation to the disclosure's context: the therapist makes an effort to make sense of the client's experience of burnout. The interaction feels natural, empathic, and coherent. In particular, the therapist communicates her understanding of what the client is saying. She communicates that the feeling makes sense, that she accepts it.

In contrast, in the second example the therapist seems more disconnected. The evoking ("What else are you feeling?") still possibly makes sense, but the attempt at rule 3 ("Thank you for expressing your emotions.") seems arbitrary and inexplicable—even socially awkward—in the context. In turn, the client expresses confusion.

It seems more likely, then, that the client will continue to open up in the first example. However, all of this interpretation comprises only guesses about what is likely to be reinforcing, and we can only really know if the therapist's response is reinforcing by observing the client's behavior over time. But these intuitions we're sharing, about which interaction seems more natural, empathic, and coherent—and more likely to be reinforcing—are key proxies or indicators that we use to track and moderate our efforts to reinforce CRB2.

Specifically, we propose the following guidelines when it comes to evaluating your reinforcing behavior:

You can't tell whether a response is reinforcing based only on its form.

Seeing more of the context allows for a fuller interpretation of the function of a behavior, but your conclusion is still only a guess.

Interactions that involve understanding and acceptance are more likely to be reinforcing, especially for vulnerable disclosure.

You might recognize the last point from chapter 4, on the awareness, courage, and love framework. We'll return to this point later in the chapter. For now, we'll explore in more detail how to approach the task of responding in reinforcing ways based on sensitivity to context and attuning to the client.

BALANCING AUTHENTICITY AND STRATEGY

FAP requires you to be deliberate about noticing CRB2 and responding in reinforcing ways. It also requires you to be natural and attuned in the way you do that.

You may notice that there's potentially tension between responding naturally (authentically) versus responding deliberately (strategically). Specifically, if you are deliberate, you have to choose your response. If you are natural, your response should be spontaneous. What if your natural response is not likely to reinforce the client's CRB2?

For example, consider a client whose CRB2 is being more assertive:

Client: Can we schedule an extra session this week?

Therapist: (Thinking about how he is already overbooked, feeling his stress level rising...)

If the therapist follows the FAP rules in a mechanical way, he might reply, "Yes, of course. I'm glad you're asking for what you need." If he is understandably human and unable to mask his hesitation to committing to another session, that response might come across as strained or inauthentic. The client, in turn, may or may not pick up on that incongruence, and this may have an effect on how reinforcing the interaction is. At an extreme, the client could walk away thinking, *So, being assertive is about "guilting" people into doing things they don't really want to do?* However, it would seem countertherapeutic if the therapist was completely authentic to his own reaction: "I can't do an extra session this week. I'm overbooked."

Thankfully, as you well know, the conversation doesn't stop with one interaction. There are many ways to respond to this situation, many of which stand a good chance of reinforcing the client's assertiveness—even if the therapist doesn't grant an extra session. Balancing competing interests in compassionate, empathic ways is core to human social skills in general. In this situation the therapist must balance attention to the client's needs, the significance of her request in the context of what she is working on in therapy, and his own needs. An emotionally congruent response balances these considerations. For example, if the therapist really can't fathom scheduling another session, he could say something like this:

> Oh, man…I can't do an extra session this week. I'm overbooked. I hate to say that to you because I know what you must feel like asking this of me. If it were any other week, I would say yes. I'm just really, genuinely pushed to my edge this week. Can we talk about another way of getting you the support you need? Or maybe we can schedule something for earlier next week?

In this statement, the therapist recognizes the intent and vulnerability and validity of the request, and in response he reciprocates that vulnerability with his own statement of needs. It's easy to imagine that the client hearing this statement would remain willing to make requests of the therapist. Now imagine that the client really is in crisis and the therapist is slightly more willing to schedule:

> I'm hesitating just because I'm really booked. But, you know what, it's important that we work on this now while the iron is hot. I'm glad you're asking for this. Let's figure out a time for Thursday afternoon.

Here the therapist is emotionally congruent about his hesitation. But he also then moves to address the meaning of the request of the client.

As we claimed early in the book, way back in chapter 1, when you genuinely understand and care for the client's progress and growth, your own reactions will tend naturally to align to serve the client's well-being. Balancing our various reactions and responses is a form of interpersonal psychological flexibility in which multiple factors and streams of experience are observed and accepted, but the most important considerations guide action.

In fact, this formulation allows us to venture a working definition of "authenticity": responding in a way that is congruent to and communicative about all the different pertinent aspects of a context, including their relative importance.

Variable Responsiveness

Let's talk next about another way that authenticity and strategy (for example, the strategy of reinforcing CRB2) potentially conflict with each other. The conflict is that the ideally reinforcing response may not match your natural, spontaneous response. The ideally reinforcing response is defined by this behavioral principle: consequences that produce reinforcement are contingent on the behavior they reinforce. In other words, the reinforcing consequence only (or nearly only) occurs in response to the behavior, and it marks a deviation from the situation before that behavior occurred. But your natural response may not be naturally contingent in that way.

This example may make the principle—and the conflict—more concrete. Think about a pigeon in an operant learning chamber. When the button is pecked three times in a row quickly, the pigeon gets a delicious piece of food. However, if the pigeon receives lots of food regardless of whether he pecks the button or not, there is no incentive to peck the button. As you can see, the food only results in a greater frequency of button pecking if the food *only* arrives when the button is pressed. This example illustrates how consequence (food) has to be contingent upon the behavior (pecking) in order for reinforcement (increase in rate of pecking) to occur. "Contingent" means "depends on."

In therapy, understanding, acceptance, and responsiveness are the main offerings you have that are reinforcing. Considering the pigeon example above, does this mean you should withhold these things until a CRB2 occurs in session? Thankfully, adult social interaction is more complex and less black-and-white than the simplified situation of the pigeon. The contingencies are more flexible; there are multiples streams of behavior and contingencies. Still, in the therapy relationship, it can be helpful to vary your response to CRB2, marking it as distinct in some way. In other words, if you do rule 3 in much the same way—with the same voice tone, same affect, same posture, and so forth—as you do everything else in therapy, you risk diminishing the reinforcing value of your response.

Thankfully, variability is a natural, authentic part of responsiveness in a close relationship. When you understand and care about another person, you naturally respond differently, with variability, to moments that you recognize as significant. In those moments, simply expressing your reaction in an attuned, empathic way will often supply enough variability to reinforce behavior. Your emotional response, after all, is naturally contingent on the behavior to which you're reacting.

At the same time, part of being naturally responsive involves modifying, extending, or suppressing natural responses in subtle or not so subtle ways so that our response functions in the most effective way in the moment. A very obvious example is how adults modify their expression of emotions when talking to children. We use a simpler emotional vocabulary and may exaggerate certain facial expressions. This is a prosocial, empathic act (at least some of the time).

We might also do this with other adults when we know they are emotional or otherwise in a frame of mind such that a more reserved or ecstatic response won't reach them. When a friend is fearfully on the verge of taking a big career risk (and you believe the risk is the right step, and the fear is irrationally high), you probably won't say, "Well, you'll probably be okay. Go for it." That response is rational but not emotionally attuned to your friend's needs. If you take the time to think about what your friend is going through and needs from you, you may realize that your response needs to be crystal clear and more intense in order to cut through the emotional noise. You may be more likely to say something like "You've worked hard for this opportunity. All the signs you can see say this is the right moment. And I believe in you. Take the leap."

In other words, even if you don't naturally feel that intensity, by tuning into what the other person needs it becomes natural to express it. We naturally vary our responses based on what other people need from us. This is an essential part of responsiveness. We aim to provide what other people need, not just what would be congruent and authentic for us if we weren't in touch with their needs. In fact, being in touch with the needs of others directly shapes our own emotional responses.

In FAP, variable responsiveness—based on empathy concerning the needs and experience of others—supplemented by attention to behavioral principles, is a big part of what guides our adherence to rule 3: reinforce CRB2.

Recognizing Assumptions

We've found it useful, when generating the needed empathy for clients with vulnerable CRB2, to ask ourselves this question:

What assumptions do I bring to this interaction that the client does not because of his or her history?

For example, you might have these assumptions:

- Feedback is healthy and nonthreatening.

- Expressions of praise or affection are genuine, not loaded with ulterior motives.

- Expression of emotion is healthy and builds relationships.

- Asking for needs to be met is reasonable and important.

Clients with painful interpersonal histories, however, might intellectually grasp these assumptions without experiencing—especially in a moment of emotion and vulnerability—their truth in any meaningful way. Clients might even hold conflicting assumptions:

- Feedback is about domination.

- Expressions of praise or affection are manipulative.

- Expression of emotion is weak and risky.

- Asking for needs to be met is unreasonable and fruitless.

When you can recognize the assumptions that clients hold (emotionally if not rationally) or do not hold, you can be responsive in more effective ways. For example, you can make explicit your prosocial assumptions about the therapeutic interaction. Imagine that the client who is asking for an extra session has a long history of key people in her life ridiculing or dismissing her requests. Your response might take into consideration her past experience of making requests and make clear your wishes: "It's important to me that you make these requests when you have them. And given your history, your anxiety about doing so absolutely makes sense to me."

Being Less Responsive

There is an exception to the above guidelines about responsiveness and variability. Sometimes the most reinforcing way to respond to a client's vulnerability is to do very little at all (at least from your perspective).

Imagine a client who—as a result of her family who ridiculed and ignored her when she expressed emotions—has adopted a stance of emotional disconnection. Others experience her as distant, disconnected, even ominous at times. Gradually, over the course of many months, she comes to trust you enough to express sadness and disappointment when describing a recent and upsetting experience with her parents. And imagine that—even though she can't say this to you—she is as disconcerted by her own emotions as she is by the experience she had with her parents.

If you are too responsive in that moment, shining the light of attention too brightly or responding with your own emotions, you might risk disrupting the sense of security and trust that allowed her emotions to emerge in the first place. If instead you remember that this behavior of expressing emotions was routinely punished in the past, and you respond to the interaction in a more reserved manner, the mere absence of the feared consequence might be extremely significant. By simply maintaining your warm, open, empathic stance, the client experiences a discrepancy between historic consequences and what is happening in the moment. It is as though the client opens a door to a room she feared held a monster only to discover the room is empty. Many FAP therapists have had clients describe to them how responding minimally in certain therapeutic relationships helped them: "It was nothing that you did in particular that made me feel so welcome here. It was simply the way you listened. It was what you didn't do. That made all the difference for me."

One Last Comment

Another important aspect of ensuring variability in your responsiveness to CRB2 is making sure you are *not* overly responsive to CRB1. If you have a habit of responding with a grin or a nod to every client request, to the extent that there is relatively little natural range in your responsiveness (you're already at a high end of responsiveness with grinning and nodding), then you might consider finding a slightly more neutral baseline stance.

REINFORCING COURAGE WITH LOVE

You don't dispense M&Ms or offer a client cash for therapeutic progress. You offer the only thing you have to offer in the moment: your natural responsiveness as a human being. Outside the moment, outside the therapy hour, the world picks up where your responsiveness left off. The hope is that the new ways of being that are shaped within therapy take root and are nourished (reinforced) by natural consequences outside of therapy. For instance, you hope that the client who has become more skillfully assertive with you will become so with his wife, and that she will respond in reinforcing ways to his assertiveness (that is, his assertiveness leads to a good outcome). But, in the moment in therapy, your responsiveness as a human being is the one thing you have to offer.

Let's now return to the awareness, courage, and love (ACL) model to further flesh out what we propose are essential aspects of responsiveness and of being reinforcing in the therapeutic relationship. As we mentioned at the beginning of this book, responsiveness has a very significant influence over behavior. These elements of responsiveness are of general value in the therapeutic relationship, but they are especially relevant when the behavior you are responding to is courageous.

In the following sections, we zero in on and discuss therapist responses to three behaviors that can fit under the umbrella of "courage": choosing to experience vulnerability and emotion, offering self-disclosure, and asking for a need to be met. We hypothesize that the types of responses specified by the ACL model tend to naturally reinforce these courageous behaviors. The responses can be summed up in three sentences that, in turn, describe the ACL therapeutic stance:

- I see you.

- You are safe here.

- I will give you, to the best of my ability, what you want to receive.

Choosing to Experience Vulnerability and Emotion

We tend to be more willing to remain vulnerable and experience emotion when the person we're communicating with offers safety and acceptance in return. In this way, safety and acceptance can reinforce vulnerability as a CRB2. "Safety" and "acceptance" are vague terms, essentially metaphorical. A lack of safety does not literally indicate danger. Instead we are talking about a more general sense of social safety: that is, an absence of judgment and the availability of empathic concern.

Imagine you make an error at work. You report the error to your supervisor, and he responds this way: "What were you thinking? I can't trust you people to do anything, for Christ's sake. You're going to feel this one, my friend." Ouch. There's no physical threat, but the experience of vulnerability, or shame, or guilt, or anger is probably intense. You're not likely to continue making vulnerable disclosures to this supervisor.

In contrast, imagine this response: "Oh, man. I'm glad you came to me. Let's talk about what happened. First of all, are you okay?" Notice that there's an appropriate expression of concern and orientation toward learning, and the tone is entirely different. You are much more likely to report future errors to this supervisor. (This example also highlights how a reinforcing response is not necessarily a happy or positive-affect response.)

Safety and acceptance are communicated through voice tone, body posture, eye contact, and facial expressions as much as through words. If you don't believe this is true, try sitting bolt upright and expressionless the next time a client is saying something vulnerable.

For therapists then, when client vulnerability is involved in CRB2, it's important for us to communicate safety and acceptance. This can be easy to forget. Sometimes therapists get caught up in being clever or wanting to do something sophisticated or active or "helpful." When you find yourself doing any of these things, slow down and make safety and acceptance crystal clear, both nonverbally and verbally. Communicate acceptance nonverbally through a steady gaze; an open, relaxed posture; and effort to understand the client's experience and needs. Judgments and evaluations should be absent. Verbally, you can use the words "safety" and "acceptance" explicitly if they fit the moment; for example, "I want you to know that when you do this, you are totally, 100 percent safe with and accepted by me." Or you might reflect a positive perspective at a moment when the client fears judgment and feels most vulnerable: "What I see in this—and it actually might be counterintuitive for you—is your strength and commitment to being honest. Everything you're feeling makes sense to me, and I want you to know I see you really fighting to live your values."

Let's consider a client who ends a disclosure with a clear statement of vulnerability:

You know, I haven't noticed it before, but your table lamp is exactly like a lamp my grandmother used to have. I remember it because we would always sit at that table doing puzzles together. I don't even know why I'm sharing this with you; I am just sharing it. I feel weird about sharing it. It makes me nervous somehow.

Given Madelaine's difficulty with self-disclosure, and the vulnerability she feels when doing so (such that we could say her avoidance of self-disclosure likely functions, in part, to avoid vulnerability), the therapist's goal is twofold: to recognize that sharing information like this is an instance of choosing to experience vulnerability and emotion, as well as an instance of offering self-disclosure; and to respond with safety and acceptance as well as with understanding and empathy.

Here are several examples of how Madeleine's therapist might respond in that moment:

Therapist: Madelaine, let me pause here for a second. I want you to know, first, that you're doing the thing we've been talking about, and I love the words you used for it: "just sharing." This is exactly what we've been talking about. So I want you to know that when you share like this, you're totally safe with and accepted by me. I loved hearing this brief story, and I want more. I can imagine you sitting with your grandma, doing a puzzle, with the light of this lamp over you. It's really nice.

Therapist: Madelaine, as I listen to you just share this story, I feel a warmth, love even, spreading across my face. Can you see it on my face? Can you see in my eyes how much I enjoy your story and how safe you are with me to talk about this?

Therapist: That's supercool. I think it would make a great puzzle lamp. I also like hearing about your grandmother. What was it like being with her?

As always, the "best" response is authentic and strategic in the context.

Offering Self-Disclosure

Self-disclosure is perhaps the bedrock of social communication. We talk about ourselves, and we want people to listen. We want to be heard, seen, and understood.

Self-disclosure is, of course, also a bedrock of psychotherapy. It's what clients do for much of the time in every single session. And if they have trouble with self-disclosure, therapy tends to focus there first. In turn, providing understanding, empathy, and validation is the bedrock for how therapists respond to client self-disclosure. That is—in the terms of the awareness, courage, and love model—we suggest that understanding, empathy, and validation function to reinforce self-disclosure. This natural relation between self-disclosure and understanding is deeply interwoven into all well-functioning social interactions and therapy sessions. To notice how fundamental it is, imagine a conversation in which you felt significantly misunderstood. Where did it lead?

Despite the fact that self-disclosure is fundamental to social relations and therapy, we often encounter clients who have difficulty with it. For example, some clients struggle to express feelings or events or attitudes in ways that are clear to others. These struggles might arise for a variety of reasons (for instance, a sense of anxious vulnerability). In FAP terms, we can treat difficulties with self-disclosure as CRB1. In turn, with CRB2 related to self-disclosure, it's important to communicate understanding and empathy clearly as part of our natural responsiveness.

Consider Madelaine again—her spontaneous statement that "You know, I haven't noticed it before, but your table lamp is exactly like a lamp my grandmother used to have. I remember it because we would always sit at that table doing puzzles together. I don't even know why I'm sharing this with you; I am just sharing it."

The therapist recognized this as CRB2 related to self-disclosure, specifically because it was spontaneous and Madelaine admitted that she didn't know why she was sharing it. This freedom of "just sharing" was important for Madelaine because previously she'd been quite constricted about what she shared. In response, the therapist communicated understanding in a simple way: "It's sweet for me to hear you say that. I used to play puzzles with my grandmother too, and it always felt peaceful. Did it feel like that for you too?" These words extend empathy toward the feelings that Madelaine may have about her memories.

If this point seems obvious, it's because empathy is a fundamental and well-practiced skill for therapists. For contrast, imagine a response that completely misses the point of Madelaine's disclosure: "Maybe you find it more interesting to talk about furniture than the stuff we've been working on here?"

Asking for a Need to Be Met

The third subcategory of courage is asking for a need to be met. This category is interesting from a FAP perspective because, at a simple level, the most natural reinforcing response when someone asks for something is generally to give them what they ask for. But obviously this isn't always possible. So how does one respond?

Consider Yolanda, a client who has had great difficulty asking others for support and asking for her needs to be met in any way at all. In the middle of therapy, she asks her therapist, "When therapy ends, could we get together for a cup of coffee every now and then?" Although this type of request is generally problematic, Yolanda's therapist recognizes that, for Yolanda, it's CRB2. It's an ethical issue for the therapist, of course, but that doesn't mean it's CRB1 for the client to ask. (Though perhaps there's an element of CRB1 in not being attuned to the awkwardness of asking your therapist out to coffee.) This tension creates a dilemma, as the therapist recognizes the impossibility of giving Yolanda what she has asked for. How would you respond? Here's a sample response:

> It means a lot to me that you're asking that, because I know what it means to you. You know, when therapy ends, my caring for you won't end. I will be eager to get updates from you and check in, and if that could take the form of meeting for coffee, that would be great. There are some complications about meeting a former client for coffee, which I'd like to share with you a little later, but the important thing right now is for me to let you know that the caring I have for you won't end just because therapy ends.

Perhaps this isn't a perfect response, but it works well enough in the moment and fits this therapist's boundaries. The key thing we want to point out is that the therapist delays having a conversation about ethics and post-therapy friendships in the moment. That's an important conversation to have with Yolanda, but the therapist recognizes that, in the moment, the conversation could function to punish the CRB2 of a vulnerable request. Further, there is no harm or ethical dilemma associated with waiting to have that discussion.

Most of the time, meeting a client's needs is less complicated. Clients often make requests about the process of therapy, therapy logistics, and so on, and CRB may occur in the context of those requests (including avoidance of making them). Consider Zoreh, a client who has great difficulty with self-disclosure and making requests. Arriving for her session one day, she says, "I'm feeling really wiped out today. Can we have a less intense session?" For any given client, this may or may not be CRB2, but because of Zoreh's difficulty with self-disclosure, for her it's CRB2 to say, "I'm feeling really wiped out." And because of her difficulty with making requests, it's a CRB2 for her to ask, "Can we have a less intense session?" As always, a potentially reinforcing response can take a variety of forms:

Yes, we can have a less intense session. I want you to know that when you ask for what you need, I really respect your needs, whatever they may be, and promise to do the best I can to meet them. My heart is with your heart in this.

Heck yes! Of course.

Again, the "best" response is authentic and strategic in context. Of course, understanding and acceptance are fundamental pieces of what we give clients in therapy in response to the unspoken requests of self-disclosure and vulnerability.

NOTICE YOUR EFFECT

Imagine yourself dribbling the ball in a soccer game. You don't just kick or nudge the ball. You watch the ball and constantly adjust your movement to keep the ball moving, to respond to opponents and teammates, and, in turn, to judge at a high level whether your movements and the movement of the ball are heading toward the larger goal. There is no dribbling possible without this constant monitoring.

Similarly, as therapists, we don't just respond to what we perceive as CRB. We watch how the behavior shifts and moves in response to our responding. You only know, for instance, whether your attempts at rule 3 are working by observing what happens to the behavior you seek to reinforce. In turn, you only know if increases in those CRB2s move the client toward his clinical goals by observing that process.

This multilayered awareness of how processes are moving—beyond the basic interpersonal attunement we ask you to bring to the therapy relationship—is fundamental to FAP. There is a deep interdependence, in particular, between rule 3 (reinforce CRB2) and rule 4 (notice your effect) because you only know if you are reinforcing CRB2 by noticing your effect.

This noticing takes two primary forms:

1. Checking in verbally, in the moment and over time

2. Observing the client's behavior

Verbal Check-Ins

One way to check in on your effect is to ask, "What was that like?"

For example, you might ask about the client's experience in a particular interaction (setting a therapy agenda, debriefing the week, processing a disagreement between the two of you) in a single session. Of course, you can't expect the client to reply in FAP terms, "Well, you very effectively reinforced my CRB2 just then." But the client's response will give you some indication of whether the interaction was on the right track.

You can also check in on broader sections of therapy. The questions of the session bridging form, introduced in chapter 7, help you check in on a session-by-session basis. You can also check in about a particular phase of therapy:

We've been working really hard on you making assertive requests from me these last weeks. How is that going from your perspective? Is this productive?

Or you can check in about therapy as a whole:

Let's step back and look at how our work's going. How are we on track in your view? Are there any things that we're not attending to enough?

Observing the Client's Behavior

Observing the client's behavior is, of course, a broader category of noticing your effect; checking in verbally with a client also involves *observing* their behavior in response to you. If the overarching goals of therapy are increasing CRB2 and the corresponding progress with presenting problems, there are a variety of signs that indicate these things are happening:

- You might notice subtle changes in the client's way of engaging with you or the tone of the sessions. For example, sessions might feel less conflictual and more rewarding.

- You might notice the complete absence of old struggles. For example, homework might be completed reliably (whereas in the past it was rarely completed). The client might present and reiterate clear agendas for each session (whereas in the past there was great murkiness).

- You might also notice critical turning-point moments, in which the way a client responds to a given situation strikes you as markedly and dramatically different from how the client would have responded in the past. For example, Gareth will never forget the client who complained and insisted for weeks that he should provide better tools to immediately relieve the client's suffering. One evening, that same client—reaching out for support from a moment of excruciating pain—took a breath and sighed. "You know, what I've realized is that your field is just not very advanced. You don't actually have tools to help me. I get that. And I appreciate you for being here to listen to me and do what you can." In that moment, the struggle took a drastic turn toward acceptance that persisted and grew profoundly over the months that followed.

SUMMARY

- The aim of responding to CRB2 is to reinforce—that is, increase the likelihood that the behavior is repeated in the future.

- Whether or not your response is reinforcing cannot be determined by the form or appearance of the response. You can only know if your response is reinforcing by watching how the client's behavior changes over time.

- That said, responses that are empathic, accepting, and responsive are more likely to be reinforcing.

- Ensure that your responses to client CRB are authentic, built on genuine empathy, and attuned to your client's needs and goals and values.

CHAPTER 10

Balance Structure and Flow— The Logical Interaction

Behavior is a difficult subject matter, not because it is inaccessible, but because it is extremely complex. Since it is a process, rather than a thing, it cannot easily be held still for observation. It is changing, fluid, and evanescent, and for this reason it makes great technical demands upon the ingenuity and energy of the scientist.

—B. F. Skinner

Going into each therapy session, the therapist was not focused on Nick's CRB1 and CRB2. Nor was he thinking about what intervention he was going to practice that day. His focus was much more human: What is Nick experiencing now? What does he need from me right now? Where are we going together? What structure or framework can I provide to get us there? Is there anything important that we're not talking about? In other words, the therapist attuned to Nick and the work of therapy, not the arbitrary features of a therapy framework. There were many times when the best focus was uncertain and Nick's responses surprised the therapist, but the therapist's flexibility in how he responded and directed Nick kept them moving forward.

At the same time, the therapist and Nick gradually built a very clear—and individualized—framework to understand what Nick was working on. The framework encompassed what Nick was striving to be in life as well as what he was working on in evocative moments in therapy, such as when he disagreed with the therapist, when he needed something different, and when the therapist challenged him in a new way. Through their process they created structure.

Both of these elements—structure and flexibility—helped their therapy progress. The glue binding these elements was the relationship, the flow of behavior—moment-by-moment attunement, responsiveness, and vulnerability—between Nick and the therapist.

In this chapter, we consider structure and flexibility, the two sides of the coin that make up the FAP process. On the one hand, there is the orderliness of principles. If you step back and survey everything we've covered so far in this part of the book, you might see that three key elements, or processes, form the structure of FAP, all of them shaping client behavior and driving the client toward clinical goals:

- Creating a connected therapeutic relationship characterized by mutual vulnerability and responsiveness (or awareness, courage, and love)

- Engaging in functional analysis as a primary avenue for case formulation

- Shaping clinically relevant behavior in session via the five rules of FAP

On the other hand, the messiness of process is a whole other thing. Anyone who has seen a neatly ordered treatment protocol fall apart upon contact with a client can attest to this. Process requires responsiveness, improvisation, and iteration.

The practice of FAP is balancing these two sides of the coin. The balance—being in a genuine, vulnerable, interpersonal process while also engaging in functional analysis and keeping some level of awareness of the rules of FAP—can be a little overwhelming at first. It may feel like trying to pat your head and rub your belly...while also jumping rope. Any new therapy feels this way.

A useful metaphor for staying grounded in the therapeutic interaction while keeping an eye on functional analysis and the five rules of FAP is based on the notion of the *participant observer* in anthropology. We can use a metaphor to define this concept. If the in-the-moment therapy process is a roller coaster (and sometimes it is), being a participant would be like riding on the roller coaster completely immersed in your experience. You feel the clunk of the cars, the weight of the collar, the anticipation as the cart crests the climb, and the rush of the wind and the dive of your insides as you plunge. You are in deep contact with the experience of the ride, but possibly at the cost of a broader or more flexible perception of the action.

In contrast, being an observer would be like standing on the ground, clipboard in hand, taking careful notes about what you can see but being fairly removed from the action. You might miss important details from this distance. The stance of the participant observer bridges these two extremes: you're on the roller coaster while also maintaining a mindful awareness of the experience, the surroundings, and how this moment fits into a broader context.

FAP asks you to be a participant observer in the therapy process. The five FAP rules are a tool, simple enough to remember at high speed, to help you along the way. Once you're familiar with them, you can begin to let them go and instead flow in the moment, returning to them for guidance as needed. In other words, the rules shouldn't interfere with your interaction; they should help nudge it in productive directions.

In this chapter we'll talk about putting the whole process of FAP together from the perspectives of participant and observer, balancing flexibility and structure. We start with a tool for thinking about the flow of the five rules in an organized way: the logical FAP framework (Weeks, Kanter, Bonow, Landes, & Busch, 2012).

THE LOGICAL INTERACTION

We introduced the five rules of FAP in chapter 5, and we've covered aspects of the first four in the second part of the book so far. We'll now bring all these rules together—along with rule 5 (support generalization), which we'll discuss again in chapter 12—to describe what has been called the *logical FAP interaction*, which is a structure for thinking about FAP process. In the discussions to come, we'll refer to this as the *logical interaction*.

In logical FAP interactions, all five rules play out, roughly in sequence, in a single session, putting the entire FAP model into play. Experienced FAP therapists who know and apply the rules well often create FAP interactions that roughly follow this sequence because there's a logical, natural flow to doing so. This isn't coincidental; the rules were written with this logic in mind.

Typically, a logical FAP interaction starts at the beginning of the session with client and therapist discussing out-of-session material—for example, what happened in the client's life over the past week. Imagine a client, working in sales, who is struggling to visit his customers each day (the examples that follow truncate the process):

Client: It was difficult to put myself out there this week. I spent so much time just sitting in the car.

As out-of-session targets are discussed, the therapist looks for and illuminates parallels between these targets and in-session processes (rule 1). Consider this example:

Therapist: I notice you seem reticent to talk even sitting here. You're looking off out the window.

The parallels, which can be established more or less explicitly, aid in identifying CRBs that may be occurring in the moment. The therapist can also evoke CRBs more directly if the parallels aren't sufficiently clear (rule 2):

Therapist: What did you feel coming here today? How did you feel about picking up this conversation with me?

In turn, when CRBs are actively in the room, occurring in the moment between client and therapist, the dance of FAP really gets going. Often, clients respond to rule 2 (evoke CRB) with CRB1, so the therapist must evoke again, fine-tuning the approach to discover or elicit CRB2:

Client: Not much. Same stuff, different day. [CRB1.]

Therapist: I wonder though. I sense something else there.

Client: I just feel heavier than normal. I'm not sure what happened. [CRB2.]

Once the client has exhibited CRB2, the therapist now aims to provide reinforcement (rule 3), making the session a positive, memorable learning experience for the client—one that not only shapes the client's CRB2 but also increases intimacy and strengthens the bond within the therapeutic relationship. At this point, hopefully a positive cycle develops in which the therapeutic response produces more CRB2, which occasions more reinforcement, and so on. The therapist may then engage in rule 4, inquiring about the client's experience in the session and noticing how the client responds across the session:

Therapist: What was it like having me challenge you to open up today?

Client: It was good. I feel pretty different now. [This matches the therapist's perception that the client is less withdrawn.]

Toward the end of the session, the focus shifts toward how the CRB2 that was shaped in session can be generalized out of session (rule 5):

Therapist: What will you take forward from this session? What did we do today that you could remember to do moving forward this week?

FAP IN ACTION

To give you a better sense of the possibilities for a realistic flow across a logical interaction, below we present a more extended example. The client, Katie, and her therapist are discussing a party at which Katie was talking with a woman named Angela whom she was attracted to. Katie said she'd wanted to tell Angela about her feelings, but she felt panicky and confused and experienced what she called a "cloud or rush" feeling. This feeling made her feel very vulnerable, and her urge was to try to avoid it. As a result, she didn't tell Angela that she was attracted to her. Based on these out-of-session experiences, the primary CRB targeted for the session was disclosing vulnerability and emotion to another. The CRB1 was avoiding this disclosure, and the CRB2 was any form of approaching this disclosure, even with anxiety and discomfort in the moment.

As a special challenge to you, we removed our annotations of the rules from the following transcript. We invite you to make your own annotations. In particular, look for examples of the five rules, of CRB1, and of CRB2. To check your answers, you can download a fully annotated transcript at http://www.newharbinger.com/33513.

Therapist: When did the panic and confusion start?

Client: The night before, when Angela said she had a crush on me.

Therapist: So ever since then you just felt confusion about her?

Client: Yeah.

Therapist: Okay. So right now, as you think about it, are you as confused and unaccepting?

Client: Yeah. (*Laughs.*)

Therapist: Okay.

Client: I feel a lot of pressure in those kinds of situations to perform very smoothly and not let my confusion or anything like that really show.

Therapist: What would happen if you did?

Client: I don't know. My gut feeling is that if I show that kind of a weakness, people won't like me. At the time, I was just thinking, "I've just got to get through this," and kind of realizing that I had a couple of goals. I guess I was just trying to get through as fast as I could but still trying to hit those goals.

Therapist: So, what were the goals, exactly?

Client: I guess to not fuck up. (Laughs.) To not show that I was so confused or anything like that.

Therapist: So would it help if during that kind of situation you were able to keep in mind, "This is what I'm scared of: if I show my confusion she'll reject me." I realize that at the time it's not that clear, and that only as you're talking about it now are you getting a little clarity on what exactly happened. Still, would it be helpful to you to have that in front of you at the time?

Client: I think I'd probably start bawling.

Therapist: If you were more aware of your confusion?

Client: Yeah, if I was that aware of it. It's so intense. The only way I've dealt with it is by not dealing with it, not even seeing it.

Therapist: And what are you basing that on, that you'd start bawling?

Client: Um, because I feel like doing it now.

Therapist: So, as you're becoming aware of it now, some of the feelings are coming out right now?

Client: Yeah, I guess. It's hard to say, because I feel so far away... Do you know what I mean? Like, it seems really far away.

Therapist: Okay, let me ask you a different question. So are you more present now? You're crying a little bit...

Client: Yeah, I guess.

Therapist: Okay, you're more present now. I mean, it's definitely on a continuum, right?

Client: Right. (Starts to cry a little bit.)

Therapist: You're more present.

Client: Right.

Therapist: So are some of your worries coming up right now? I mean are you worried about how I'm seeing you?

Client: I'm definitely struggling with the showing-emotion thing.

Therapist: So what are you worried about right now?

Client: Right now? *(Sighs.)* I think it's not wanting to be one down—like somehow there's this tallying going on that gives people power.

Therapist: So you feel vulnerable?

Client: No, I feel kind of like a goalie. *(Laughs.)* I feel like I'm not just vulnerable, but...

Therapist: Under attack?

Client: Yeah. I feel like there's this wall and it's crumbling down, and I've got to keep people from getting in because it's dangerous.

Therapist: And you're feeling that a little bit right now with me.

Client: Yeah. And even talking about it...the calmer I can be talking about it, the more okay it is. The more analytical I can be talking about it, the more okay it is.

Therapist: So is there any way right now, with me, you could not do that?

Client: What do you mean?

Therapist: Is there any way you could maybe ask me something—rather than avoiding, just sort of checking with me about it? I mean, if your fear is that by showing your emotions right now you're vulnerable and a little under attack, is there any way you could stay with the feelings and talk to me about them?

Client: *(Laughs.)* I was thinking I could ask you about what you're thinking about me, but then I'd have to believe what you say.

Therapist: Right. And you might or you might not.

Client: Honestly, the safest thing feels like throwing up as many walls as I possibly can.

Therapist: Well, there are a couple of options here. One is that your fears are true. That you started crying just now, that you're showing a little more of yourself, and that now you're potentially in more danger with me because of it. That somehow I'm going to reject you, or not understand, or do something that's going to hurt you because of this. So if that were true, it would be best to get away from this as fast as possible. That's one possibility. But the other option is that this may not be true. And maybe you could find out by staying with this. The big point is this: Is there anything you can do right now to check in with me? To check out your fear? To not just throw up walls but actually say, "Well, maybe my fear's not real. Maybe he is safe and won't hurt me."

Client: Well, the only thing that comes immediately to mind is asking what it means to you that...that...

Therapist: That you're crying? That you're...

Client: Not just that I'm crying, but that I'm sitting over here feeling so much.

Therapist: Okay. I understand the question.

Client: But I really don't want to ask that.

Therapist: Why not?

Client: Because I don't want to care. It shouldn't matter.

Therapist: Okay. Why shouldn't it matter?

Client: Because I should be above caring what other people think.

Therapist: Why should that be the case?

Client: Um, because that's the smart way to be? And you're stupid if you don't?

Therapist: Why?

Client: I don't know why. (Laughs.) It just is.

Therapist: Caring allows you to...

Client: There's no point in it. Other people can't do anything for you. They're unreliable and dangerous, so you shouldn't care.

Therapist: Okay, well, you asked me what it means to me, what you were doing a few minutes ago, and then kind of took it back a little bit, but I'm going to just ignore that part of it.

Client: (Laughs.) Why?!

Therapist: The truth is, I can't help you with everything. I mean, we have a limited relationship in some ways, but I still want to tell you how I feel in response to just what you're going through. It pulls at my empathy and it warms me up to you. I feel a sense of caring for you when I see you like this, and I think—and this is the truth—I really like this person and I hope I can help her. I see that you're struggling, and it feels a little sad for me, just because you're sad and I like you, so it makes me a little sad. That's just my first pass at sharing my reactions.

Client: That's very, very, very hard to hear.

Therapist: Me saying this is hard for you to hear? What's hard about it?

Client: Before I get to that, when you were saying it, all I could think was, "You don't think I'm crazy?"

Therapist: (Pauses and makes prolonged, warm, consistent eye contact.) Do I think you're crazy? No. Why would I think you're crazy?

Client: (Cries in earnest.) Because I have all this shit going on!

Therapist: And that makes you crazy because…?

Client: (Continues to cry.) Because I can't handle it. Or because I have it—because I have all of this shit going on. So you don't think I'm crazy?

Therapist: (Pauses and makes prolonged, warm, consistent eye contact again.) No.

Client: (Still crying.) What are you thinking?

Therapist: Are you worried that I'm thinking something particular, are you just curious, or…

Client: Yeah. I guess.

Therapist: Well, I must admit that part of what I was thinking is that I wish this session had more time. And…um…I'm also thinking that it's good that you're struggling with this the way you are. I'm thinking this is good for you.

Client: Is it? How so?

Therapist: Let me ask you a question that might help you respond: How do you feel right now?

Client: Relieved. Exhausted. (Therapist nods.) Definitely nervous, but intense. I came through that one okay, but am I going to be able to keep doing this okay?

Therapist: Okay. But what if you stick with what just happened? You started out feeling emotional, showing that a little bit, and having some fears about it, but you stayed with it with me, and once you heard what I was really thinking, it seemed like you believed me, based on the reaction you had. It kind of opened up a lot for you, and you really expressed yourself. Now you feel relieved and a little safer, but also still have some nervousness. So you feel safer by not avoiding and by checking out what I am thinking. I think that's the lesson for you.

Client: For me, feeling safer seems more connected to your reaction and less about not avoiding—instead checking out what you are thinking. Do you know what I mean?

Therapist: Well, if I had reacted differently you wouldn't feel safer. And if you hadn't asked, you might not have known.

Client: Right.

Therapist: Right. And so the question is, how are people out in the world going to react? Right? You know how your mom and dad will react. They're the ones who instilled this in you in the first place. *(Client nods.)* But the question is, what do you do with the rest of the world, with people like Angela? I mean that's why I brought this up—to help you with Angela. So, what can you do with those feelings of confusion and how unsafe it feels to show some of this to somebody like Angela? Hopefully that's where this will lead you. And we're running out of time, so I think I have to just leave it as a question for you.

As you might guess from this transcript, as you become more familiar with using the five rules and the logical interaction, you will develop an intuitive sense of how to pace a session based on where you are in the sequence. In turn, you will exhibit a good deal of flexibility while retaining structure in each session.

Using a semistructured interaction is one useful method for practicing logical interactions—and, in connection, all of the FAP skills. You can practice this interaction with other therapists learning FAP, or with clients (use your clinical judgment about how and when to do so). Below is a sample flow of questions you might use. Don't feel constrained to stick to this exact wording—you will need to flex and bend to make the interaction flow.

What's something important or distressing that is coming up in your life right now?

What do you need to do—what is your 2—in that context?

How could you practice a version of that 2 with me, right here and right now?

[Continue to evoke until CRB2 occurs. Then offer a genuine rule 3 response.]

What was it like to have this interaction with me?

What will you take from this interaction?

Here's an example of a semistructured interaction:

Therapist: What's something important or distressing that is coming up in your life right now?

Client: Okay, let me see… I think what's most important is something I've been struggling to deal with. My aunt has cancer. I just learned about it a couple of weeks ago. She lives on the East Coast. And I've been avoiding reaching out to her. We were really close when I was little, but I've not talked to her much since moving out here.

Therapist: What is most important for you to do with her?

Client: I just need to reach out to her and tell her that I'm sorry, that I'm here. That I love her.

Therapist: I see how much she means to you. I hear that what you most want to do for her is reach out and speak honestly from your heart about what she means to you. Do I have that right?

Client: Yes.

Therapist: Would you be willing to talk to me, from your heart, right now, just as you want to talk to her?

Client: Sure...but I don't know what to say.

Therapist: Tell me what our interaction right now means to you.

Client: It means a lot. To be listened to. I sense your caring—that you're listening to me and understanding what's most important to me.

Therapist: You are important to me. I want to hear what's important to you. And for your aunt to hear that from you too.

Client: Yeah. That's what I want.

Therapist: What was it like to have this interaction with me?

Client: It focused me on what mattered. I can feel now what I need to say to her. Before it's like there was a wall up.

Therapist: I'm glad you can feel what you need to say. What is most important for you to remember from this interaction?

Client: Just that I can say directly, honestly, what she means to me. Thank you.

THERAPIST MISTAKES

One crucial thing to remember about the loopiness of the therapy process is this: therapists make mistakes. It's inevitable. For example, you might assign a useless homework assignment, miss a fundamental aspect of the client's history, double-book an appointment, or trigger an unexpected panic attack by asking a client to practice mindfulness of breath.

In our view, because mistakes are inevitable, and because how you work through them can destroy or fuel therapy, making mistakes is a critical part of therapy—or any relationship for that matter.

No one is perfect. And because each of us is in our own skin, none of us can completely know the inner world of others, including clients. To some extent, then, relating to another is always an act of reaching out into uncertainty. As we reach out to connect, the ways we fail to make contact can be just as edifying and instructive as the ways we do make contact. And if we chose not to reach out because of the risk of failure, we wouldn't connect at all. Being committed to reaching out means trying and failing to connect at times.

In turn, building lasting relationships requires becoming resilient to failures, mistakes, and missteps. What's crucial is how we negotiate those mistakes. When we negotiate them well, we can actually strengthen a relationship, deepening the bond and building trust that the bond won't be broken by mistakes.

As much as we may wish to present a professional front of expertise, therapy is innately prone to missteps and failure. This is a matter of empirical fact. No one looking at the success rates of even the most robustly effective therapies can claim otherwise. If the issues for which people seek help in treatment were easily amenable to change, therapists wouldn't be needed.

Expertise, then, doesn't lie in perfection; it lies in the ability to relate to clients in ways that allow therapist and client to collaboratively create a path to change—a path that traverses hills and valleys of mistakes and uncertainties as well as victories and clarity. And when you stick with clients through the vicissitudes of the process of change, you also gift them with the profound experience of what it means to be in a resilient relationship. You do more than teach them about it; you share the experience with them.

So don't fear mistakes in therapy. They provide an opportunity to be human and to teach something profound. In FAP terms, they provide an opportunity to evoke all sorts of CRBs: how does the client relate to your shortcomings? How does she express dissatisfaction or disappointment? How does she ask for what she needs? How does she forgive, collaborate, or rebuild trust?

What to Do with Mistakes

Ideally, you'd notice therapeutic missteps in the moment and address them right away, perhaps saying something like "You know, what I just said made no sense. Let me try it again." An advantage to this kind of statement is that it also communicates that making mistakes (and acknowledging them) is acceptable.

Of course, no one has the presence of mind to catch all mistakes in the moment. You can address missteps after the fact, including in the next session: "I was thinking about what I said to you last week—the way I painted a picture of why you're seeking treatment now. As I thought about that and some of the things you've said, I think I've gotten you wrong in some ways. So I want to acknowledge and apologize for that. I think I see more clearly now why you're here, and here's what I think is important..." It's okay to ask for a do over, and always give clients permission for do overs. After all, "do over" is just another name for "learning and growth."

Therapist mistakes can play a role in getting therapy stuck. It's important to clearly acknowledge when this is the case in the type of evocative conversation we outlined for getting unstuck in chapter 8. For example, you might say, "I've played a role in how we've gotten stuck. I've backed off too easily when you pushed back or were uncertain. And I didn't clearly get what you needed in those moments. I'm sorry about that, and I want to do better."

Apologizing can be a hard thing to do well. In our opinion, a good apology includes two elements. The first is fully taking responsibility. You may rightly believe that you weren't entirely to blame for the problem, but a good apology will still focus on your responsibility. This allows the other person to focus on his responsibility, without the added pressure of blame. The second element is promising to do better. Of course, you may make the same mistake again—you are human, after all—but you can still commit to doing better.

Here's an example that incorporates both elements: "I want to say how sorry I am. I see now that I've been really pushing you and not seeing how hard you've been trying. I've been interpreting your frustration as just more of the problem, rather than taking responsibility for how I've been causing it by not fully understanding what you need. I want to do better. I can't guarantee that I'll never make this mistake again, but I can promise to you that I will really try." This kind of honest apology tends to not only repair a rupture in the moment, but it may also serve as a great model, helping clients learn to apologize more skillfully.

If mistakes and apologies are particularly fraught territory for you, as a therapist or in your personal life, take some time to reflect on the following questions. You might consider asking colleagues to do this exercise with you, sharing your answers with one another.

What did you learn about mistakes in your family as you were growing up? How were mistakes dealt with? How does your personal history with mistakes affect the way you deal with your mistakes as a therapist?

What therapeutic mistakes have you made? (Examples include empathetic failures, boundary violations, forgetting appointments, starting sessions late, or letting sessions run long.)

What do you feel in general when you make mistakes? How about when you make mistakes with clients?

What have clients been upset with you about or complained to you about? (Bear in mind that these things can reflect client vulnerabilities as well as mistakes on your part.)

What can you do or have you done to repair your missteps with clients?

What are your T1s and T2s in regard to your therapeutic mistakes?

The Bony Truths About Therapy

If you have trouble accepting these ins and outs of the therapy process, we find it's helpful to rehearse and reflect upon some of the bony truths about therapy. These truths don't fit the optimistic picture sometimes presented at professional meetings, but they are nevertheless the reality of our work. As you review this list, notice where your mind or heart rebels. How can you make a home in that place?

Clients are doing the best they know how and yet they are often struggling.

Clients are exactly as they should be, given their history.

Even the most stubborn, frustrating, or senseless behavior makes sense at a certain level for the individual engaging in it.

It's more important for therapists to be helpful than to be right.

You can't force clients to do what you think they should do.

The practice of therapy has many shortcomings and limitations, as do therapists.

Despite your shortcomings or limitations, it's your responsibility to be the best therapist you can be. Solving problems that stump you *is* the work of therapy.

You may make mistakes in therapy, and a client might reasonably feel hurt or frustrated by you.

Therapy has a substantial failure rate.

When you try to correct an issue in a certain way and it doesn't work, sometimes you need to stick with it.

The process of therapy is often painful and uncertain before it is successful.

The thing that's most difficult for a client is often exactly what the client most needs to work on.

It's your responsibility to teach what's most difficult, which often requires that you understand what's needed in a very clear and experiential way. You might need to face your own scary demons to accomplish this.

SUMMARY

- The FAP process balances structure and flexibility.

- The structure of the five FAP rules is encapsulated in the logical interaction, which flows from rule 1 to rule 5 in a single interaction.

- At other times, the therapy process demands improvisation, iteration, and following a nonlinear path through trial and error.

- Therapist mistakes can be a crucial part of the therapy process and the progress that is made within it. Take responsibility for your mistakes, and model for the client flexible habits of accountability, honesty, and commitment.

- The flexible, challenging process of therapy can be just as evocative for therapists as it is for clients. Observe your T1s and T2s.

CHAPTER II

Understanding in Motion—Case Conceptualization with FAP

It is the province of knowledge to speak, and it is the privilege of wisdom to listen.

—Oliver Wendell Holmes

Make a list of the next five clients you will see. Type or write their names on a blank page. Do it right now. Pick one client with whom progress seems particularly slow or uncertain. Then consider these questions for that client:

- What does this person most need to do in life right now? (Be as behaviorally specific as possible. Remember that behavior includes seemingly insubstantial things such as accepting, believing, envisioning, and so on.)

- What is most important for this person to practice doing, in the moment in therapy, to get the most out of the next session?

  - What does the client need to accept and experience?

  - What does the client need to think about? Ask for? Feel? Attend to?

  - What does the client need to do?

- What does this person do that most undermines or impedes progress in therapy?

- What is the function of this particular behavior? (Describe from the client's perspective.)

- How does that behavior make complete sense, given the client's history?

- What are the most important things for you to do in this therapy session with the client?

- What must you be willing to experience and accept in order to do those things?

These questions might not prove useful or insightful for all clients. Perhaps you are already making terrific progress with several clients. Perhaps there are other clients with whom these are exactly the right questions—exactly the right focus—and you know it. Perhaps you are stumped about how to answer these questions for other clients.

These questions are, in many ways, the core case conceptualization questions of FAP. We have found that these questions—or variants of them—are often helpful, especially when therapy is stuck or unfocused. They fit nicely with the principles and case-conceptualization strategies of other treatment models, and they focus your attention on concrete behaviors and on how those behaviors will show up in the therapy process. Ultimately, of course, you will be the best judge of when or how these questions will be useful (though you might benefit from consulting with someone who can offer a perspective outside your own).

We want to offer the following definition of *case conceptualization* in terms of FAP because it might differ from the definitions you've learned for other types of therapy:

FAP puts understanding in motion. How you work with clients in the moment is guided by your understanding of them as individuals within their present-moment context: what they need from you, what they need in life, what works for them. That understanding evolves through the therapy relationship. Case conceptualization is, in essence, an evolving, ongoing process of understanding clients that prepares you for and steers you during in-the-moment interactions with them. The process of case conceptualization isn't something a therapist keeps close to his or her chest or hidden in a secret folder, and it isn't shrouded in jargon. In FAP, case conceptualization is a transparent, caring conversation about the behaviors at issue in therapy.

As you know, in FAP this process centers on functional analysis. In chapter 3 we outlined the general principles of functional analysis from the FAP perspective (these principles are another version of the questions above):

- Orient to the key behaviors and contexts that are related to the client's presenting problems.

- Clarify the function of those behaviors.

- Look for the functional classes involved.

- Define improvements.

- Notice clinically relevant behavior in the moment. Define how problem behaviors (CRB1) and improvements (CRB2) might show up in the therapy relationship.

- Understand your own key behaviors that either interfere with (T1) or support (T2) the client's process of change.

- Shape and refine your understanding of the above over time.

In this chapter, we expand on these fundamental ideas to describe how they inform the process of case conceptualization across therapy.

EXPANDING FUNCTIONAL ANALYSIS TO CASE CONCEPTUALIZATION

As with just about everything in FAP, case conceptualization can take many different forms depending on the client, the context, and your personal style. Case conceptualization may involve spending a great deal of time on functional analysis, or it may proceed rapidly. An effective conceptualization can vary from highly precise and complex to highly generalized and simple. Ultimately, the quality of the case conceptualization depends on its function—how well it works to achieve the aims of therapy—rather than its form. In other words, evaluate your case conceptualization by how well it's working.

Under that umbrella, there is one outcome of case conceptualization that tends to be a key performance indicator in FAP: the conceptualization allows both client and therapist to identify instances of CRB as they happen. (Perhaps this is only a key indicator in FAP because you can't do FAP without being able to see CRBs. There are, of course, other ways to achieve therapy outcomes besides FAP.) More generally, when case conceptualization is on track in FAP, the following conditions tend to arise:

Therapist and client agree that certain problematic interpersonal behaviors are related to the presenting problem.

Therapist and client mutually recognize instances of CRB1 as they occur in session.

Therapist and client agree that CRBs identified in session (both CRB1 and CRB2) are functionally related to problem behavior outside of session.

The therapist works to manage the therapy process effectively, engaging in more T2s and fewer T1s.

The therapist's attention to CRB1 and CRB2 is balanced, such that the client feels both recognized for progress and appropriately challenged to keep moving forward.

The process of addressing CRBs in session (supported by homework assignments) yields insight and motivates the client to change functionally related problem behaviors in daily life, thus validating that the case conceptualization is useful in focusing the therapeutic process.

There are many ways to achieve these ends. To illustrate FAP's flexibility in another way, consider these summaries of case conceptualization. (A summary of a case conceptualization in FAP lists problems, CRBs, T1s, and T2s and serves as a quick reference guide for therapist and client. Remember, the summary is not the process of case conceptualization; it's an *outcome* of that process.) The summaries are diverse in the type of language they use and the level of precision they employ, but they may all adequately function to focus therapist and client attention in the process of therapy.

Example 1: Relatively Metaphorical Language

Client's out-of-session problems: Avoiding risk, holding back, putting her wall up

CRB1: Avoiding risk, holding back, putting her wall up

CRB2: Taking risks, moving beyond her comfort zone in opening up, exploring the wall and being willing to lower it

Generalized CRB2: Taking strategic risks, opening up, dropping the wall a little bit (especially when talking with men)

T1: Holding back, allowing the wall to stay up

T2: Addressing how the connection feels, exploring why the client feels she needs the wall, gently inviting the client to put up a window instead

Example 2: Less Metaphorical Language

Client's out-of-session problems: Avoiding expression of needs at work and with his partner, overcommitting to helping others

CRB1: Focusing on what the therapist thinks he should do, avoiding expression of his needs, overcommitting to therapy tasks that don't serve his needs

CRB2: Tuning in to and expressing what he needs based on what works or doesn't work for him, making realistic commitments to therapy tasks that serve his needs

Generalized CRB2: Expressing clearly and proactively what he needs, saying no when meeting a request isn't workable

T1: Playing into and reinforcing the "good client" routine

T2: Slowing the process down to help the client contact his needs, exploring his fear of expressing his needs, and identifying realistic commitments

Example 3: Using the ACL Model—Elaborate Conceptualization

Client's out-of-session problems: Lacking awareness of others' needs and her impact on others, especially family members; being excessively critical; tending to respond with punishment when family members express vulnerability; being unable to respond to family members with love; being unable to help family members feel safe when they're vulnerable

CRB1: Lacking awareness of her impact on the therapist, focusing on problem solving, tending to avoid discussions of emotion or reacting to discussions of emotions with hostility

CRB2: Having an increased awareness of the therapist's feelings and her impact on the therapist, being able to stay focused on emotional topics without becoming hostile or sarcastic, accepting feedback from the therapist when she feels hostile, developing the ability to signal safety and acceptance when the therapist challenges her

Generalized CRB2: Becoming more aware of the emotional needs of family members; being able to respond with patience, love, and safety when family members express vulnerability

T1: Letting the client problem solve, avoiding challenging the client to stay with emotions when she becomes hostile and sarcastic, judging the client

T2: Directly expressing sadness and fear to the client when she reacts with hostility, persisting with a compassionate approach even in the face of punishment, remembering that the client is always doing the best she can in the moment

Example 4: Using the ACL Model—Simple Conceptualization

Client's out-of-session problems: Not noticing what he needs (awareness), not asking for what he needs (courage)

CRB1: Not noticing what he needs (awareness), not asking for what he needs (courage)

CRB2: Tuning into himself, noticing his needs, and/or asking (awareness/courage) for what he needs

Generalized CRB2: Tuning into himself, noticing his needs, and/or asking (awareness/courage) for what he needs

T1: Not pausing to create space, bowling over the client's needs

T2: Creating space, inviting requests

Notice that not all aspects of the functional analysis are addressed explicitly in these case conceptualization summaries. For instance, the specific context, and especially the particular reinforcers in that context or learning history, aren't included. The main purpose of such summaries is simply to cue both therapist and client to remember and attend to key behaviors.

THE FULL PROCESS OF CASE CONCEPTUALIZATION

Whether the process of case conceptualization is brief or extended, linear or nonlinear (and whether the summary describing problem behavior and CRB is elaborate or simple), it typically involves three key steps, which we'll briefly review in the following sections:

1. Arrive at an initial working formulation.

2. Test the working formulation.

3. Refine the formulation.

Step 1: Arrive at an Initial Working Formulation

The first step of case conceptualization is to come up with an initial best guess about what the client's key problem behaviors are and what the corresponding CRBs are—that is, how do behaviors related to the client's presenting problems occur here and now in the therapy relationship. Arriving at this initial formulation of CRB involves three substeps:

A.   Identify problem behaviors and their functions.

B.   Define functional classes of problem behavior.

C.   Identify CRB1 and CRB2 as instances of those problematic functional classes.

SUBSTEP A: IDENTIFY PROBLEM BEHAVIORS AND THEIR FUNCTIONS

Imagine you have a client named Chris who wants help improving her mood. She reports that relationships are a major stressor for her, and she reveals that most of her current interactions are conflictual or distant and generally precede her episodes of low mood, whereas more positive interactions tend to improve her mood.

In order to orient yourself to the specific behaviors involved in "low mood," you next define in greater detail what the client is doing before, during, and after she experiences "low mood." For instance, you determine what she does when she has a low mood. Does she withdraw from all social interaction? Does she drink more alcohol and watch more television? Does she procrastinate work?

Imagine you discover that Chris tends to isolate when her mood is low. She doesn't return phone calls. She stops cleaning the house. She stops preparing food. She is much more likely to call in sick at work. In turn, these behaviors result in a mounting sense of being overwhelmed about all the things she hasn't done—all the ways she is failing.

Inquiring about the function of these painful problem behaviors, you assume—consistent with the framework of behavioral activation (Martell, Addis, & Jacobson, 2001)—that their key function is avoidance of something aversive. So you ask Chris, "If you weren't avoiding, what would you have to face that might be even more uncomfortable or painful?" The conversation that follows reveals that Chris feels intense shame about her low mood and her failure to respond to friends, such that if she were to talk to someone on the phone, she fears she would feel intense vulnerability. She describes that drinking alcohol and watching television are the only ways she can temporarily escape her painful feelings of shame.

At this stage, early in treatment, you are using a variety of tools and streams of information to shape your initial analysis of the problem behaviors and their functions. You consider what Chris reports to you verbally. You might also use psychometric instruments or interviews. Transcripts of text messages, e-mails, and other virtual communications can provide an amazingly useful natural record of how the client interacts with others. (You might also see discrepancies between the client's self-reporting and what you observe in these interpersonal interactions.)

No doubt you will also notice that, for any given presenting problem, there are numerous behaviors involved. For instance, in addition to the simple pattern of avoidance detected for Chris, you might learn that she

has a limited sense of her values or goals, leading to reduced motivation to face difficult situations;

tends to make critical misattributions about the reactions of others (she thinks they are judging her, for instance);

has difficulty recognizing and making sense of her painful emotions (for example, differentiating sadness from shame from anxiety); and

lacks the social skills to constructively express her needs to others who could offer support.

Given this complexity, what is the right focus? At this early stage, the "right" focus will always be a moving target. You are observing the flow of behavior, and you don't know yet what changes will lead most effectively to the best outcome. All you have is your best guess.

The right focus, then, is often defined by what seems workable in the moment. A workable focus tends to have a few features: First, there's a good empirical or assessment-based reason for thinking the target will be fruitful—in other words, moving that target will result in clinical progress. Second, the client is motivated and able to work on that target. A useful question to ask clients is "What situation or situations, if we changed them now, would have the biggest impact on your well-being?" The answer can help you get at whether or not you have a workable focus. (Keep in mind that clients who are stuck might have ideas about what they need to do that are in fact part of the problem. For instance, Chris might tell you that she "just needs to get up enough willpower to get some things done," even though every effort she has made to drum up willpower has resulted in greater self-criticism and shame.)

SUBSTEP B: DEFINE FUNCTIONAL CLASSES OF PROBLEM BEHAVIOR

As you get a sense of the flow of behavior related to presenting problems, common functions tend to come into view. For instance, with Chris you notice that the common thread across all of her behaviors is avoiding situations in which she will be judged as deficient, either by herself or by others.

In turn, seeing a functional pattern can help clients gain insight, as they often aren't aware that a behavior has a similar function in different situations. Clients also may not realize that behaviors that outwardly appear quite different often serve the same function. For example, upon reflection Chris discovers that one way she avoids the judgment of others is by committing to too much at work (she thinks that if she always says yes, others will respect her more). She also discovers that she avoids asking her long-term partner to make a deeper commitment in the form of marriage because she fears her partner will judge her as needy, even though there is no evidence of that. Though the form of her behavior in these two contexts is quite different, both situations involve rigid behavior that functions to avoid incurring the judgment of others.

As another example, consider a man who spends long hours toiling away in a career that he knows won't satisfy him in the long run. He may not see how this behavior resembles how he approached life as an opiate addict. However, in both cases he's avoiding the pain and uncertainty of striving for a more meaningful life and facing his hopelessness about ever achieving that.

SUBSTEP C: IDENTIFY CRB1 AND CRB2 AS INSTANCES OF THOSE PROBLEMATIC FUNCTIONAL CLASSES

The assessment process in substeps A and B unfolds while you interact with the client. As we described in chapter 7, on beginning therapy, throughout that interaction you observe the client's behaviors in the moment, the effects those behaviors have on you, and the effect you have on the client. What you observe in the moment helps you make hypotheses about the client's behavior as it relates to his or her presenting problems; for example, "You seem X to me. Is that related to your struggle in daily life?" As the functional analysis becomes clearer, you will also start to see CRB—behaviors occurring here and now that are functionally related to the client's problems.

Imagine Chris describes a conversation with her partner that didn't go well, in which she confronted her partner's procrastination regarding the planning of a vacation they had agreed to earlier in the year. As she describes the conversation, you notice that her tone of voice is slightly exasperated and she talks about her partner in judgmental ways. This is surprising to you, because you've tended to think of Chris as more passive and avoidant. You're also slightly confused by her narrative, and when you ask for clarification, she seems irritated. You might then ask, "I wonder…the way our conversation feels right now, is this what it felt like when you were talking to your partner? As you tell me the story, is that how your tone of voice sounded then, as well?"

If Chris admits that her tone was probably quite negative, you have crucial information about what happens in relevant interactions: When Chris feels that her needs aren't met, she communicates her frustration ineffectively, and she isn't aware of the negative impact of her tone of voice. This perpetuates a pattern in which others resist or avoid her, which, in turn, leads to Chris feeling ashamed and self-critical and avoidant of these sorts of interactions with others. You can then ask yourself what other behaviors fit this pattern. You also now have a clear sense of the CRB related to this pattern.

In exploring possible CRB, or the links between what you notice in the moment and the client's presenting problems, it's often helpful—especially early in therapy—to focus on moments when the client seems more emotional, more avoidant, less socially skilled, or disconnected from you. Keep in mind that the context of therapy is filled with interpersonal challenges that may parallel the challenges the client faces in daily life, and because of this, therapy may evoke these difficulties. Consider some of these challenges that therapy may involve for clients:

Having obligations or commitments to another person

Interacting with someone who's more educated or higher on a perceived social ladder

Vulnerably sharing emotions, experiences, or facts

Having an opportunity to trust or depend on someone

Relating to someone whom they pay to serve them

Relating to an expert whom they expect to have answers to their problems

Making needs or requests known

Coping with disappointments or unmet expectations

Collaborating on a difficult, uncertain task

Wanting to know more about the other person

Feeling seen, validated, or cared about

Wanting more time than the other person can give

Feeling gratitude or appreciation

Wondering if the other person is being honest or authentic

Wanting to be more special than others (for example, not just one of many clients)

Facing a time-limited relationship

In some cases, both CRB1 and the related CRB2 will rapidly become evident. In other cases, you'll be able to see the CRB1 clearly but be uncertain about a more workable CRB2. In the latter situation, you'll enter into a design or discovery process guided by this key question: What behaviors will be more effective and functional in the contexts in which this client is struggling? It might take time for you to understand the struggle and the client's life situations well enough to see the path clearly.

In turn, understanding the client's CRB1 and CRB2 will help you identify the key behaviors you must engage in to be an effective therapist for this client. What must you do to evoke CRB2? What patterns and behaviors must you watch out for because they will undermine therapy progress? For example, with Chris you might need to be firm but calm when inviting her to express her needs in session. You might also need to be patient, helping Chris find the language to articulate her needs and forgiving her when she is overly vague or harsh. This stance might be challenging, especially if you are very goal directed in your own life and in how you conduct therapy. To maintain an open, inviting stance, you may need to accept some uncertainty and lack of focus in the therapy process as Chris finds her way.

Step 2: Test the Working Formulation

Remember, the right case conceptualization is the one that works. You can only know if something works by testing it. Therefore, after arriving at an initial working formulation, the next step is to test it. One simple form this testing takes is to formulate CRB2 that can be evoked and reinforced in the moment, then assign homework based on practicing that same behavior in other contexts. Then, observe the results: Is the client able to achieve the change? Does the change produce the desired effect? And if there seems to be a negative outcome (for example, the client feels bad), is it actually a negative outcome?

Of course, the testing process is not always so focused and simple, so it's important to keep in mind that the process, more broadly speaking, is to proceed with therapy, inquiring whether the formulation leads to progress in therapy as you go along. You might swing a strike. Or you might get a hit, but the hit, in turn, may lead to a new focus.

For example, with Chris you might choose to focus on increasing her ability to compassionately and effectively assert herself with others—despite her fear of their negative judgment—because there are several painful situations in which her own needs are being trampled. In service of that focus, you compassionately challenge her (rule 2, evoke CRB) to be more direct with you about what kind of guidance she needs (CRB2) to most effectively build assertiveness skills and be willing to practice them. In the following weeks, she has several conversations—with her partner, with her supervisor—that go well. She feels a sense of relief in those relationships. She immediately discloses, however, that the much deeper issues she has been struggling with involve whether to even stay with her partner and in her current job. While it's perhaps true that her increased assertiveness facilitated her honesty about those doubts, the focus now shifts from the CRB of assertiveness to willingness to be vulnerable in discussing her longing for deeper changes.

Step 3. Refine the Formulation

The initial working formulation of the problem gets you started. It facilitates client buy-in and creates a sense of collaboration and understanding. However, as therapy proceeds, the testing process may reveal that the initial formulation is less than accurate or less than useful. You will then need to refine and evolve and reformulate your formulation through ongoing assessment and dialogue.

This is especially likely when clients are inaccurate or unreliable reporters of what happens to them outside of session and why. With such clients, it can take time to gain the needed clarity in conceptualization. In turn, the process of sharpening the conceptualization helps to focus therapy and hone the client's self-awareness.

In-session work can be especially fruitful for refining the formulation because of the clarity with which you can see and experience client behavior in the here and now. And as your understanding of individual clients and their problems and life situations evolves, so might your understanding of the significance of what you observe in session. Sometimes the behavior will strike you as unique or odd, but you won't know for a while whether it is clinically significant. Only with time do the pieces of the puzzle start to fall together. This is a natural evolution of the therapy process as you get to know a client over time, and it's a key aspect of case conceptualization in FAP. With Chris, for instance, perhaps it takes a while to understand that her slight edge of defensiveness and judgment of others—visible even in your first meeting—is related to her clinical issues. (It may also take a while to build enough rapport that you feel confident Chris will accept your feedback.)

ACCEPTING THAT THE PROCESS ISN'T LINEAR

It may take time for an effective conceptualization to come into focus. While you're searching for clarity, both you and the client may experience challenges within the therapy relationship. For example, the client may doubt whether therapy can help her. She may wonder if she is "unfixable." She may be frustrated by your inability to find a more direct path. You in turn may wonder about your competence to help this client.

These experiences can be useful for case conceptualization because you can observe how the client responds to such challenges. In fact, difficulty tolerating the necessary trial and error of change could be part of the pattern that keeps a client stuck. Addressing how clients cope with change, with obstacles to change, and with the frustration of failed efforts can be extremely therapeutic. In some cases, this direct focus on process is crucial for progress in therapy.

Imagine that a wave of hopelessness arises for Chris after she discloses to you that she has been contemplating leaving her partner and her job. She tells you that she fears therapy can't help her with big decisions and, in fact, such decisions are no-win situations for her. You may spend several weeks floundering, trying to find a way that seems to support Chris with her fear. Through that struggle, however, you might eventually discover something critical about how Chris approaches big decisions: she expects there to be a perfect answer that entails her not feeling any uncertainty or conflict. Once you recognize that key belief, you can work on a more flexible and accepting approach to her decisions. (Of course you are welcome to identify that hang-up more quickly. Our point is that it's helpful to accept the fact that sometimes clarity takes time.)

EXAMPLES OF CASE CONCEPTUALIZATION OVER THREE DIFFERENT TIME FRAMES

In the final sections of this chapter, we provide several extended examples of case conceptualization to illustrate the range of settings in which it occurs. We start with a single conversation focused on functional analysis. We'll then present case conceptualization from a relatively short-term case, closing with a description of a complex, multiyear course of therapy.

FAP in Action: Functional Analysis in the Moment

When clinicians first learn functional analysis, they sometimes have difficulty putting the principles into practice in session. Even if the goal outcome of functional analysis is fairly targeted (for instance, identifying CRB), it's important to know that the process itself can be quite flexible, conversational, and completely jargon-free, as the following dialogue illustrates. In this example, the client is a woman struggling with a severe anxiety disorder. She has just described how this anxiety worsens when her parents come to visit.

Therapist: So, when you're with your parents, what sorts of things come up?

Client: Well, I'm worried that they must be judging me because I just stay in bed all day and don't really do anything.

Therapist: You've said your dad was pretty critical when you were young, too. Does that still continue?

Client: No, he's actually better now. He used to get really angry. He was critical of me all the time. I remember him yelling at my mom.

Therapist: What else do you remember?

Client: One time we were on a summer vacation when I was a teenager, and I was trying to get a really dark tan. He said that if we were in the South and I was that tan, I'd have to sit in the back of the bus.

Therapist: Wow. That's problematic on so many levels.

Client: I have lots of stories like that.

Therapist: What would you do when he said things like that?

Client: I felt terrible…ashamed.

Therapist: And did you still want to be close to him? To have his approval?

Client: Of course I did. I always wanted his approval.

Therapist: How did you cope with that? It must have been really painful.

Client: I pulled back. I hid a lot. I did my best to please him. I don't know…

Therapist: It seems you learned that you're likely to be judged when you're close to other people—and it's as though your anxiety is really tuned in to that threat. You're calibrated for the relationship with your dad, where there actually was a lot of threat. But now the anxiety has a life of its own. You want connection. Over and over you've told me that's what you want. But there's so much anxiety around that, around being vulnerable with people, especially those who matter to you. So it's easier to pull back and stay separate. And when you do get closer to someone, there's a good chance your fear will spike, so you very well may feel worse. What do you think about what I'm saying?

Client: Well, I know it makes sense. But I'm not convinced that there aren't really threats with other people too.

Therapist: Oh, there might be. They might judge you. They might not. That uncertainty seems to be what's really scary for you. I mean, imagine if someone judged you and you could just react like, meh…whatever. That would be a huge change, right? But what happens now is that all your alarms go off. It's like a catastrophe. It's hard to connect when you're having the feeling that some kind of catastrophe is happening.

Client: Even when I do connect, I say to myself, "If this person is nice to me, it's because they think I'm ugly. They're taking pity on me."

Therapist: Yes. And if they weren't nice, the explanation would be similar. But instead of pity, they're disgusted by you.

Client: Yes.

Therapist: See how you end up back in the same spot? You get relief when you withdraw, when everything is coherent. Like you said, it feels better to think people find you ugly. But then no new information or experience gets in. It's a closed system.

Client: I guess so.

Therapist: Can you say more?

Client: I get what you're saying. I just don't trust it all yet.

Therapist: It makes sense that you don't. I don't either yet. We're figuring it out together.

Client: Even as we're talking now, it's like I feel that fear a bit, and I get stuck on it. Part of me is distracted with it. I want to hide.

Therapist: Yes. And what do you notice?

Client: I just want you to know that fear is there. I always think something is going wrong with me.

Therapist: You've said it's uncomfortable to be here, talking to me. And sometimes these fears come up. What else does the fear say?

Client: Well, I wouldn't want there to be something wrong without me catching it. I wouldn't want you to judge me without me knowing about it. Like even a minute ago, I was wondering if you could see what's wrong with my hair.

Therapist: So, normally, would you tell someone about your fear?

Client: No.

Therapist: In this context, I'm glad you're telling me. It helps me understand you. It makes sense given what we're talking about. In our work, I want to help you feel willing to be open with me in a way that doesn't involve pulling back and hiding.

To summarize, this dialogue starts with a description of an old dynamic between the client and her dad: she doesn't disclose vulnerable information to him because she fears his reaction. Then the client discloses the same urge to avoid showing up in the moment ("I want to hide."). Based on this conversation, functional thinking leads the therapist to hypothesize that the client reacts to fear of judgment by avoiding vulnerable disclosure. In turn, the client's preoccupation with her appearance likely also functions to help her avoid or cope with that vulnerability and fear of judgment (similar to the way a compulsion functions in relation to an obsession in obsessive-compulsive disorder). This thinking allows the therapist to notice that the behavior of disclosing fear, and potentially meeting judgment, is a change—a possible CRB2.

Notice that there are still many uncertainties. For example, does the client struggle with reassurance seeking (in addition to her avoidance of vulnerability)? Is she seeking reassurance by mentioning that she wonders if the therapist noticed anything about her hair? What kind of vulnerable disclosure would it be effective to increase in her daily life to move her toward the goal of better relationships? What kind of willingness or acceptance will be needed to move in that direction? All of these issues might be addressed with time. The conversation above simply illustrates one moment in the process of case conceptualization.

FAP in Action: Ongoing Case Conceptualization Over a Short-Term Treatment

Tony is a thirty-eight-year-old married banker who, in his first session, said he felt burned-out in his work. He expressed frustration about his supervisors ("They're so incompetent sometimes") and his colleagues ("They're like children"). Below we describe the evolution of the case conceptualization across Tony's relatively short-term treatment.

Based on the idea that anger often reflects frustrated or unmet needs, the therapist first asked Tony about how well his needs were met at work and how effectively he expressed his needs, both proactively and when they weren't met. Tony reported that he tended to avoid speaking up until he reached his boiling point, after which he communicated with a lot of anger.

The therapist also discovered that Tony persevered in a lot of friendships that weren't very satisfying to him or apparently to the other person, and that many of these friendships fizzled out after a few months, while those that lasted involved ongoing conflict. This also related to how he expressed (or didn't express) his needs, as most of his difficulties with friends revolved around their failure (in his view) to be considerate of him. Ultimately, it seemed that Tony invested a lot of energy in relationships that arguably provided the opposite of what he needed: stress instead of support, and conflict instead of understanding. Based on what was happening at work and in his friendships, in the first session, the therapist decided to initially focus treatment on how Tony expressed his needs.

For the first several sessions, Tony participated in an agreeable but unfocused way. He was pleasant to the therapist, even while talking at length about his frustrations with people outside of session. When the therapist pointed out this discrepancy ("How is it that we get along so well, yet you have so many frustrations with others in your life?"), Tony said, "Well, you haven't done anything to disappoint me." The therapist also noticed that Tony wasn't very clear about what he wanted to focus on in each therapy session, even when prompted. He tended to spend a lot of time telling detailed stories about events in his week. After several sessions, the therapist pointed this out: "It's curious to me that you say I haven't disappointed you, yet you've also rated the helpfulness of our sessions as moderate. It seems like you hired me for a good reason, and my job is to help you.

I want to help you. Yet I notice that your needs often seem quite vague to me when you're here. I find myself losing track of what you need and what we're working on. I have the sense that if I let you, you'd tell stories for the entire session, then thank me, and then rate the helpfulness of the session as moderate. And I sense that you'd be satisfied to go on that way for a while. But we wouldn't really get anywhere. Is that right?"

Tony smiled and replied, "Yep, that's pretty much right. That's what I did with my last therapist." This led to a conversation about how Tony—at least until he reached his boiling point—made his social interactions smooth and easy by putting his own needs aside. He said it felt awkward for him to ask for things directly, and that in the short term it was easier for him to cruise along without making his needs known. At the therapist's invitation, Tony committed to work toward expressing his needs more clearly, both in the therapeutic relationship and in other contexts. The therapist in turn provided a concrete framework for assertiveness skills.

In the first few weeks after this discussion, Tony practiced expressing what he needed in several crucial conversations with colleagues. The conversations worked well enough, in that he got what he needed in the moment, but he still felt ongoing resentment toward his supervisors, and his burnout didn't decrease markedly. As the therapist explored this, Tony mentioned a couple of work commitments—extra assignments he had volunteered for—that were stressing him out on a weekly basis. This in turn led to a discussion about Tony's overall workload. It emerged that Tony was dramatically overcommitted and spread thin over several projects he was not enjoying but felt obligated to complete. Tony hadn't realized that these commitments likely played a key role in his burnout until the therapist asked about this possibility directly. Tony responded, "Doesn't everyone have too much work to do?"

Based on this new information, the therapist helped Tony craft requests for the relevant supervisors to renegotiate these commitments, and although Tony felt considerable anxiety about initiating these conversations, he committed to doing so. He was also more direct with his therapist in asking for her support in preparing for these conversations, which she recognized as CRB2. As a result of all of this work, over the next few weeks Tony fundamentally restructured how his time was allocated at work, and his burnout improved rapidly and substantially.

In the next phase of therapy, Tony expressed deeper needs, opening up about ongoing frustrations and conflicts in his closest relationships, including his marriage. Together, Tony and his therapist discovered that he had a pattern of holding high expectations of those closest to him and that, as in professional relationships and friendships, he typically didn't express his needs with respect to these expectations very clearly; then when his loved ones failed to meet his unexpressed needs, he tended to either blow up with anger or withdraw. All of this was functionally similar to his behavior in other contexts. But with loved ones, a different type of behavior also manifested: Tony worried a lot about their well-being and success, and in response to this worry, he tended to pressure them to change their behavior in ways he thought they should. Not surprisingly, this usually resulted in conflict or distance in the relationship.

As the therapist explored this dynamic, she discovered that Tony was the oldest of several children, and that during his childhood he often felt compelled to take care of his siblings because his parents were fairly neglectful. As a child, he felt proud of the responsibility he carried, and he wanted—but didn't receive—recognition and appreciation for the parental role he played. At the same time, he had considerable anxiety about his responsibility for his siblings, and he mainly managed them through nagging and threatening.

This pattern of behavior was understandable in the context of Tony's childhood situation. However, in his adult life, it wasn't functional. The conversation in which this pattern came fully to light functioned as a huge CRB2, with Tony deeply expressing his wish to fundamentally change how he related to those closest to him. Just a few days afterward, Tony had a conversation with his wife in which he broke a long-standing avoidance of talking about the elephant in the room: their relationship. He acknowledged that putting pressure on her to behave how he wanted wasn't helpful, and he apologized for not being more sympathetic. He also clearly expressed his own needs and vulnerability. The result was that he immediately felt closer to his wife than he had in a long time.

FAP in Action: Case Conceptualization Over the Long Term

Tony's case is a relatively straightforward, brief treatment, with the case conceptualization evolving over a couple of months. Now we'll offer an example of case conceptualization that evolved over almost three years. Nick was struggling with more severe problems—chronic depression, anxiety, interpersonal difficulties, and dependence on alcohol—and had been referred to treatment after hospitalization for being suicidal.

EARLY TREATMENT (DURATION: TWO MONTHS)

Initially Nick was suspicious of therapy and withheld most of the details of his emotional experience. During the first two months of treatment, he gradually opened up and described intense loneliness, despite having fairly frequent social contact. The therapist's attempts to use activity scheduling failed. During this phase, Nick's CRB1s included avoiding the therapist by skipping sessions and withholding feedback when interventions weren't helpful. His CRB2s included honest disclosure and making his needs known to the therapist.

PHASE 2 (DURATION: FOUR MONTHS)

As Nick disclosed more, it became clear that he met criteria for borderline personality disorder. This was a significant realization for him. The therapist identified deficits in emotion regulation, social perspective-taking, and social skills more generally, and then she intensively assessed Nick's history, focusing on his interpersonal relationships and pursuit of goals. This revealed that many of Nick's actions were based on perceived obligations to others and to a very rigid code of how people should behave, which his parents had imposed upon him from an early age. One function of this code was to help him decide how he should relate to others in order to avoid shame and faux pas. Yet it also became clear that he had a very difficult time taking others' perspectives; as a result, he couldn't make sense of other people's behavior when it broke the code, and he felt angry, anxious, and puzzled much of the time.

This lack of understanding and disappointment with others—and basic lack of perspective taking—meant his relationships were frustrating and lacked depth. He resented (and envied) others for what he perceived as their superficiality and failure to adhere to the code. These feelings emerged in the form of ranting in session, and although this was uncomfortable for the therapist at times, it was also important, as the therapist recognized the ranting as a likely starting point for shaping CRB2s related to honest emotional expression and expression of needs. This frustration also motivated Nick to work with the therapist to develop basic behavioral strategies to address painful conflicts, including ending several dysfunctional relationships and starting to engage with his family members differently—in more assertive or flexible ways.

In this phase, Nick's CRB1s included demanding overly simplistic solutions from the therapist ("You need to tell me how to fix this!") and sticking rigidly to his code in session, rather than thinking beyond it. His CRB2s included expressing feelings and needs openly, orienting toward problems and situations he wanted to solve (instead of complaining), sticking with the process even when it involved challenges or uncertainty, and inquiring about and accepting the therapist's perspective on what might be helpful.

PHASE 3 (DURATION: EIGHT MONTHS)

Six months into therapy, Nick's suffering had eased somewhat, and he was experiencing significantly less conflict. However, he still hadn't achieved any substantial changes in his life, and he was painfully lonely, which led to a deeper feeling of hopelessness, increased suicidal thinking, and increased conflict with his therapist centered around the demand that she provide more effective solutions. During these times of high distress, he engaged in some skills practice based on dialectical behavior therapy (DBT), albeit reluctantly and without much benefit.

His therapy seemed to reach a turning point through a series of very raw discussions focused on the process of change. In these discussions, his therapist said, with considerable emotion, "Change won't happen unless you change how you're living more fundamentally. It involves opening up to a way of living that's scary to you—facing the anxiety of letting go of the code to become who you really want to be. If you don't do this, you'll probably keep feeling the same way." This may sound harsh. But in the context, it was exactly this directness that motivated Nick to let go of what was not workable, to let go of how he had been living previously, and to move toward accepting the need for deeper change—and all the anxiety and grief that came with these changes.

After working through that conflict in the therapy process, they discussed Nick's pattern in conflicts, which usually left him feeling completely alienated from the other person—including the therapist. They committed to work on maintaining an understanding of and connection to each other through any conflict that arose between them. This work led to Nick experiencing things with the therapist that he had never experienced before: being understood and cared for despite his anger and high levels of conflict, and persevering through conflict to reestablish a connection.

This new interpersonal process in session functionally mirrored, at a very high level, what Nick needed to achieve in his life outside of session: pushing through discomfort and fear to find a more authentic way of living and connecting with others.

To consolidate the case conceptualization, the therapist and Nick defined two different ways of being: one based on the code versus one based on genuine desires and needs. They named living by the code Hans because the name signified duty and obligation, and they named living based on genuine desires and needs Bowie because the name captured how Nick secretly wished to live: as a rock star who is creative, gregarious, and free of conventions. During this phase, Nick's CRB1s included escalating his demands, anxiety, and suicidal thinking in order to get his therapist's attention; avoiding or suppressing his genuine desires and wishes about how to live; and attacking or judging others. His CRB2s included expressing his needs vulnerably and directly, taking into account his impact on the therapist; accepting uncertainty; accepting care from the therapist; and disclosing his genuine wishes about how he wanted to live.

PHASE 4 (DURATION: THIRTEEN MONTHS)

Fourteen months into treatment, Nick committed to radically changing how he was living life. This change centered on altering how he presented himself to others (literally, how he dressed and spoke), participating in social activities he was interested in but Hans forbade, and learning to speak and relate as Bowie rather than as Hans. For the first time, Nick started to spontaneously report feeling hopeful. In the context of his compelling desire to live like Bowie would, Nick became much more motivated to practice a variety of DBT emotion regulation skills, with a particular focus on actively managing his anxiety.

As Nick implemented these changes, the therapeutic relationship became progressively deeper and more solid based on mutual respect, understanding, caring, and commitment to this crucial but difficult task of living in line with his values as Bowie. Nick's CRB1s included "being like Hans," seeking reassurance or black-and-white answers, and suppressing his needs. His CRB2s included taking risks to express and embody who and what he wanted to be; accepting uncertainty; taking the therapist's perspective; and sharing his appreciation for the therapist.

PHASE 5 (DURATION: SIX MONTHS)

By phase 5, through a lot of hard work (much is left out of the condensed story we offer here) and after twenty-seven months of therapy, Nick had achieved several life goals he had believed were impossible. He no longer felt terrified or enraged during interactions with his family. He was in a committed and stable romantic relationship. And beyond his partner, he had a strong, local community of friends. He was also spending most of his time doing activities he valued. To prepare Nick for the end of treatment, during this phase the therapist focused on dealing with the so-called normal challenges of living, such as what to do when work conflicts with romantic relationships or how to talk about the future with your partner.

SUMMARY

- Case conceptualization in FAP is based on ongoing functional analysis that unfolds in the therapeutic relationship.

- Case conceptualization, like the therapy process in FAP, is iterative and collaborative. It only needs as much precision as is required to efficiently achieve a positive therapy outcome.

- The case conceptualization might identify out-of-session problems, CRB1s, CRB2s, out-of-session goals, T1s, and T2s.

CHAPTER 12

Solidify Change with Homework and Experiential Exercises

This is the real secret of life—to be completely engaged with what you are doing in the here and now. And instead of calling it work, realize it is play.

—Alan Watts

"What you did with me in session today was so powerful. The way you 'dropped the wall'—and yet I could see you staying in contact with me, even with your anxiety, through your eye contact. I have the sense it took a lot of courage and trust to take that leap."

"Yes. I feel really proud about it. I feel like I'm doing something I've not let myself do for so long."

"I'm glad to be here with you. And I'm curious, as we come into our last ten minutes today, are there places in your life this week, with other people, where it could be useful, or powerful, to drop the wall in a similar way? Maybe not 100 percent like you did with me. But maybe 10 percent? Or 30 percent? Do you know what I mean?"

"Yes, absolutely. What comes to mind is, I have a volunteer group meeting on Wednesday. There's a new member, a guy who I've only met briefly before, but I've heard so many good things about him. I've already been anticipating feeling really insecure and closed up. I'd like to try dropping the wall some more with him. Just being real."

In this vignette, the therapist reinforces the progress the client makes in the session, but, rather than stop there, she suggests the client take this behavior to the outside world. This is a form of homework, one of the topics of this short chapter. Homework in FAP is a tool for rule 5 (support generalization). We also present a small set of experiential exercises in this chapter that might be useful in FAP. We've combined these two topics in one chapter for a few reasons. First, many experiential exercises are suitable as homework assignments. Second, good, functionally attuned homework assignments and experiential exercises are defined by a common quality: they provide an effective context for evoking CRB2 and for receiving reinforcing consequences for that behavior. We encourage you to think about them in this similar way, as further practice in developing functional thinking.

HOMEWORK

Homework is often a crucial therapy tool. In FAP, it's a tool for following rule 5, support generalization. Rule 5 is about providing a means for transferring in-session behavior change to other contexts in the client's life. In that sense, homework is simply a cue or framework for doing certain things in certain situations.

As a general rule, homework is assigned every session. This guideline is rooted in FAP's foundation in behavior therapy. The goal of therapy is to change how clients are functioning in their lives. Homework is about making the process of change deliberate, active, and strategic. At the same time, homework need not be overtly focused on action. It can target a broad range of behaviors: noticing, reflecting, thinking, feeling, as well as taking action.

Individualizing Homework

Homework should be individualized to the client's behavioral goals and contexts. This might mean adapting one of the exercises we offer, or it might mean designing homework assignments from scratch. You can let go of rigid formats for homework activities (as in, "You've got to do it this way because that's what the manual says") and instead flexibly attend to the functional question "What will work for this client this week?"

The simplest homework is to practice CRB2 outside of session. As an example, for the client in the opening vignette of this chapter, the homework is simply practicing the behavior of courageous self-disclosure, first undertaken in session, when opportunities to do so naturally arise. The client identifies a natural setting where she wants to practice CRB2 (and based on contextual understanding, the therapist and client together are confident that the client can be successful in that context), but she also has freedom to improvise. Alternatively, the homework could entail having very specific conversations and conducting them in a very particular way, perhaps even starting with a prepared script.

It's important to strike the right balance between structure and flexibility. Homework is often most effective when clients own the process of creating it and are encouraged to adapt it to the situations they face and in ways that seem to work. Keep in mind that sometimes it takes time to build the confidence and skills to make such adaptations. In contrast, when clients take on rote assignments in a rote way, they're more likely to give up when the assignments don't seem to achieve the desired change or it's not clear how to adapt the assignment to reality. A *structured* assignment should be targeted to a very specific context in which the client needs structure; or it should be able to be completed independently of context (for example, simply filling out a worksheet). A *flexible* assignment should be given when the client will succeed with that flexibility (even if it is somewhat challenging; for example, if the client is working on the behavior of making decisions under conditions of uncertainty, she might be slightly uncomfortable but perfectly capable of enduring the discomfort).

Finally, remember that assigning homework is another aspect of the therapy process, in which a range of CRB (or T1s and T2s) might be evoked. This applies not just to assigning homework, but also to whether and how clients complete it. Throughout the therapy process it's important to debrief about homework assignments and revise them to be more focused and effective.

Integrating these considerations, here are some questions that can keep you and your clients on track in regard to homework.

Is the homework feasible and realistic? As a general rule, an intense, important assignment that clients don't complete isn't as useful as a more modest assignment that they will actually do.

Does the homework address important behavioral targets? Homework that doesn't challenge clients to try something new isn't particularly useful either. Homework should be feasible but should also target the most important behaviors and push clients to try new things. The outcome of homework should be something new.

Is the client's commitment (or lack of commitment) to the homework CRB? For some clients, compliance with homework is CRB1—part of a pattern of overcommitment and underexpression of needs that tends to create frustration and burnout. For them, assigning homework can provide a context in which they are invited to practice the CRB2 of making realistic commitments and being direct about their needs. For other clients, failure to follow through on homework assignments is an important CRB1, though this may, of course, reflect similar deficits in expressing their needs prior to agreeing to an unrealistic commitment.

Are you collaborating on homework in a way that builds the client's mastery? Clients should actively keep track of what does and doesn't work in regard to homework, not just whether they did it or not. Similarly, ideally they will become increasingly autonomous in designing and debriefing their homework, reflecting increased skill at self-management.

Keep in mind that homework that doesn't turn out the way you or the client thought it would isn't necessarily "failed" homework. It can still provide invaluable learning. Among other things, "failed homework" provides an opportunity to see and engage with how the client responds to setbacks and learns from them.

Three Common Types of FAP Homework

In this section we present three standard types of FAP homework: keeping a behavior log, engaging in specific conversations, and connecting with the therapist outside of session.

KEEPING A BEHAVIOR LOG

The concept of a behavior log is simple: in a diary, clients track behaviors relevant to therapy goals between sessions. Use any format that works for a given client: a journal, a structured form, a spreadsheet, and so on.

Many potentially useful target behaviors can be tracked in this way, including engaging in vulnerable self-disclosure, expressing emotions, offering or requesting feedback, making requests or expressing needs, or approaching significant conflicts or disagreements. Of course, you can also target more specific contexts or actions in keeping with the case conceptualization.

One common focus for behavior logs is risk; in fact, we often ask clients to keep a "risk log" in which they keep track of interpersonal risks. In FAP, taking risks means approaching interpersonal situations that clients might otherwise avoid; it doesn't mean engaging in reckless or destructive actions. Risks are strategic. That said, engaging in a deliberate practice of risk-taking will involve occasional "failures" in the sense of not getting the desired results. Therefore, encouraging clients to engage in this kind of risk-taking typically involves both experiencing the benefits of risks, as well as learning to cope with and respond to failure or disappointment in new ways. In the bigger picture, the function of risk-taking extends beyond immediate results as clients engage in an overarching practice of pursuing goals or values despite the chance they might encounter obstacles or failure.

For some clients, tracking risk is exactly the wrong homework. For example, clients who are too impulsive, tend to lack awareness of the appropriateness of their behavior, or are unlikely to experience a positive response should not track risks. For these kinds of clients, it might be better to keep an "impact log" (What impact do I think I have on others?) to build skill with seeing other perspectives. Behavior logs can be used to track any behavior that fits the case conceptualization and CRB2, from a "loving others log" to a "self-care log" to a "proud-moments log." We tend to favor tracking CRB2 (improvements) over CRB1 (problem behavior) because it is generally more appetitive to track improvements.

Besides making behavior change visible and providing you the opportunity to respond to progress, the log provides a window into the client's daily life, potentially revealing features of his or her behavior you might not otherwise notice: absence of emotion, an excessive focus on negative events, avoidance of important relationships or issues, and so on. The way the client writes the log can also reveal CRB.

ENGAGING IN SPECIFIC CONVERSATIONS

Success in a single important conversation can have a massive positive impact on the trajectory of a relationship. For example, talking about a long-avoided issue with a friend, discussing the idea of having children with a partner, making plans for the holidays with a difficult family member, giving feedback to a partner about the impact of his drinking, or asking for a raise or change of focus at work can dramatically alter a client's life. As therapists, we are perfectly situated to help clients craft and engage in these conversations.

The first step of this multilayered homework assignment is to identify a crucial conversation. Then work with the client toward the goal of making the conversation happen in a successful way. Preparation is key. Sometimes the words or tone that the client needs to bring to the conversation will already have happened in the therapy relationship as CRB2. In that case, the instruction is to "do what you did with me in that conversation." Sometimes it takes a while to shape up the CRB before you and the client are confident he will be successful.

You may also need to prepare the client in more direct ways to create a bridge between in-session work and the conversation itself. For instance, you might collaboratively create a thirty-to-sixty-second script for an opening statement to begin the conversation. You may want to coach the client in important aspects of the conversation in a more didactic way, such as remembering to validate or not casting blame. Remember that tone and body language are sometimes more important than what is said. It can also be useful to attend to the setting of the conversation; for example, depending on what will work best, you may want to suggest e-mail or written form for some conversations rather than face-to-face, or vice versa. (E-mail is often solid ground for learning because it provides the opportunity to really craft a message.)

Some therapists are hesitant to provide such highly directive guidance about how to engage in conversations. However, when clients lack the skills to converse effectively and yet a conversation needs to happen, teaching the needed skills directly can be extremely helpful and more efficient than waiting for clients to discover the skill for themselves. There are, of course, many different resources available for training in social skills and communication, including books related to psychology, self-help, and business. You can use these resources to train yourself. You can also recommend that clients use them as appropriate. (Susan Scott's 2002 book *Fierce Conversations* is a favorite of the authors.)

CONNECTING WITH THE THERAPIST OUTSIDE OF SESSION

Although FAP homework often focuses on client interactions with significant people, in some contexts it may be helpful to choose homework that involves interacting with the therapist outside of session. Technology has made this kind of connection immensely easier. However, two important caveats are in order: First, and obviously, any technology used for therapy purposes should comply with relevant laws and your professional and organizational guidelines. Second, it's important that this kind of contact not exceed the therapist's limits, and that any CRB1 or T1 be addressed. (This practice mirrors the skill coaching elements of dialectical behavior therapy.)

Caveats aside, out-of-session contact with the therapist can be a strategic way to provide the client an additional bridge between therapy and daily life. It gives the therapist an opportunity to respond in reinforcing ways to behaviors when and where they happen. For instance, consider a client who's working on noticing and approaching moments of happiness; his homework assignment might be to notice and take pictures of things that make him happy and then send the pictures to his therapist in the moment via text message. The therapist can then respond as befits the case conceptualization or her guidelines. As another example, the homework for a client struggling with disconnection might be noticing her disconnection in the moment and then reaching out to her therapist with a short e-mail ("I'm feeling disconnected now."), thereby creating connection in moments of disconnection.

EXPERIENTIAL EXERCISES

The remainder of this chapter offers a small sample of experiential exercises that can be useful vehicles for implementing the five rules of FAP in session; or they can be used as homework assignments that set the stage for in-session work. We recommend viewing them as templates for adaptation or as inspiration for creating client-specific exercises or homework. Before we turn to the specific exercises, there are a few things to consider prior to using them.

Keeping Exercises Relevant

There has been some debate in the FAP community about experiential exercises—specifically, whether they're clinically useful. The main concern of detractors is that exercises are a weird or artificial context detached from normal interpersonal interactions, and because of that, behavior shaped by exercises can't really transfer to other settings. In other word, they're irrelevant. And, even worse, they argue that exercises may actually do harm; for instance, an exercise might encourage intense emotional disclosure that would be disastrous if replicated in a professional meeting. There's also a more general concern that using structured exercises could insidiously lead therapists away from functional attunement—that is, being aware of what clients are experiencing and need in the moment. In other words, the therapist might become more concerned about the goal of the exercise than about the client.

Although these are valid concerns, at its core FAP is about using any therapeutic tool, including exercises, in a way that's functionally attuned, embedded in a working functional analysis, and oriented toward transferring behavior shaped in the here and now to relevant settings in the client's life. If therapists keep that orientation in mind, the "unnatural" nature of experiential exercises (or any other aspect of therapy, for that matter) can in fact serve several useful functions. One is that exercises sometimes offer an expedient way to evoke a behavior that might not otherwise occur naturally but would function well in a given situation. For instance, consider a client who would benefit from practicing giving and receiving appreciation. In this case, you might introduce the exercise "sharing appreciations" (which we present shortly): "In the service of practicing positive connections, let's end each session by exchanging appreciations. This is also a good way to let me know in the moment what's most important or effective about what we did today. How about if we take turns and share one or two appreciations each. Would you like to go first?"

In this case, the exercise is essentially a directive and evocative (in the sense of rule 2) intervention. The method of evoking, and the exercise itself, can be somewhat unnatural; for example, it's unlikely that clients will receive direct requests to exchange appreciations in other contexts (although this is actually a very useful interpersonal strategy). However, the behavior that's shaped in the exercise (giving and receiving appreciation) can function well in a variety of real-life contexts.

Selecting Useful Exercises

The same functional analysis that guides the selection of any intervention in FAP should be used to choose exercises. The primary question to ask yourself is, how can this exercise evoke CRB2 for a given client? Different exercises tend to evoke different CRB2s for different clients. In turn, once the target CRB2 is evoked, ensure that it's reinforced, whether it be within the exercise itself or while debriefing the exercise afterward.

Sometimes it's useful to discuss with the client in advance what the exercise will evoke and what the client should focus on in the exercise. For example, depending on a given client's case conceptualization, you might ask one of the following questions:

How can you engage in this exercise in a way that's meaningful to you?

How can you remain connected with yourself and others if the exercise elicits strong emotion?

How can you be more aware and accepting of whatever feelings come up for you during the exercise?

What do you want to do in the presence of any emotions that come up during the exercise?

How do you want to explore emotional topics and share about them in the context of this exercise?

Then, when you debrief exercises, help clients assess what they experienced, whether the target CRB2 was evoked, and what they experienced as a result.

Specific Exercises

The following sections briefly describe specific exercises, or general types of exercises, commonly used by FAP therapists. The last three exercises invite deeper reflection, so they are more often assigned as homework. A critical part of each one, however, is sharing and processing the work in session.

INTENTIONAL SHARING

Clients often begin sessions by describing (or venting about) events that happened since the last session. The intentional sharing exercise offers a way to structure and contain such sharing and to encourage CRB2 during the process. To put this exercise into action, invite clients to begin sessions with a mindful, succinct (one-to-five-minute) update about what they experienced over the previous one to two days, with a focus on describing specific emotions they experienced. For example, "I woke up feeling anxious about my presentation. It went really well, though, and afterwards I felt proud—excited. Then I got a message that a dear friend is really sick. I felt stunned. Then really sad..." If it seems helpful for increasing reciprocity and connection, you can offer a brief personal update as well.

Common CRB1s evoked by this exercise include sharing too much; not sharing enough; offering descriptions of emotion that are thin, confusing, minimal, and so on; avoiding the discussion of more emotional situations; skimming over significant experiences; or failing to remember or attend to significant events. Sometimes it is useful to cue the client to stay focused on emotions as he's talking. At other times it's more effective to wait until the client is finished before offering your feedback (for example, "I noticed that you tended to drift away from emotions and toward storytelling. Did you notice that?").

The intentional sharing exercise can be practiced in other relationships as well, though clients don't need to signal that they're doing an exercise and can instead talk in a more natural way; however, they should remain mindful of their emotions. Clients are often surprised by the amount of change they experience regarding the level of connection to others they feel when they adopt this focus.

SHARING APPRECIATIONS

In the sharing appreciations exercise, set aside time—for example, at the end of each session—for the deliberate exchange of appreciation. This may be particularly valuable for clients with CRB1s related to difficulty accepting compassion or appreciation from others or asking for appreciation.

You can invite the client to go first or second. For your part, share something the client said or did in the session that you appreciate, or something you appreciate about the client in general:

I appreciate the way you slowed me down, listened to me, and helped me see more clearly what I need to do.

I appreciate how open you were in sharing things you felt uncertain or vulnerable about. I appreciate that you let me see you clearly.

I appreciate how hard you are working in your life at this point.

Of course, appreciation is just one type of feedback that can be shared. If relevant to the client's CRB, it may be useful to target constructive criticism or asking for a need to be met; for example, instead of exchanging appreciation you could ask, "How could we have made the session better today?"

TIMED WRITING EXERCISES

Timed writing can be used in session or assigned as homework. In this exercise, clients are given a set amount of time, such as three minutes, to write whatever comes to mind without censoring. Choose the topic based on the client's CRB. You can ask her to write about a specific topic that the two of you are addressing in therapy (for example, what she feels shame about, the fear of closeness, or feelings toward a parent). Alternatively, you can ask the client to write about whatever is on her mind. Other than a time limit and the task being written rather than oral, the exercise is a lot like free association, with the aim being to express feelings and thoughts that may be more difficult to contact and express under typical social conditions. In other words, the timed writing task is often about evoking vulnerable disclosure.

It can be helpful to provide stem phrases for clients to work with. Here are a few suggestions, though of course you can use others:

I'm sad that… (or I'm hurt that…)

I'm angry that…

I miss…

I'm relieved that…

I'm grateful that…

I'm sorry about… (or I regret…)

I wish I had…

I wish [someone significant] had…

I forgive [someone significant] for…

Please forgive me for…

I never told [someone significant] that…

[Someone significant] never told me that…

What I learned from my relationship with this person is…

I will always remember… (or I will never forget…)

I want [someone significant] to know…

If only I could…

LIFE HISTORY

You may assign the life history exercise—the same one we gave you in chapter 6—as homework for your clients. (Many FAP therapists assign this exercise as standard homework in preparation for or immediately following the first session of therapy.) By sharing their stories, clients reveal a lot about their history as well as potential CRB related to vulnerable disclosure. It's important to be sensitive to the demands of this exercise; it may be incredibly intense—even unthinkable—for some clients. Adjust the level of disclosure or detail you ask for based on the client's needs and current tolerance for vulnerability.

COMPILING AN INVENTORY

Compiling an inventory about a particular type of experience is similar to writing a life history. For example, you might invite a client who seems to be carrying a lot of avoided grief to write a history focused on experiences of loss. This can be a useful way to evoke vulnerable disclosure alongside the processing of sadness and the experiences of loss. You might ask clients to consider one of these examples:

From your earliest memories to the present, what are the losses (big and small) that you've endured in life that stand out to you?

What has made you sad, broken your heart, or left a gap in your life?

What has been missing in your life?

What losses do you think should or could evoke a response in you now but don't?

What do good-byes bring up for you?

Other useful inventories include accomplishments, close relationships, appreciation, and shameful experiences.

NURTURING CONNECTION

For some clients, nurturing connection with an important person can be a useful homework assignment. First, the client needs to identify a specific person he'd like to be closer to; then he asks that person if she'd be willing to have a conversation (or perhaps a conversation that repeats weekly or monthly) to share and connect on an emotional level. Here are some potential questions the client might pose:

What was the best thing that happened to you this past week?

When did you feel closest to me this past week? Why?

When did you feel most distant from me this past week? Why?

What are you excited about or looking forward to doing in the near future?

What are you concerned or worried about?

What have you recently felt grateful for? Why?

Is there anything you're avoiding saying or communicating to me? If so, what is it?

What have you appreciated about me this past week?

What have you appreciated about yourself this past week?

Is there anything else you want to tell me?

Initially, you might ask clients to answer these questions with you reciprocally before doing the assignment with others.

SUMMARY

- Homework in FAP supports the generalization of CRB2 in the client's daily life outside of session.

- Homework design is based on functional thinking. Homework creates a context that evokes target behavior in target contexts.

- Common types of homework assignments include behavior logs, engaging in specific conversations, and connecting with the therapist outside of session.

- Experiential exercises in FAP, like homework, are designed to evoke and provide an opportunity for reinforcing CRB2.

CHAPTER 13

Marking the End of Therapy

Great is the art of beginning, but greater is the art of ending.

—Henry Wadsworth Longfellow

Too often, therapy tapers off, trickles out, or cuts off. After a decrease in the frequency of sessions, the client doesn't respond to a final message. Or, the client goes on a trip or adventure, crossing the threshold of a major life event, with the vague promise of picking up sessions again in the fall, and then that doesn't happen. Or, there is a more deliberate termination session, but it is slightly awkward and anticlimactic. Client and therapist have already withdrawn from each other.

Yet endings—including coping with endings and fear of endings—are important parts of relationships. They may also be related to clinical issues, either directly or indirectly. For example, some clients with a history of abandonment or unreliable caregivers will begin to fear the ending of therapy when they begin to attach to the therapist. Some clients will avoid getting close to you because of this, or they will withdraw or decompensate as the ending draws nearer. Even though other clients may ostensibly handle the ending well, they may walk away with lingering uncertainty about the therapeutic relationship: Did he really care? What did he think of me? Was he happy to move on to work with other people? This is not always a problem, of course, but as with everything else in FAP, we want to look at endings functionally and ask this: What does the ending mean— how does it function—for this person?

Further, ending therapy may also be difficult for therapists, especially if a strong relationship has been formed, and it might evoke various T1s as a result. For instance, you might become less responsive to a client as you anticipate her departure. While the manner in which therapy ends should primarily serve the client, the therapist may have important needs as well, and therefore the FAP stance toward endings is designed to encourage both CRB2 and T2.

ISSUES EVOKED BY THE END OF THERAPY

For many clients, the end of therapy brings up feelings and memories of previous transitions and losses. With these clients, you can use the termination of therapy to further build skills for coping with loss and endings. Of course, when coping with loss is a central therapy target, it will be addressed much earlier in treatment. (For some clients for whom loss is central, the imagined future termination of the therapy relationship might be explored from very early in treatment. For example, "Loss is such a core part of your daily life. As we begin our therapy relationship, what comes up for you about the fact that one day our work together will also end?")

Relationships in the outside world frequently don't end well. Sometimes they end with anger or conflict, and sometimes people just gradually slip apart without ever saying good-bye. If these have been a client's primary experience with endings, it may be valuable to strive for a deliberate, meaningful termination of therapy in which the client clearly identifies and experiences the CRB2s she might engage in to make the ending of therapy satisfying and memorable; this skill can then be generalized to future good-byes with others. In cases like this, as painful as it might be, the important part of an ending is to express everything that is important and constructive to express— appreciations, regrets, wishes. The goal is often to end with the sense that *I told her everything it was in my heart to say. I held nothing back about what this relationship meant to me.*

For other clients, the most important aspect of ending therapy is addressing the transition from interdependence with the therapist to relative independence. The absence of a weekly therapy meeting—especially when the therapy has been long-standing—can be a tremendous loss of support or stability. Consider whether the goals of therapy have been adequately addressed and whether the client has set up adequate support. It may be important to assess whether the client is expressing his needs in regard to terminating therapy and seeking other forms of support.

Here are some other common CRBs that may show up around ending therapy, any of which may also show up for therapists:

Avoiding talking about the end of therapy

Distancing from the therapist in anticipation of the ending, usually to avoid the pain of termination

Becoming more anxious or demanding in response to fear of termination

Experiencing or creating more problems so therapy can continue

Being overly preoccupied with the ending

Rushing through the ending to get it over with

Failing to adequately plan for termination, such as considering whether the client has enough support

Overpreparing or otherwise being overly cautious about ending therapy

Because endings affect everything that follows, ending poorly can tarnish all of the progress that was made. Ending well helps to ensure that the work you did together has sustained impact.

END-OF-THERAPY LETTER TO CLIENT

It's amazing that many courses of therapy end without any concrete record of what was learned. The therapy is later lost in time. To mark endings explicitly and create a lasting record, we recommend writing an end-of-therapy letter to clients. It helps to make the process of termination explicit, open, and focused on the most important CRB2s, while also producing a concrete, durable record of the most important lessons of the therapy. If you wish or think it would be beneficial, you can also invite clients to write a similar letter for themselves, for you, or both, according to their needs. For instance, clients whose CRB2s involve communicating to others might find it meaningful to write a letter to the therapist, and clients whose CRB2s involve self-care, self-compassion, or self-direction might benefit from writing a letter to themselves.

Because the intent is for the client to keep the therapist's letter for a long time, take care with what you write. In addition to addressing what you want to say now, also consider what reminders the client may benefit from in one, five, or twenty years. The letter may include any or all of the following components, as appropriate. We tend to include most of them in every letter:

The client's goals and progress in therapy

The client's unique and special qualities and what you appreciate about her

Interactions you had with the client that stand out, what impacted you personally, what you enjoyed

What you'll take away from your work with the client, what you'll remember about him, how you're different as a result of having worked with him

What you want the client to take away from her work with you, what's important for her to remember

Any regrets you have about your work together

Your hopes and wishes for the client

What you'll miss about the client

Any parting advice about what to watch out for in the future, how to prevent relapse

The process of writing and sharing the letters can help organize the process of saying good-bye for both therapist and client, and doing so may also deepen the experience of therapy. Once you've written the letter, read it out loud to the client in session. If the client has written a letter, she can read it out loud as well. This can be an extremely evocative interaction. After reading the letters, exchange them, and recommend to the client that she keep your letter to refer to in the weeks, months, and years to come.

Here's a sample letter:

Dear [Client],

I remember when you said to me, with some fear and shame, that you are "too intense." I started looking for this intensity after that. Part of me was waiting for you to get angry or superopinionated or demanding. But mostly I knew none of that would happen. Because instead of grating or out-of-control intensity, what I kept seeing in you was strong feeling, commitment, integrity, trustworthiness, and a fundamental orientation toward connecting with others and with your world.

What I also saw—and you felt—alongside those qualities was a lot of fear and self-doubt. However, even here, in session, with your most difficult thoughts about yourself, you had the impulse of clear seeing and compassion.

And what I think we came to see clearly is how your view of yourself as intense comes from particular places and times. Maybe we could call these places and times "interactions between you and your family when they were at their most limited and you were at your most vulnerable." There doesn't need to be any loss of compassion for anyone arising from this understanding. Actually, you could feel even more compassion from this recognition.

From that understanding, you could say everything we worked on together was about getting you free of that story that you're intense, helping you to see how some interactions pulled you out of you as your best you, and then returning you to you through "I-am-you-are"; risk logs; and "appreciating yourself as a sunset, not a math problem."

The most powerful thing you did—and the best example of you being you—was asking me for more presence and focus and direction in our work via the session bridging questions and in our e-mail exchanges. Here is what is so cool about that: you were very afraid and yet simultaneously also very yourself and connected to yourself when you asked these things of me. Despite your fear borne from the story that you're too intense and that men won't care and won't respond to you, you listened to your own voice, and because of that you forged a real connection with me. Your intensity led you toward me, not away.

Above all, I hope you move forward from our work with the experience that your intensity can lead you toward others and draw people in, not just push you or them away. I also hope you recognize that there is a whole lot more to you than intensity. Your intensity contains sensitivity, compassion, generosity, flexibility, and so on. Let your intensity become your presence and your commitment to yourself. There will always be rough edges for us to work on in ourselves. But we are more capable of doing that work when we have gentle tools—like fine sandpaper and soft cloths—as well as heavy hands and sledgehammers.

All things pass and come to an end. And as our time together in this therapy comes to a close, you're helping me remember that what matters most is not that we drag things on and on or experience lots of the same moments together. What is far more precious and persistent is the quality and integrity of our contribution and connection to others. You brought an incredible quality and integrity to this work.

For these reasons, our work together these last months will be truly memorable for me.

With great admiration and care,

[Therapist's name]

END-OF-THERAPY QUESTIONS FOR CLIENTS

We've developed a set of questions that can assist with processing the end of therapy. Reflecting on and responding to these questions can help clients consolidate their gains and also facilitates saying a meaningful good-bye. If you invite clients to write a good-bye letter to you, you might also recommend that they incorporate their responses to these questions into that letter:

What thoughts and feelings do endings in general bring up for you?

What thoughts and feelings are you having about the end of this therapy relationship with me?

What have you learned? What's been helpful for you in this therapy?

What are you aware of about yourself that you weren't aware of before?

What courageous actions on your part stand out to you the most?

How has your ability to be loving changed, or how have your relationships changed?

What are the most important skills you've learned that you want to keep implementing in your life?

What do you like and appreciate about yourself? What are you grateful for in your life?

What stands out to you most about your interactions with me?

What do you like and appreciate about me? What will you always remember about me?

What regrets do you have about the therapy or what do you wish had gone differently?

What situations, thoughts, or behaviors make you vulnerable to feeling [state the client's presenting problems here], and how can you deal with them to decrease the severity of these feelings?

What are some things you can do to maintain your gains from therapy and continue to improve your life?

What do you feel most vulnerable about saying to me as you say good-bye?

SUMMARY

- The endings of relationships are significant episodes in the history of many clients.

- The ending of therapy offers an opportunity to work therapeutically with what is evoked in the client and to ensure that the ending is as focused and therapeutic as possible.

- The end-of-therapy letter is a useful tool for making the ending process explicit and open.

Conclusion

As to the methods, there may be a million and then some, but principles are few.
The [person] who grasps principles can successfully select his [or her] own methods.
The [person] who tries methods, ignoring principles, is sure to have trouble.

—Harrington Emerson

Some have said that FAP boils down to a way of being with a client in a therapeutic relationship. Think of it like this: when one *does* all the things contained in these pages, a way of being in relationship emerges. Echoing the Bertrand Russell quote that opened this book—"Neither love without knowledge, nor knowledge without love can produce a good life"—this way of being balances the "love" of an open, empathic, compassionate stance with the "knowledge" of functional thinking and contextual behavioral science (CBS). The aim is a therapeutic relationship, one that flows with the moment, always asking, "What is needed for this person in this moment?"

Here is a poem, written by Gareth, that describes this stance:

The FAP Therapist's Prayer

May I see and hear myself.
May I see and hear this person in front of me.
May I remember what it feels like to stand on the edge of growth.
May I be open, and through my openness invite the same.

May I hear the past speaking in the present
and the longing for a future.

May I accept not knowing what the next step is
and stand with this other person
as they find their next step.

May I take risks, big and small,
to suggest the next step,
may I offer challenges, big and small,
without imposing my opinion.
May I continue to listen as my opinions rise and fall.

May I welcome whatever arises,
with concern or comfort
or courage or camaraderie, as is needed.

May I speak to this, here and now,
slipping into the pool of
what is real and simple between us,
whether it is warm or cold.

May I find and feel and serve
what matters to this person,
this unique person
and their piece of the universal.

May I know the road this person walks,
as best as one can,
so I can speak their truth like a
loving novelist.

May I voice the truths that
have fallen silent.

May I communicate my affection,
generously,
without obligating the other to me.
May my compassion set this person free.

May my compassion set me free.
May I do my own work
and offer all of this to myself.

In this book we've laid out the basic ideas and practices of FAP. We have taken the title of the book (and of the series in which this book belongs) to heart: we have made our presentation as *simple* and clear as possible. Much of our presentation mirrors the way we teach FAP in workshops, classrooms, and group or individual consultations. We included both the theoretical and practical, bottom-line clinical teaching that we believe clinicians most crave.

At the same time, we resisted the urge to portray FAP and the process of therapy as being simpler than they really are. That wouldn't be doing you any favors. As we wrote at the beginning, neither the theory nor the book is the therapy itself. It's up to you to *apply* the ideas and practices we have provided, and there are lots of ways to do that. We tried to make things simpler, but that does not mean the work is easy. The ideas we've given point the way and grant great flexibility in how you walk the FAP way. The bottom line is this: if you are

1. taking a CBS stance toward therapy;

2. understanding what happens in the therapy process in terms of function;

3. participating in an aware, courageous, and loving therapeutic interaction; and

4. using your interaction to shape the behaviors that you determine are functionally related to the client's clinical issues, then you are doing FAP.

As you practice, your ultimate guide should be the process of therapy and your interaction with your client and your grasp of the contexts in which you are working. FAP is about that process. What is real there? The work is not perfected, and rarely is it completed. It is practiced. It is not laid out ahead of time. It is lived. We don't dictate to our clients—we relate. Relating is where the change process lies.

It's inevitable that there are aspects of the FAP practice we have not covered adequately. There are things we do in practice or teach to consultees that we've not thought to cover here. Please do reach out to the FAP community if and when you need help.

May your practice be enriched by the principles of FAP. The remainder of this conclusion offers a few suggestions and wishes as you carry these principles forward into your practice.

DELIBERATE PRACTICE

There are ways of practicing that are more effective than others. In particular, time spent in practice by itself is not the most important factor for skill development. It matters that you practice deliberately (Ericsson, Krampe, & Tesch-Romer, 1993):

- Attend to specific behaviors and contexts that challenge your performance.

- Practice the desired improvements.

- Monitor the outcomes of your practice and adapt your practice based on what you observe.

This process need not be complicated. In fact, the simpler you can make the practice process the more likely you are to persist with it amidst the demands of a busy professional life. Picking something and working on it with the minimal deliberate practice for viable implementation is more effective than spending hours preparing and finding just the right target. Pick something and go. The process of practice will be more instructive than your contemplation at the outset.

Consider this example of deliberate practice:

Let's say you want to work on inquiring more directly about CRB as it happens in the moment.

Decide when you will practice this. Perhaps you will practice it with all clients, or perhaps with only those with whom you struggle to inquire.

To orient yourself to the practice as you first begin, come up with a couple of questions to help you inquire about CRB: "What did you feel just then?" "Is what is happening right now like what happens with her?" And so forth.

The entire planning process above might take five minutes. After you have a plan, remember to actually do the practice. A simple visual reminder on your laptop or therapy clipboard or whiteboard might be sufficient: "practice" or "evoke."

After each session in which you deliberately practice, or at the end of the week, reflect on how the deliberate practice went. What went well? What would you like to improve for next week? Don't be discouraged by mistakes. You can learn as much from mistakes as from success, if not more. Incorporate what you learn into the deliberate practice and repeat. Five minutes of reflection about your deliberate practice per week, compounded over months and years of practice, can make an immense difference in your performance. At the end of each chapter in this book, we offered summaries of the key things to do and remember. These may serve as a checklist of competencies for your practice of FAP.

CONSULTATION GROUPS

Practicing with other professionals is probably the most popular way to learn FAP. You might form or join an existing FAP consultation group or integrate FAP principles into your existing consultation work. Sharing the learning of FAP with other professionals offers the opportunity to practice the principles in the context of genuine interactions with your colleagues.

The most important, nonnegotiable practices that must be part of any FAP consultation group are authenticity and attending to the actual process of relating to each other. You should know the 1s and 2s of each other, and you should practice vulnerable disclosure with each other. Elephants in the room should be discussed. All members should be committed to stepping outside of their comfort zones in service of building skills. At the same time, keep in mind that everyone starts where they are, and vulnerability should be consensual and freely chosen.

Here are some other useful practices for group consultation:

- Sharing logs (for example, risk logs) and briefly reflecting—verbally or in writing via e-mail or social media—on a partner's log

- Case presentation and role-playing

- In vivo process work (for example, processing avoidance, conflict, and so forth in the consultation group)

- Experiential exercises and debriefing conversations

Obviously this topic warrants much more discussion than can be provided here. A growing number of FAP trainers and practitioners who have started consultation groups can provide guidance and other resources.

THE FUTURE OF FAP

FAP is evolving through the efforts of many people and organizations worldwide, including the Center for the Science of Social Connection led by Jonathan Kanter, Mavis Tsai, and Bob Kohlenberg at the University of Washington in Seattle.

There are three key things that FAP needs in order to evolve successfully:

1. **Science:** As we noted in the introduction, the science supporting FAP as an intervention (not the basic learning principles themselves) is underdeveloped. FAP does not

meet conventional criteria for "evidence-based treatment" status. That continues to be a challenge for FAP practitioners and researchers.

2. **Innovation:** We need to develop innovative applications (for example, protocols, manuals, specific processes) for FAP principles that lend themselves to scientific evaluation and that pinpoint where and how FAP principles are most likely to add clinical value.

3. **Community:** Because community is the foundation for innovation and science, our hope is that this book will inspire the FAP community to innovate its principles and create the scientific research that is needed to validate this approach to therapy. We hope the community will actively evolve FAP into something more impactful and valuable.

May we be there for each other.

Acknowledgments

GARETH HOLMAN

There are many people who helped create this book, not only by shaping the words and ideas that went into it, but also by helping me grow over the last couple of years. Compiling this list, I feel like a very lucky man: Jen Loser, for presenting the idea that creativity is an act of love at just the right moment. Jonathan Bricker, for offering reassurance—when I was deciding whether or not to take on this project—that the book could offer a worthy contribution, despite the absence of strong evidence base for FAP. "It will be beautiful as a clinical guide." Neil Kirkpatrick—the most effective (or at least opinionated) behavior therapist I know—for sorting out the initial hairy draft of chapter 1 in a profoundly useful way. Yvonne Barnes-Holmes, Carmen Luciano, Niklas Törneke, Joe Oliver, John Boorman, Miles Thompson, Nic Hooper, Kelly Wilson, and Louise McHugh, for inspiring me with the clarity and passion of your work during the 2015 ACBS conference in Berlin. The book crystallized in huge leaps during that week. Tien Mandell, for your original work and your challenge to clarify and make FAP theory useful.

Michael Vurek, Tore Gustafsson, and Marie Blom, for your comments and support on some early chapters. Marie Blom, in particular, for finding the wonderful Virginia Woolf quote that opens part 2. Fabian Olaz, for sharing your friendship and your growth with me. We are on the roller coaster together. Benjamin Schoendorff, for your kind words. Joanne Steinwachs, for "No picking and choosing." Rachel Collis, for a real, true working relationship. Daniel Maitland, for honesty, an open mind, integrity, and hard work. Angela Cathey, for persisting and believing. Russell Kolts, for compassion and visions of paddleboards. Jenn and Matthieu Villatte, for friendship and what feels like sibling affiliation. Glenn Callaghan, for believing that this can be done right. Chris Hall, for friendship and a view from outside. All the members of the FAP community, for caring about this work. My clients and consultees, who have been my most valuable education and purpose. Kelly Koerner, Linda Dimeff, Katie Patricelli, and Tim Kelly at the Evidence Based Practice Institute, for teaching me so much and then setting me free.

Catharine Meyers, Heather Garnos, Katie Parr, and Jesse Burson at New Harbinger, for giving me this opportunity and then supporting me, with great patience and cheer, along the road it took to get here. Jasmine Star and James Lainsbury, for brilliant editing and holding my hand. Bob Kohlenberg and Mavis Tsai, for being my professional parents. This book is my real dissertation. Jonathan Kanter, for being my companion and friend as FAP evolved these last years.

And to my family, I love you.

Sarah and Jackson, I love you.

JONATHAN KANTER

I would like to acknowledge the important contributions to my thinking about FAP, and personal support, from Alessandra Villas-Bôas and Glenn Callaghan; the love and support of my wife, Gwynne Kohl; and my inspiration to see joy and beauty in all things large and small, Zoe Kanter.

MAVIS TSAI

I would like to thank my University of Washington FAP practicum co-instructors over the years— Mary Plummer Loudon, Gareth Holman, Andrew Fleming, Julia Hitch, Hilary Mead, and Daniel Maitland—for helping me create a profound learning environment where everyone's wounds are validated and our gifts are nurtured. Laura Brown, Julie Gottman, Barbara Johnstone, Kelly Koerner, Linda Luster, Joanne Steinwachs, and Jennifer Waltz are soul sisters. I am incredibly grateful to the consultees and students who have shaped who I am—many of you have become mighty FAP companions who inspire my mind and heart. And to Bob—you are the love and light of my life, and that will never change.

ROBERT KOHLENBERG

Thinking about relationships from way back that have planted the seeds and set the conditions that eventually led to FAP: Loren Acker, Ivar Lovaas, Steve Hayes, and Barbara Kohlenberg. Those of you who know the history of FAP also know how the sacred relationship between Mavis and me was and is at its core. I also want to acknowledge the contributions of my coauthors, Jonathan, and of course Mavis again, and especially Gareth, who was the inspirational driving force and main contributor to this book.

Additional Reading

Aron, A., Melinat, E., Aron, E. N., Vallone, R. D., & Bator, R. J. (1997). The experimental generation of interpersonal closeness: A procedure and some preliminary findings. *Personality and Social Psychology Bulletin, 23*(4), 363–377.

Kanter, J. W., Landes, S. J., Busch, A. M., Rusch, L. C., Brown, K. R., Baruch, D. E., et al. (2006). The effect of contingent reinforcement on target variables in outpatient psychotherapy for depression: A successful and unsuccessful case using functional analytic psychotherapy. *Journal of Applied Behavior Analysis, 39*(4), 463–467.

Kanter, J. W., Tsai, M., Holman, G., & Koerner, K. (2013). Preliminary data from a randomized pilot study of web-based functional analytic psychotherapy therapist training. *Psychotherapy: Research, Theory, Practice, Training, 50*(2), 248–255.

Kanter, J. W., Tsai, M., & Kohlenberg, R. J. (Eds.). (2010). *The practice of functional analytic psychotherapy.* New York: Springer.

Kohlenberg, R. J., Tsai, M., Kuczynski, A. M., Rae, J. R., Lagbas, E., Lo, J., & Kanter, J. W. (2015) A brief, interpersonally oriented mindfulness intervention Incorporating Functional Analytic Psychotherapy's model of awareness, courage and love. *Journal of Contextual Behavioral Science, 4*(2), 107–111.

Kolts, R. (2016). *CFT made simple: A clinician's guide to compassion-focused therapy.* Oakland, CA: New Harbinger.

Maitland, D., Kanter, J., Tsai, M., Kuczynski, A., Manbeck, K. Kohlenberg, R. J. (in press). Preliminary findings on the effects of online Functional Analytic Psychotherapy training on therapist competency. *The Psychological Record.*

Nelson, K. M., Yang, J. P., Maliken, A. C., Tsai, M., & Kohlenberg, R. J. (2014). Introduction to using structured evocative activities in Functional Analytic Psychotherapy. *Cognitive & Behavioral Practice, 23*(4), 459–463.

Skinner, B. F. (1974). *Walden two.* Indianapolis, IN: Hackett.

Tsai, M., Fleming, A., Cruz, R., Hitch, J., & Kohlenberg, R. (2014) Functional analytic psychotherapy (FAP): Using awareness, courage, love, and behaviorism to promote change. In N. C. Thoma & D. McKay (Eds.), *Working with emotion in cognitive behavioral therapy.* New York: Guildford.

Tsai, M., Gustafsson, T., Kanter, J., Plummer Loudon, M., Kohlenberg, R. J. (in press). Saying good goodbyes to your clients: A Functional Analytic Psychotherapy (FAP) perspective. *Psychotherapy.*

Tsai, M., Kohlenberg, R. J., Kanter, J. W., Holman, G. I., & Loudon, M. P. (2012). *Functional analytic psychotherapy: Distinctive features.* London: Routledge.

Tsai, M., Mandell, T., Maitland, D., Kanter, J., & Kohlenberg R. J. (in press). Reducing inadvertent clinical errors: Guidelines from functional analytic psychotherapy (FAP). *Psychotherapy.*

Tsai, M., McKelvie, M., Kohlenberg, R., & Kanter, J. (2014). Functional analytic psychotherapy: Using awareness, courage, and love in treatment. Society for the Advancement of Psychotherapy. http://societyforpsychotherapy.org/functional-analytic-psychotherapy-fap-using-awareness-courage-love-treatment.

Tsai, M., Yard, S., & Kohlenberg, R. J. (2014). Functional analytic psychotherapy: A behavioral relational approach to treatment. *Psychotherapy, 51*(3), 364–371.

References

Alves de Oliveira, J., & Vandenberghe, L. (2009). Upsetting experiences for the therapist in-session: How they can be dealt with and what they are good for. *Journal of Psychotherapy Integration, 19*(4), 231–245.

Aron, A., Aron, E. N., & Smollan, D. (1992). Inclusion of other in the Self Scale and the structure of interpersonal closeness. *Journal of Personality and Social Psychology, 63*(4), 596–612.

Barnett, P. A., & Gotlib, I. H. (1988). Psychosocial functioning and depression: Distinguishing among antecedents, concomitants, and consequences. *Psychological Bulletin, 104*(1), 97–126.

Beck, J. G. (2010). *Interpersonal processes in the anxiety disorders: Implications for understanding psychopathology and treatment.* Washington, DC: American Psychological Association.

Beidas, R. S., & Kendall, P. C. (2010). Training therapists in evidence-based practice: A critical review of studies from a systems-contextual perspective. *Clinical Psychology: Science and Practice, 17*(1), 1–30.

Biglan, A. (2015). *The nurture effect: How the science of human behavior can improve our lives & our world.* Oakland, CA: New Harbinger.

Bonow, J. T., Maragakis, A., & Follette, W. C. (2012). The challenge of developing a universal case conceptualization for functional analytic psychotherapy. *International Journal of Behavioral Consultation and Therapy, 7*(2–3), 2–8.

Buechner, F. (1991). *Telling secrets.* New York: Harper Collins.

Bugental, D. B. (2000). Acquisition of the algorithms of social life: A domain-based approach. *Psychological Bulletin, 26*(2), 187–209.

Busch, A. M., Kanter, J. W., Callaghan, G. M., Baruch, D. E., Weeks, C. E., & Berlin, K. S. (2009). A micro-process analysis of functional analytic psychotherapy's mechanism of change. *Behavior Therapy, 40*(3), 280–290.

Cacioppo, J. T., Hawkley, L. C., Crawford, E., Ernst, J. M., Burleson, M. H., Kowalewski, R. B., et al. (2002). Loneliness and health: Potential mechanisms. *Psychosomatic Medicine, 64*(3), 407–417.

Cacioppo, J. T., & Patrick, W. (2008). *Loneliness: Human nature and the need for social connection.* New York: Norton.

Callaghan, G. M. (2006). The Functional Idiographic Assessment Template (FIAT) system: For use with interpersonally based interventions including functional analytic psychotherapy (FAP) and FAP-enhanced treatments. *Behavior Analyst Today, 7*(3), 357–398.

Cassidy, J., & Shaver, P. R. (1999). *Handbook of attachment: Theory, research, and clinical applications.* New York: Guilford.

Dahl, J., Plumb-Vilardaga, J., Stewart, I., & Lundgren, T. (2009). *The art and science of valuing in psychotherapy: Helping clients discover, explore, and commit to valued action using acceptance and commitment therapy.* Oakland, CA: New Harbinger.

Dunbar, R. 2010. *How many friends does one person need?* Cambridge, MA: Harvard University Press.

Ericsson, K. A., Krampe, R. T., & Tesch-Romer, C. (1993). The role of deliberate practice in the acquisition of expert performance. *Psychological Review, 100*(3), 363–406.

Esparza Lizarazo, N., Muñoz-Martínez, A. M., Santos, M. M., & Kanter, J. W. (2015). A within-subjects evaluation of the effects of functional analytic psychotherapy on in-session and out-of-session client behavior. *Psychological Record, 65*(3), 463–474.

Ferriss, T. (2007). *The four-hour workweek: Escape 9–5, live anywhere, and join the new rich.* New York: Crown.

Gilbert, D. T. (2002). Inferential correction. In T. Gilovich, D. W. Griffin, & D. Kahneman (Eds.), *Heuristics and biases: The psychology of intuitive judgment.* Cambridge, UK: Cambridge University Press.

Gilbert, P. (2010). *Compassion focused therapy: The CBT distinctive features series.* London: Routledge.

Harari, Y. N. (2015). *Sapiens: A brief history of humankind.* New York: Harper.

Haworth, K., Kanter, J. W., Tsai, M., Kuczynski, A. M., Rae, J. R., & Kohlenberg, R. J. (2015). Reinforcement matters: A preliminary, laboratory-based component-process analysis of functional analytic psychotherapy's model of social connection. *Journal of Contextual Behavioral Science, 4*(4), 281–291.

Hayes, S. C., Barnes-Holmes D., & Roche, B. (Eds.). (2001). *Relational frame theory: A post-Skinnerian account of human language and cognition.* New York: Plenum.

Hayes, S. C., Barnes-Holmes, D., & Wilson, K. G. (2012). Contextual behavioral science: Creating a science more adequate to the challenge of the human condition. *Journal of Contextual Behavioral Science, 1*(1–2), 1–16.

Hayes, S. C., Levin, M. E., Plumb-Vilardaga, J., Villatte, J. L., & Pistorello, J. (2013). Acceptance and commitment therapy and contextual behavioral science: Examining the progress of a distinctive model of behavioral and cognitive therapy. *Behavior Therapy, 44*(2), 180–198.

Hayes, S. C., Strosahl, K., & Wilson, K. G. (1999). *Acceptance and commitment therapy: An experiential approach to behavior change.* New York: Guilford.

Henrich, J. (2016). *The secret of our success: How culture is driving human evolution, domesticating our species, and making us smarter.* Princeton, NJ: Princeton University Press.

Holt, Lunstad, J., & Smith, T. B. (2012). Social relationships and mortality. *Social and Personality Psychology Compass, 6*(1), 41–53.

Holt-Lunstad, J., Smith, T. B., & Layton, B. (2010). Social relationships and mortality: A meta-analysis. *PLoS Medicine, 7,* e1000316.

Hooper, N., Erdogan, A., Keen, G., Lawton, K., & McHugh, L. (2015). Perspective taking reduces the fundamental attribution error. *Journal of Contextual Behavioral Science, 4*(2), 69–72.

Hooper, N., & Larsson, A. (2015). *The research journey of acceptance and commitment therapy (ACT).* New York: Palgrave Macmillan.

Horowitz, L. M. (2004). *Interpersonal foundations of psychopathology.* Washington, DC: American Psychological Association.

Horvath, A. O., Del Re, A. C., Flückiger, C., & Symonds, D. B. (2011). Alliance in individual psychotherapy. *Psychotherapy, 48*(1), 9–16.

House, J. S., Landis, K. R., & Umberson, D. (1988). Social relationships and health. *Science, 241*(4865), 540–545.

Jones, E. E., & Harris, V. A. (1967). The attribution of attitudes. *Journal of Experimental Social Psychology 3,* 1–24.

Kanter, J. W., Holman, G. I., & Wilson, K. (2014). Where is the love? Contextual behavior science and behavior analysis. *Journal of Contextual Behavioral Science 3*(2), 69–73.

Kanter, J. W., Schildcrout, J. S., & Kohlenberg, R. J. (2005). In-vivo processes in cognitive therapy for depression: Frequency and benefits. *Psychotherapy Research, 15*(4), 366–373.

Kanter, J. W., Landes, S. J., Busch, A. M., Rusch, L. C., Brown, K. R., Baruch, D. E., & Holman, G. I. (2006). The effect of contingent reinforcement on target variables in outpatient psychotherapy for depression: An investigation of functional analytic psychotherapy. *Journal of Applied Behavioral Analysis, 29,* 463–467.

Kiecolt-Glaser, J. K., Loving, T. J., Stowell, J. R., Malarkey, W. B., Lemeshow, S., Dickinson, S. L., et al. (2005). Hostile marital interactions, proinflammatory cytokine production, and wound healing. *Archives of General Psychiatry, 62*(12), 1377–1384.

Kohlenberg, R. J., Kanter, J. W., Bolling, M. Y., Parker, C. R., & Tsai, M. (2002). Enhancing cognitive therapy for depression with functional analytic psychotherapy: Treatment guidelines and empirical findings. *Cognitive and Behavioral Practice, 9*(3), 213–229.

Kohlenberg, R. J., & Tsai, M. (1991). *Functional analytic psychotherapy: A guide for creating intense and curative therapeutic relationships.* New York: Plenum.

Landes, S. J., Kanter, J. W., Weeks, C. E., & Busch, A. M. (2013). The impact of the active components of functional analytic psychotherapy on idiographic target behaviors. *Journal of Contextual Behavioral Science, 2*(1–2), 49–57.

Leach, D., & Kranzler, H. R. (2013). An interpersonal model of addiction relapse. *Addictive Disorders and Their Treatment, 12*(4), 183–192.

Levin, M. E., Luoma, J. B., Vilardaga, R., Lillis, J., Nobles, R., & Hayes, S. C. (2016). Examining the role of psychological inflexibility, perspective taking, and empathic concern in generalized prejudice. *Journal of Applied Social Psychology, 46*(3), 180–191.

Linehan, M. M. (1993). *Cognitive behavioral treatment of borderline personality disorder.* New York: Guilford.

Maitland, D. W., & Gaynor, S. T. (2016). Functional analytic psychotherapy compared with supportive listening: An alternating treatments design examining distinctiveness, session evaluations, and interpersonal functioning. *Behavior Analysis: Research and Practice, 16*(2), 52–64.

Maitland, D. W. M., Petts, R. A., Knott, L. E., Briggs, C. A., Moore, J. A., & Gaynor, S. T. (in press). A randomized controlled trial of functional analytic psychotherapy versus watchful waiting: Enhancing social connectedness and reducing anxiety and avoidance. *Behavior Analysis Research and Practice.*

Mangabeira, V., Kanter, J. W., & Del Prette, G. (2012). Functional analytic psychotherapy (FAP): A review of publications from 1990 to 2010. *International Journal of Behavioral Consultation and Therapy, 7*(2–3), 78–89.

Martell, C. R., Addis, M. E., & Jacobson, N. S. (2001). *Depression in context: Strategies for guided action.* New York: Norton.

McEvoy, P. M., Burgess, M. M., Page, A. C., Nathan, P., & Fursland, A. (2013). Interpersonal problems across anxiety, depression, and eating disorders: A transdiagnostic examination. *British Journal of Clinical Psychology, 52*(2), 129–147.

Meltzoff, A. N., & Moore, M. K. (1977). Imitation of facial and manual gestures by human neonates. *Science 198*(4312), 75–78.

Oshiro, C. K. B., Kanter, J. W., & Meyer, S. B. (2012). A single-case experimental demonstration of functional analytic psychotherapy with two clients with severe interpersonal problems. *International Journal of Behavioral Consultation and Therapy, 7*(2–3), 111–116.

Pettit, J. W., & Joiner, T. E. (2006). *Chronic depression: Interpersonal sources, therapeutic solutions.* Washington, DC: American Psychological Association.

Pincus, A. L. (2005). A contemporary integrative interpersonal theory of personality disorders. In M. F. Lenzenweger & J. F. Clarkin (Eds.), *Major theories of personality disorder* (2nd ed.). New York: Guilford.

Polk, K. L., & Schoendorff, B. (Eds.). (2014). *The ACT matrix: A new approach to building psychological flexibility across settings and populations.* Oakland, CA: New Harbinger.

Polk, K. L., Schoendorff, B., Webster, M., & Olaz, F. O. (2016). *The essential guide to the ACT matrix: A step-by-step approach to using the ACT matrix model in clinical practice.* Oakland, CA: New Harbinger.

Porges, S. W. (2001). The polyvagal theory: Phylogenetic substrates of a social nervous system. *International Journal of Psychophysiology, 42*(2), 123–146.

Ramnero, J., & Törneke, N. (2008). *The ABCs of human behavior: Behavioral principles for the practicing clinician.* Oakland, CA: New Harbinger.

Reis, H. T. (2007). Steps toward the ripening of relationship science. *Personal Relationships, 14*(2), 1–23.

Reis, H. T., Collins, W. A., & Berscheid, E. (2000). The relationship context of human behavior and development. *Psychological Bulletin, 126*(6), 844–872.

Scott, S. (2002). *Fierce conversations: Achieving success at work and in life, one conversation at a time.* New York: Berkley.

Skinner, B. F. (1953). *Science and human behavior.* New York: The Free Press.

Sober, E., & Wilson, D. S. (1998). *Unto others: The evolution and psychology of unselfish behavior.* Cambridge, MA: Harvard University Press.

Törneke, N. (2010). *Learning RFT: An introduction to relational frame theory and its clinical applications.* Oakland, CA: New Harbinger.

Truax, C. B. (1966). Reinforcement and nonreinforcement in Rogerian psychotherapy. *Journal of Abnormal Psychology, 71*(1), 1–9.

Tsai, M., Callaghan, G. M., & Kohlenberg, R. J. (2013). The use of awareness, courage, therapeutic love, and behavioral interpretation in functional analytic psychotherapy. *Psychotherapy, 50*(3), 366–370.

Tsai, M., Kohlenberg, R. J., Kanter, J. W., Kohlenberg, B., Follette, W. C., & Callaghan, G. M. (2009). *A guide to functional analytic psychotherapy: Awareness, courage, love, and behaviorism.* New York: Springer.

Twain, M. (1894). *The tragedy of Pudd'nhead Wilson.* New York: Charles L. Webster.

Vandenberghe, L., & Silvestre, R. L. S. (2014). Therapists' positive emotions in-session: Why they happen and what they are good for. *Counseling and Psychotherapy Research, 14*(2), 119–127.

Vilardaga, R., Estévez, A., Levin, M. E., & Hayes, S. C. (2012). Deictic relational responding, empathy, and experiential avoidance as predictors of social anhedonia: Further contributions from relation frame theory. *The Psychological Record, 62,* 409–432.

Villatte, M., Villatte, J., & Hayes, S. C. (2015). *Mastering the clinical conversation: Language as intervention.* New York: Guilford.

Weeks, C. E., Kanter, J. W., Bonow, J. T., Landes, S. J., & Busch, A. M. (2012). Translating the theoretical into practical: A logical framework of functional analytic psychotherapy interactions for research, training, and clinical purposes. *Behavior Modification, 36*(1), 87–119.

Gareth Holman, PhD, is a Seattle-based psychologist and consultant. Holman is partner at OpenTeam—a consulting firm that helps business and leadership teams communicate openly and cooperate effectively towards their purpose. His private practice focuses on improving relationships and communication, and he trains and consults with therapists and coaches worldwide who are practicing functional analytic psychotherapy (FAP) and related behavioral therapies.

Jonathan Kanter, PhD, received his doctorate in clinical psychology from the University of Washington in 2002. He is currently research associate professor and FAP term professor in the department of psychology at the University of Washington, where he directs the Center for the Science of Social Connection. The center's research focuses on FAP and other interventions based on a contextual-behavioral understanding of social connectedness and intimate relations in areas of public health significance where relationships matter, such as psychotherapy and racism. Kanter is regarded as a leader in research on FAP, and is regularly invited to lecture, provide workshops, and provide consultation on FAP internationally.

Mavis Tsai, PhD, is cofounder of FAP, and director of the FAP Specialty Clinic at the University of Washington. Tsai has an international following as a trainer, consultant, and clinician.

Robert Kohlenberg, PhD, is cofounder of FAP and professor of psychology at the University of Washington.

Foreword writer **Steven C. Hayes, PhD**, is Nevada Foundation Professor and director of clinical training in the department of psychology at the University of Nevada. An author of forty-one books and nearly 600 scientific articles, his career has focused on analysis of the nature of human language and cognition, and its application to the understanding and alleviation of human suffering and promotion of human prosperity. Among other associations, Hayes has been president of the Association for Behavioral and Cognitive Therapies, and the Association for Contextual Behavioral Science. His work has received several awards, including the Impact of Science on Application Award from the Society for the Advancement of Behavior Analysis, and the Lifetime Achievement Award from the Association for Behavioral and Cognitive Therapies.

Index

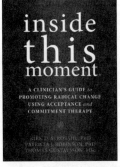